Contents

Key findings
Social attitudes in an age of austerity

In a period of extended recession, and with the Coalition government having embarked on a severe programme of cuts to public services, we ask how the British public is reacting. Are people looking to the state to protect public services and social welfare, or are they turning away from government being the answer? With nearly three decades of data covering three recessions and five prime ministers, British Social Attitudes is uniquely placed to answer these questions.

Role of the state

There are initial signs of increased concern about the impact of public expenditure cuts on public services such as health and education. But there is also a longer-term hardening of attitudes towards redistribution and welfare.

The proportion calling for the government to **increase taxes and spend more** on health, education and social benefits rose for the first time in nine years – up five points to 36%. The principle of a tax-funded health service available to all is supported by a clear majority: 73% oppose the idea of the NHS being "available only to those with lower incomes".

Set against this, neither redistribution in general nor **welfare benefits** in particular are as popular as they once were. During the previous recession in 1991, 58% agreed that "government should spend more on welfare benefits even if it leads to higher taxes" – more than double the proportion who think this now (28%).

Social divisions

There are signs of increasing social divisions, particularly in terms of attitudes towards welfare recipients and immigrants.

The **most vulnerable in the labour market** are viewed far less sympathetically than before, despite Britain's current economic difficulties. This change predates the recession, and the trend has continued in recent years. From 2008–2011, even support for more spending on benefits for disabled people unable to work fell from 63% to 53%.

There is increased concern about **immigration**, another trend that predates the recession. The proportion thinking that "Britain's cultural life is generally undermined" by immigration has increased, with 47% taking this view, up from 33% in 2002.

Editors:
Alison Park, Elizabeth Cle
John Curtice, Miranda Phi
and David Utting

2012 Edition

BRITISH SOCIAL ATTITUDES 29

NatCen
Social Research that works for society

At **NatCen Social Research** we believe that social research has the power to make life better. By really understanding the complexity of people's lives and what they think about the issues that affect them, we give the public a powerful and influential role in shaping decisions and services that can make a difference to everyone. And as an independent, not for profit organisation we're able to focus our time and energy on meeting our clients' needs and delivering social research that works for society.

Publication details

Park, A., Clery, E., Curtice, J., Phillips, M. and Utting, D. (eds.) (2012), *British Social Attitudes: the 29th Report*, London: NatCen Social Research, available online at: www.bsa-29.natcen.ac.uk

First published 2012

NatCen Social Research
35 Northampton Square
London
EC1V 0AX

info@natcen.ac.uk

ISBN 978-1-907236-24-2

This summary highlights public attitudes on two different themes: the role of the state, and social unity

Introduction

Four years on from the banking crisis of 2008, Britain remains less wealthy than it was before the crisis began. Growth remains elusive at best. The coalition government has embarked upon a programme of cuts the size of which has not been seen since the Second World War (Chote, 2010). The result? The British public has been presented with a rude reminder of the potential fragility of its material wellbeing.

How are people reacting in this extended period of recession and austerity? In this short summary, drawing on evidence from our 29th British Social Attitudes report, we provide some answers. The summary highlights public attitudes on two different themes: the role of the state, and social unity. In doing so, we focus in particular on two very different potential responses. The first is what we might call the social democratic reaction, in which people rediscover their faith in the role of the state. Having seen market mechanisms and private sector institutions fail so visibly, they increasingly value the state's role as a provider of important public services and necessary social protection, and perhaps even as a way of achieving a more equal society. Awareness that few people's jobs or incomes are safe leads to increased sympathy for those who have fallen on hard times, including those who require support from the welfare state. This response might see a feeling of solidarity, a sense that 'we are all in it together', and perhaps a belief that the better-off should shoulder more of the financial burden.

But one can also imagine a different reaction, one that points towards far less reliance on a centralised state. People may increasingly feel that the state is the problem and not the solution. A government that cannot pay its way is seen as profligate and wasteful, leading to an increasing desire to cut back both on taxes and on spending. There might be a growing feeling that people should look after themselves in times of trouble rather than expecting government or the rest of society to 'bail them out'. We may also see increasing social division, as people believe that others, whom they see as less 'deserving', are taking things (jobs, benefits, or access to state services) away from them.

The longevity and impartiality of British Social Attitudes puts us in a unique position to assess Britain's reaction to austerity. The survey series was created by NatCen Social Research in 1983, shortly before Margaret Thatcher's second election victory. Many key questions are repeated each year, and three decades of data now cover seven elections, five prime ministers and three recessions. This allows us to put current responses to austerity into a longer-term perspective. Perhaps what is happening to the public mood is little different from what has happened before – no more than a cyclical response to the ups and downs of economic activity. But if what we are seeing now differs greatly from the past then we may be uncovering evidence that the country wants to move in a different long-term direction.

We start by shedding light on how people view the role of the state, focusing on taxation and public services, the NHS, welfare and inequality. We then look at the extent to which austerity is drawing us together, or pushing us apart. Finally we look at what austerity means for families and explore the pressures that they are facing.

What do citizens want from the state?

Every government makes tough decisions about how much it should tax and spend. Previous research indicates that attitudes towards taxation and spending are cyclical (Soroka and Wlezien, 2005; Wlezien, 1995). So when public expenditure goes up, people's appetite for better public services is increasingly satisfied. Their support for further increases then falls away as their concern turns instead to the amount of tax they are paying. But when expenditure is reduced, support for more spending increases, as people become dissatisfied with the state of public services.

In 2011, the proportion calling for an increase in taxation and spending rose for the first time in nine years

This pattern is clearly illustrated in Figure 0.1, which shows responses to our long-running question about taxation and public spending. When British Social Attitudes first began in 1983, only one third (32 per cent) wanted to see government "increase taxes and spend more on health, education and social benefits", while 54 per cent wanted to "keep taxes and spending on these services at the same level as now". But as the efforts of the Thatcher government to curb public expenditure began to bite, so the public mood changed drastically. By 1991, when the economy was beginning to enter recession, no less than two-thirds (65 per cent) said they wanted to see taxes and spending increase. Thereafter, the figure remained consistent at around three-fifths until 2003, from which point it fell repeatedly in reaction to the substantial increases in public spending that took place under the then Labour government. By 2010, only 31 per cent wanted to see increased public spending, dipping below the figure recorded in Thatcher's heyday in 1983. But in 2011, the proportion calling for an increase in taxation and spending rose for the first time in nine years – up five points to 36 per cent – while 55 per cent would like to see spending levels stay as they are. This is a modest increase, but it could well be the first sign of a reaction against the public spending reductions that the government has begun to implement, and which are set to accumulate between now and 2017.

Figure 0.1 Attitudes to taxation and spending, 1983–2011

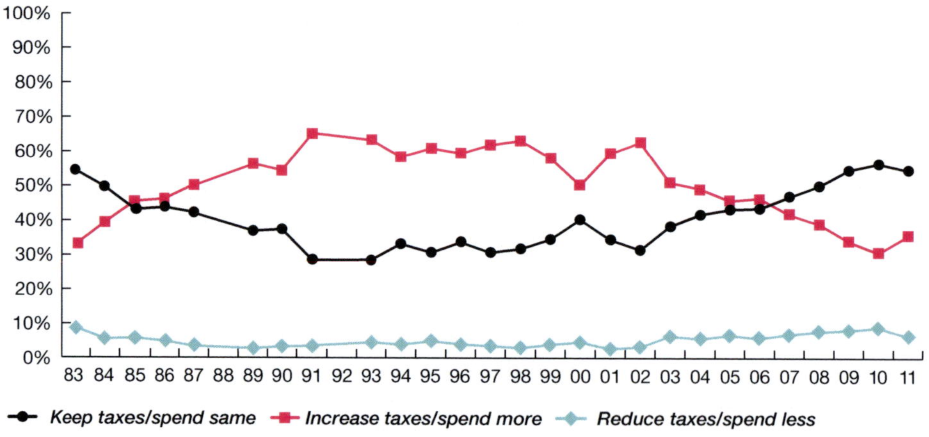

The data on which Figure 0.1 is based can be found in the appendix to this chapter

68%

choose health as their priority for more government spending

Of all Britain's public services, the NHS has a special place in the public's heart. Since the survey began, it has consistently been the most popular target for additional spending, with 68 per cent per cent choosing it in 2011 as either their first or second priority for more spending (education is the second most popular, at 61 per cent). Any possibility that the NHS might no longer be primarily a universal service free to all at the point of access meets with widespread and largely unchanging levels of opposition. As our Health chapter shows, the proportion opposing the idea of the NHS being "available only to those with lower incomes" meaning that "contributions and taxes could be lower and most people would then take out medical insurance or pay for health care" has remained consistent at around 70 per cent for more than 20 years. So when it comes to the principle of a tax-funded health service available to all, majority public opinion has remained largely unchanged.

However, the public is now showing signs of concern as to whether this principle will continue to guide the NHS in the future. When asked whether they think that "in 10 years' time the NHS will still be paid for by taxes and free to all", just under half (47 per cent) say yes while almost as many (44%) say no.

But this is not to say that the public think the NHS is perfect. Our Health chapter offers insights into a number of findings about people's views on the NHS and how it might change. We have seen satisfaction with the NHS fall for the first time in 10 years: from a high of 70 per cent in 2010 to 58 per cent now; a sign perhaps of early unease about the possible impact of funding restraint, no doubt fuelled by the recent controversy about NHS reform.

And there is an appetite for modest, though possibly not radical, change. Over half (55 per cent) believe that "a few changes" are needed to "the health care system in Britain", while another third (32 per cent) think it needs "many changes". Only small minorities (five per cent in both cases) believe either that no changes are needed or that it "needs to be completely changed".

There are signs of some support for the central plank of the coalition government's reform, a more localised system that has GPs in charge of deciding how a substantial proportion of the NHS budget should be spent. Although only a third (34 per cent) think decisions about "how money is spent on your local NHS" should be made by local GPs, even fewer (30 per cent) think that these decisions should be made by the government. The remainder opt for other forms of local decision making, by either the local council (17 per cent) or local people in general (17 per cent).

So while the public retains its support for the state funding of the NHS, there is some appetite for more localised decision making.

One British Social Attitudes finding that has attracted considerable comment over the last few years has been its identification of increased public scepticism about the benefit system and a growing concern that welfare benefits may have a counterproductive impact on their recipients. So what impact has austerity and recession had on public support for government action in this area?

On attitudes towards unemployment benefits there is little evidence of a change of mood since 2007, despite the recent recession

We would expect attitudes towards unemployment benefits to be among the most responsive to recession. Figure 0.2 shows how people have responded since 1983 when asked to choose between two statements about benefits for unemployed people: that they are "too low and cause hardship" or that they are "too high and discourage them from finding jobs". The findings show that attitudes were indeed shaped somewhat by the recession of the early 1990s, with the proportion of people thinking unemployment benefits were too low increasing from 46 per cent in 1986 to a peak of 55 per cent in 1993. But the proportion who felt this began to fall away when Labour came to power in 1997, and then continued to fall in spite of the buoyant economy of the early years of the 21st century. By 2007 the proportion feeling that unemployment benefits were too low had seemingly settled at around the 25 per cent mark. Since then there is little evidence of a change of mood, despite the recent recession; indeed our latest reading in 2011 shows that the proportion who consider unemployment benefits too low has shrunk still further (to 19 per cent). Responses to other questions, considered in our Welfare chapter, show a similar trend. So, for example, during the previous recession in 1991, 58 per cent agreed that "government should spend more on welfare benefits even if it leads to higher taxes" – over double the proportion who think this now (28 per cent in 2011).

Figure 0.2 Attitudes to unemployment benefits, 1983–2011

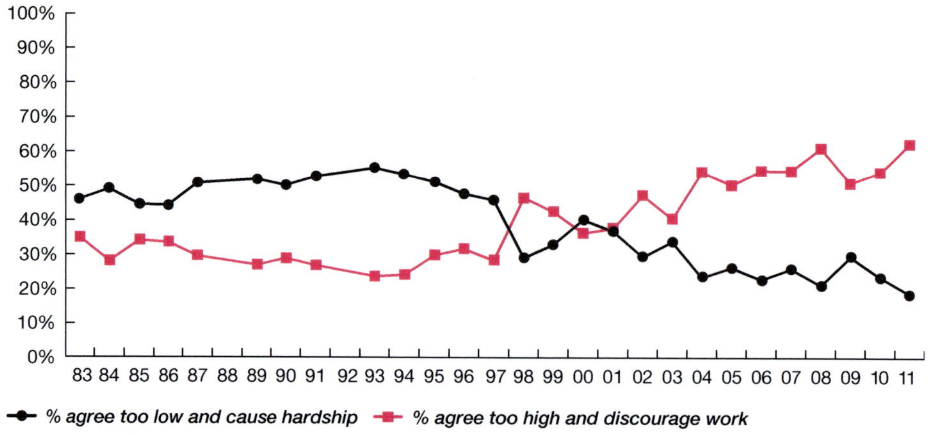

The data on which Figure 0.2 is based can be found in the appendix to this chapter

Of course some benefit recipients might be looked upon more kindly than others. The retired, for instance, are often seen to be part of a 'deserving poor' that excludes groups like single parents or the unemployed (Taylor-Gooby and Martin, 2008). Indeed the current government's attitude towards welfare appears to draw a distinction between those in retirement and others in receipt of benefits (Cameron, 2012). Table 0.1 shows how attitudes towards benefits for various groups have evolved over the last 10 years or so. It shows that people do indeed make a distinction between different groups. At one end of the spectrum there is almost universal support for increasing government spending on the benefits paid to those who care for someone who is sick or disabled (75 per cent), whereas very few people back increased spending on benefits for unemployed people (just 15 per cent). But perhaps the most striking feature of this table is the trend common to each and every group – namely that support for more spending on benefits has fallen since 1998, and in many cases quite markedly between 2008 and 2011. As we might expect from the results we have seen so far, in some cases this trend began well before the recession. So, for example, the proportion favouring more spending on benefits for disabled people who cannot work fell from 74 per cent in 1999 to 64 per cent in 2006. But it has fallen even further since then – down from 64 to 53 per cent – and the same is true for almost all the groups in the table. If anything (unlike our findings on taxation and spending), here it seems that the recession has prompted a wish to see the strings of the public purse tightened even more securely.

Table 0.1 Attitudes to government spending on different benefits, 1998–2011

% would like to see more government spending on benefits for ...	1998	1999	2002	2004	2006	2008	2011
... unemployed people	22	25	22	15	16	15	15
... disabled people who cannot work	74	74	72	65	64	63	53
... parents who work on very low incomes	70	71	71	64	68	69	58
... single parents	35	34	40	36	39	38	29
... retired people	73	71	74	74	73	73	57
... people who care for those who are sick or disabled	84	84	84	82	84	85	75
Weighted base	*3146*	*3143*	*3435*	*3199*	*3228*	*3333*	*3311*
Unweighted base	*3146*	*3143*	*3435*	*3199*	*3240*	*3258*	*3311*

37%

agree the government should redistribute income from the better-off to those who are less well-off

Britain's changing attitudes to welfare mirror another clear trend of the last two decades – a move away from a belief that government should attempt to deliver a more equal society through income redistribution. Before Labour came to power in 1997, the proportion agreeing with the view that "government should redistribute income from the better-off to those who are less well-off" consistently remained well above 40 per cent, even hovering around 50 per cent during the recession of the early 1990s. But from 1998 onwards only once has the figure been higher than 40 per cent, with 37 per cent agreeing in 2011 (Figure 0.3). While that is higher than the levels seen between 2004–2007, there's little sign here that the advent of recession – or even the public disquiet about the amounts of money paid to corporate chief executives (not least those in charge of some of Britain's banks) – has rekindled support for a more redistributive state to the levels that existed last time a Conservative Prime Minister occupied 10 Downing Street. This is also despite the fact that Labour's attempts to reduce inequality failed to reverse the large growth in inequality that occurred between the late 1970s and early 1990s (Hills et al., 2010).

Figure 0.3 Agreement that government should redistribute income, 1986–2011

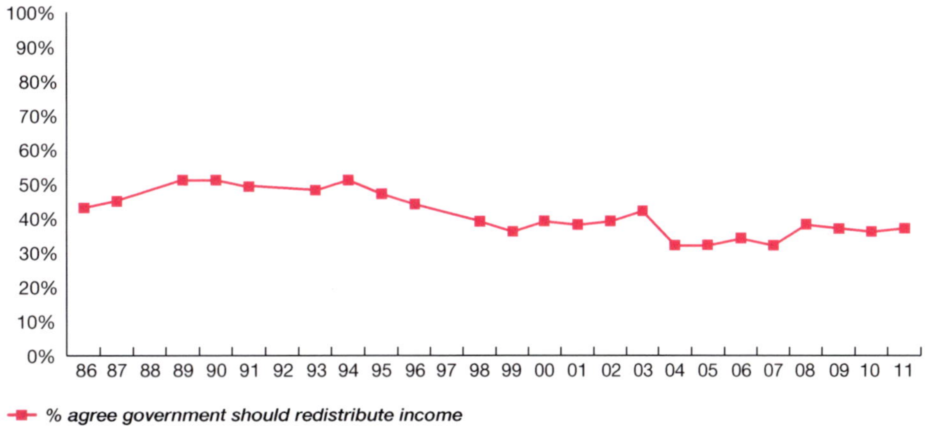

The data on which Figure 0.3 is based can be found in the appendix to this chapter

Britain clearly entered this recession less convinced than before that it was government's responsibility to alleviate inequality

Britain clearly entered this recession less convinced than before that it was government's responsibility to alleviate inequality, either through income redistribution or welfare provision.

A nation united or divided?

Earlier we wondered whether, in times of austerity, we would find evidence of growing unity, a feeling that 'we are all in it together', or instead whether there might be an increasing sense that in times of trouble people should look after their own and not expect others to help them out. On the evidence from our Welfare chapter presented earlier, it is clear that Britain entered recession far less supportive of welfare provision than it once was. This change of mood, which began under a Labour government and which recession has done little to reverse, appears to represent a fundamental long-term change that leaves Britain looking like a more individualistic society, one in which those on benefits are judged more harshly than in the past and seen as less deserving of public assistance.

In 1995, 39 per cent thought that the "number of immigrants to Britain" should reduce "a lot"; by 2011 this had risen to 51 per cent

Our Immigration chapter also helps shed light on the question of social unity or division. As an island nation with a global imperial legacy, the question of who we allow to join 'us' has a unique resonance. The chapter examines how views about migration have changed, covering a 15-year period which saw the largest inflow of migrants in British history, as well as recession and growing concern about integration among specific migrant groups. Overall, it finds an increasing desire among the public to see less immigration – in 1995, 39 per cent thought that the "number of immigrants to Britain" should reduce "a lot"; by 2011 this had risen to 51 per cent, with a further 24 per cent thinking the number should reduce "a little". It is also clear that the cultural and economic impacts of migrants on Britain are increasingly seen as negative. In 2011, 52 per cent thought "migrants coming to

Britain from other countries" were "generally bad for Britain's economy", up from 43 per cent in 2002. There was an even bigger increase in the proportion thinking that Britain's cultural life" is "generally undermined" by immigration, with 47 per cent taking this view in 2011, up from 33 per cent in 2002.

What impact has austerity had on public opinion in this area? While our data do not allow us to pinpoint precisely when these attitude shifts took place, our Immigration chapter points to one clue about the possible impact of recession on public opinion. The attitudes of different social groups towards the economic impact of immigration have become increasingly polarised over the last decade. While all groups have become more concerned, the trend has been most pronounced among those without qualifications and among less-skilled workers. While 40 per cent of people in professional occupations assess the economic impact of immigration negatively (up from 36 per cent in 2002), the same is true of 62 per cent of those in routine manual work (up from 51 per cent). A similar pattern is found for income: 39 per cent of people in the top income quartile make a negative assessment of the economic impact of immigration (unchanged since 2002), compared with 61 per cent of those in the bottom quartile (up from 47 per cent in 2002). So while economically comfortable and culturally more cosmopolitan groups show little change in their assessments of the economic impacts of immigration, economically and socially insecure groups have become dramatically more hostile.

Like our findings on welfare, this suggests a clear sense of 'them and us', in this case perhaps reflecting the dual impact of increased immigration and recession. The chapter also finds that some migrants are seen to be more easily integrated into 'us' than others – Britons are not opposed to migration across the board, but strongly favour migrants they perceive as socially beneficial and easy to integrate (for example, there is less opposition towards highly qualified professionals than there is towards unskilled labourers).

The advent of devolution in Scotland and Wales in 1999 has seen the share of public spending received by these parts of the UK come under closer scrutiny

Our Immigration chapter focuses on the boundaries of the United Kingdom and those who cross them. But of course there are other boundaries within the British Isles that are relevant to this theme of unity and division. As our Scottish independence chapter shows, the advent of devolution in Scotland and Wales in 1999 has seen the share of public spending received by these parts of the UK come under closer scrutiny. Spending per head in Scotland and Wales has long been higher than in England, a position that, it is argued by defenders of the status quo, recognises the greater needs and lower population densities of these countries (but see Holtham, 2010; McLean et al., 2008). The devolved bodies are free to determine how they will spend much of this money, a situation that has resulted in the free provision in one or more of the devolved territories of services which still have to be paid for by many people in England (university tuition and prescriptions, for example). There are clear signs that this is beginning to generate resentment in England. Before 2007 only around a quarter of people in England felt that Scotland received "more than its fair share of public spending", but in 2007 this rose to a third (32 per cent) and since 2008 has consistently been around the 40 per cent mark, standing at 44 per cent now. We cannot be sure this change has been exacerbated by the recession, but it clearly echoes earlier findings that austerity has been accompanied by decreasing support for government activity that redistributes resources from one set of citizens to another.

Families under pressure

We have already seen that, in spite of its profound consequences for people's lives, the recession has not led to increased sympathy for those who have fallen on hard times. Our Work and wellbeing chapter describes how, not surprisingly, feelings of job insecurity have become more widespread, with only around a quarter (23 per cent) saying it is "very true" that their job is secure, down from 32 per cent in 2004. This decline has been almost entirely experienced by women; in 2004 they were far more likely than men to describe their job as secure, but now there is little difference between the sexes.

1 in 5

(22%) have taken a pay cut in the last three years

Demands in the workplace have also increased somewhat. Nearly nine in ten (88 per cent) workers agree that their "job requires them to work very hard", up from 78 per cent in 2004. Meanwhile, the rewards of work have decreased; one in five (22 per cent) have taken a pay cut in the last three years, while a quarter (24 per cent) say they have "had to do less interesting work".

These trends cannot be good news for families. As well as reductions in pay and in the average number of paid working hours, more people report working unsocial hours, and there have been small but significant increases in the proportions of people saying that they worry about work when they are at home. Eight in ten (80 per cent) say they "keep worrying about work problems" when they are not working, up from 73 per cent in 2004.

British Social Attitudes has charted a huge decline over the last three decades in traditional views about gender roles (Crompton and Lyonette, 2008). This decline continues: only 10 per cent of working men and women agree that "when jobs are scarce, men should have more right to a job than women", down from 15 per cent in 2004. It is clear that the recession and its impact on households has done nothing to reinforce traditional views of men's and women's work roles, and may even have eroded them further.

Conclusions

So what's the verdict? How has the British public mood shifted in response to the most sustained recession since the 1930s? Are we seeing a renewed faith in a social democratic state, or have people lost confidence in the merits of a strong state? Is there an increasing sense of social solidarity, or are we heading in a more socially divisive and individualistic direction?

There is certainly some evidence of continued faith in the role of the state. There are initial signs of increased concern about the impact of public expenditure cuts on public services such as health and education. But these appear to be no more than a cyclical reaction to the prospect of reductions in public expenditure rather than evidence of a new public mood. It is also clear that people continue to believe in a universal and publicly-funded NHS.

Neither redistribution in general nor welfare benefits in particular are as popular as they once were

But the more striking message is a transformation in Britain's attitudes towards the creation of a more equal society, an aspiration that in part might be delivered through welfare benefits. Neither redistribution in general nor welfare benefits in particular are as popular as they once were. This is by no means a recent change and certainly predates the recession. It primarily reflects a change in public attitudes during Labour's years in power between 1997 and 2010.

These findings point towards an increased sense of 'them and us', with the most vulnerable in the labour market being viewed far less sympathetically than before, despite Britain's current economic difficulties. This sense of division is also clear in our Immigration chapter, which finds increasing concern about immigration in general, and about its economic and cultural impacts in particular. Although increased opposition to immigration predates the recession, austerity may well help explain the fact that concern about its impacts has grown the most among those who are themselves the least well-qualified or skilled. Finally, we also see evidence of geographic division, with an increasing sense of resentment in England about what is seen to be the 'unfair' share of public spending received by Scotland, something that may have been exacerbated by austerity.

Our results have clear implications for the coalition government. With less than half the Parliamentary term having passed, the number of people wanting to see more public spending is already on the increase and satisfaction with the NHS has fallen for the first time in a decade.

In contrast, there is much evidence of support for the Coalition's pledges to control welfare spending and immigration. With Ed Miliband and Labour also pledging action in both areas, these will clearly become battlegrounds in any upcoming general election, and all parties will be keen to ensure they are in tune with public concern on these key issues.

If austerity will loom large in people's memories of these times, so surely will the London 2012 Olympics. Britain's 65 medals came from across the four nations; from those educated in private schools and state schools; from those with every privilege to those brought up with multiple disadvantages. Some believe that the true legacy of the Games will be to bring Britain together once more. But for now, the 29th British Social Attitudes report tells a rather different story.

References

Cameron, D. (2012), 'Welfare speech', 25 June, London: Prime Minister's Office, available at: www.number10.gov.uk/news/welfare-speech/

Chote, R. (2010), 'Opening remarks' from Emergency Budget June 2010 Briefing, Institute for Fiscal Studies, available at: www.ifs.org.uk/budgets/budgetjune2010/chote.pdf

Crompton, R. and Lyonette, C. (2008), 'Who does the housework? The division of labour within the home', in Park, A., Curtice, J., Thomson, K., Phillips, M., Johnson, M. and Clery, E. (eds.), *British Social Attitudes: the 24th Report*, London: Sage

Hills, J., Brewer, M., Jenkins, S., Lister, R., Lupton, R., Machin, S., Mills, C., Modood, T., Rees, T. and Riddell, S. (2010), *An anatomy of economic inequality in the UK: Report of the National Equality Panel*, CASE Report 60, London: Government Equalities Office / Centre for Analysis of Social Exclusion, LSE

Holtham, G. (chmn.) (2011), *Fairness and Accountability: a new funding settlement for Wales. Final Report of the Independent Commission on Funding and Finance for Wales*, Cardiff: Independent Commission on Funding and Finance for Wales

McLean, I., Lodge, G. and Schmuecker, K. (2008), *Fair shares? Barnett and the politics of public expenditure*, London: Institute for Public Policy Research

Soroka, S. and Wlezien, C. (2005), 'Opinion-Policy Dynamics: Public Preferences and Public Expenditure in the United Kingdom', *British Journal of Political Science*, **35**: 665–89

Taylor-Gooby, P. and Martin, R. (2008), 'Trends in sympathy for the poor' in Park, A., Curtice, J., Thomson, K, Phillips, M., Johnson, M. and Clery, E. (eds.), *British Social Attitudes: the 24th Report*, London: Sage

Wlezien, C. (1995), 'The Public as Thermostat: Dynamics of Preferences for Spending', *American Journal of Political Science*, **39**: 981–1000

Appendix

The data on which Figure 0.1 is based are shown below:

Table A.1 Attitudes to taxation and spending 1983–2011

	1983	1984	1985	1986	1987	1989	1990	1991	1993
	%	%	%	%	%	%	%	%	%
Reduce taxes and spend less	9	5	6	5	3	3	3	3	4
Keep taxes and spending the same	54	50	43	44	42	37	37	29	28
Increase taxes and spend more	32	39	45	46	50	56	54	65	63
Weighted base	*1761*	*1645*	*1769*	*3066*	*2766*	*2930*	*2698*	*2836*	*2945*
Unweighted base	*1719*	*1675*	*1804*	*3100*	*2847*	*3029*	*2797*	*2918*	*2945*

	1994	1995	1996	1997	1998	1999	2000	2001	2002
	%	%	%	%	%	%	%	%	%
Reduce taxes and spend less	4	5	4	3	3	4	5	3	3
Keep taxes and spending the same	33	31	34	31	32	34	40	34	31
Increase taxes and spend more	58	61	59	62	63	58	50	59	63
Weighted base	*3469*	*3633*	*3620*	*1355*	*3146*	*3143*	*2302*	*3287*	*3435*
Unweighted base	*3469*	*3633*	*3620*	*1355*	*3146*	*3143*	*2292*	*3287*	*3435*

	2003	2004	2005	2006	2007	2008	2009	2010	2011
	%	%	%	%	%	%	%	%	%
Reduce taxes and spend less	6	6	7	6	7	8	8	9	6
Keep taxes and spending the same	38	42	43	43	47	50	55	56	55
Increase taxes and spend more	51	49	46	46	42	39	34	31	36
Weighted base	*3276*	*2130*	*2167*	*3228*	*3082*	*2184*	*1134*	*3297*	*3311*
Unweighted base	*3272*	*2146*	*2166*	*3240*	*3094*	*2229*	*1139*	*3297*	*3311*

The data on which Figure 0.2 is based are shown below:

Table A.2 Attitudes to unemployment benefits, 1983–2011

	1983	1984	1985	1986	1987	1989	1990	1991	1993
% agree too low and cause hardship	46	49	44	44	51	52	50	53	55
% agree too high and discourage work	35	28	34	33	29	27	29	27	24
Weighted base	*1761*	*1645*	*1769*	*3066*	*2766*	*2930*	*2698*	*2836*	*2945*
Unweighted base	*1719*	*1675*	*1804*	*3100*	*2847*	*3029*	*2797*	*2918*	*2945*

	1994	1995	1996	1997	1998	1999	2000	2001	2002
% agree too low and cause hardship	53	51	48	46	29	33	40	37	29
% agree too high and discourage work	24	30	32	28	46	42	36	37	47
Weighted base	*3469*	*1199*	*3620*	*1355*	*3146*	*3143*	*3426*	*3287*	*3435*
Unweighted base	*3469*	*1234*	*3620*	*1355*	*3146*	*3143*	*3426*	*3287*	*3435*

	2003	2004	2005	2006	2007	2008	2009	2010	2011
% agree too low and cause hardship	34	23	26	23	26	21	29	23	19
% agree too high and discourage work	40	54	50	54	54	61	51	54	62
Weighted base	*3272*	*3199*	*3210*	*3228*	*3082*	*3333*	*1134*	*3297*	*3311*
Unweighted base	*3276*	*3199*	*3139*	*3240*	*3094*	*3258*	*1139*	*3297*	*3311*

The data on which Figure 0.3 is based are shown below:

Table A.3 Agreement that government should redistribute income, 1986–2011

	1986	1987	1989	1990	1991	1993
% agree government should redistribute income	43	45	51	51	49	48
Weighted base	*1315*	*2424*	*2529*	*2349*	*2644*	*1327*
Unweighted base	*1321*	*2493*	*2604*	*2430*	*2702*	*1306*
	1994	**1995**	**1996**	**1998**	**1999**	**2000**
% agree government should redistribute income	51	47	44	39	36	39
Weighted base	*2957*	*3145*	*3103*	*2546*	*2478*	*2991*
Unweighted base	*2929*	*3135*	*3085*	*2531*	*2450*	*2980*
	2001	**2002**	**2003**	**2004**	**2005**	**2006**
% agree government should redistribute income	38	39	42	32	32	34
Weighted base	*2821*	*2929*	*3634*	*2610*	*3539*	*3744*
Unweighted base	*2795*	*2900*	*3621*	*2609*	*3559*	*3748*
		2007	**2008**	**2009**	**2010**	**2011**
% agree government should redistribute income		32	38	37	36	37
Weighted base		*3576*	*3963*	*2951*	*2810*	*2841*
Unweighted base		*3578*	*3990*	*2942*	*2791*	*2845*

Table and figure conventions

1. Data in the tables are from the 2011 British Social Attitudes survey unless otherwise indicated.
2. Tables are percentaged as indicated by the percentage signs.
3. In tables, '*' indicates less than 0.5 per cent but greater than zero, and '–' indicates zero.
4. When findings based on the responses of fewer than 100 respondents are reported in the text, reference is made to the small base size.
5. Percentages equal to or greater than 0.5 have been rounded up (e.g. 0.5 per cent = one per cent; 36.5 per cent = 37 per cent).
6. In many tables the proportions of respondents answering "Don't know" or not giving an answer are not shown. This, together with the effects of rounding and weighting, means that percentages will not always add to 100 per cent.
7. The self-completion questionnaire was not completed by all respondents to the main questionnaire (see Technical details). Percentage responses to the self-completion questionnaire are based on all those who completed it.
8. The bases shown in the tables (the number of respondents who answered the question) are printed in small italics. Both the weighted and unweighted bases are given.
9. In time series line charts, survey readings are indicated by data markers. While the line between data markers indicates an overall pattern, where there is no data marker the position of the line cannot be taken as an accurate reading for that year.

Contributors

David A. Alexander
Emeritus Professor of Mental Health, Former Director, Aberdeen Centre for Trauma Research, Institute for Health & Welfare Research, Robert Gordon University

John Appleby
Chief Economist at The King's Fund

Elizabeth Clery
Research Director at NatCen Social Research and Co-Director of the British Social Attitudes survey series

John Curtice
Professor of Politics at the University of Strathclyde and Research Consultant at NatCen Social Research

Christopher Dandeker
Professor of Military Sociology, Department of War Studies, and Co-Director of the King's Centre for Military Health Research (KCMHR) at King's College London

Nicola T. Fear
Reader in Military Epidemiology, and Co-Director of the King's Centre for Military Health Research (KCMHR) at King's College London

Robert Ford
Lecturer in Politics at the University of Manchester

Rachael Gribble
Research Assistant, King's Centre for Military Health Research (KCMHR) at King's College London

Anthony Heath
Professor of Sociology at the University of Manchester and Emeritus Professor of Sociology at the University of Oxford

Alun Humphrey
Senior Research Director at NatCen Social Research

Susan Klein
Professor of Trauma Research and Director, Aberdeen Centre for Trauma Research, Institute for Health & Welfare Research, Robert Gordon University

Lucy Lee
Researcher at NatCen Social Research and Co-Director of the British Social Attitudes survey series

Sally McManus
Research Director at NatCen Social Research

Gareth Morrell
Senior Research Director at NatCen Social Research

Rachel Ormston
Senior Research Director at ScotCen Social Research

Alison Park
Head of Society and Social Change at NatCen Social Research and Co-Director of the British Social Attitudes survey series

Jane Perry
Independent social researcher

Miranda Phillips
Research Director at NatCen Social Research and Co-Director of the British Social Attitudes survey series

Andrew Scott
Researcher at NatCen Social Research

Ben Seyd
Lecturer in Politics at the University of Kent

Eleanor Taylor
Researcher at NatCen Social Research and Co-Director of the British Social Attitudes survey series

David Utting
Independent writer, researcher and policy consultant

Simon Wessely
Professor of Psychological Medicine, Head of the Department of Psychological Medicine, and Director of the King's Centre for Military Health Research (KCMHR) at King's College London

Acknowledgements

British Social Attitudes could not take place without its many generous funders. A number of government departments have regularly funded modules of interest to them, while respecting the independence of the study. In 2011 we gratefully acknowledge the support of the Department for Work and Pensions and the Department for Transport. Thanks are also due to the King's Fund, the Economic and Social Research Council (ESRC), the Nuffield Foundation, Unbound Philanthropy, the Trust for London, the Joseph Rowntree Foundation, the Joseph Rowntree Charitable Trust, the Paul Hamlyn Foundation and the Diana, Princess of Wales Memorial Fund.

The Economic and Social Research Council (ESRC) continued to support the participation of Britain in the International Social Survey Programme (ISSP), a collaboration whereby surveys in over 40 countries administer an identical module of questions in order to facilitate comparative research. Some of the results are described in our Health chapter.

We are also grateful to Professor Richard Topf of London Metropolitan University for all his work in creating and maintaining access to an easy to use website that provides a fully searchable database of all the questions that have ever been carried on a British Social Attitudes survey, together with details of the pattern of responses to every question. This site provides an invaluable resource for those who want to know more than can be found in this report. It is located at www.ccesd.ac.uk/BritSocAt.

The British Social Attitudes survey is a team effort. The report editors could not do their job without the invaluable editorial support provided by the two BSA researchers, Lucy Lee and Eleanor Taylor. The survey is heavily dependent too on staff who organise and monitor fieldwork and compile and distribute the survey's extensive documentation, for which we would pay particular thanks to Sarah Allcock and her colleagues in NatCen's administrative office in Brentwood. Thanks are also due to the fieldwork controllers, area managers and field interviewers who are responsible for all the interviewing, and without whose efforts the survey would not happen at all. We are also grateful to Sandra Beeson and Sue Corbett in our computing department who expertly translate our questions into a computer assisted questionnaire, and to Roger Stafford who has the unenviable task of editing, checking and documenting the data. Many thanks are also due to BergHind Joseph who have worked with us on designing the report.

Finally, we must praise the people who anonymously gave up their time to take part in our 2011 survey. They are the cornerstone of this enterprise. We hope that some of them might come across this report and read about themselves and the story they tell of modern Britain with interest.

Welfare
Are tough times affecting attitudes to welfare?

In previous economic downturns, the public has responded with increased sympathy for welfare recipients and support for spending on welfare benefits. But as the coalition government begins to apply extensive reforms to the benefit system, is that still the case?

Role of government

Support for government's main role in providing welfare support and for increasing spending on benefits has declined markedly in the past decade.

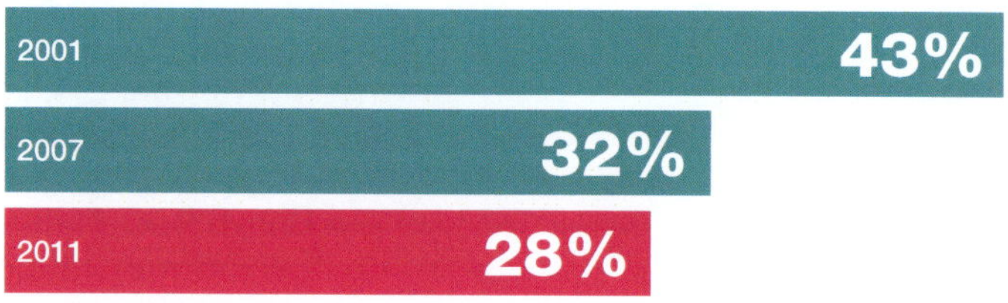

In 2001 88% agreed that government should be mainly responsible for ensuring **unemployed people** have enough to live on; 59% think this now.

In 2001 43% thought that the **government should spend more** on welfare benefits for the poor, even if it leads to higher taxes, compared to 32% in 2007 and 28% now.

Attitudes to benefit recipients

People are more sceptical about whether benefit recipients deserve the help they receive than during the last recession in the early 1990s and attitudes show little sign of softening.

In 1991, 26% agreed that, if benefits were less generous, people would stand on their own two feet. This proportion rose to 52% in 2007, before the onset of recession, and now stands at 54%.

62% agree that unemployment **benefits are too high** and discourage work, more than double the proportion who thought this in 1991 (27%) and a significantly higher proportion than said this was the case in 2007 (54%).

Author

Elizabeth Clery
Elizabeth Clery is a Research Director at NatCen Social Research and a Co-Director of the British Social Attitudes survey series

During previous times of economic difficulty, the public has tended to be more sympathetic towards benefit recipients and more supportive of increasing welfare spending

Introduction

Welfare has become a highly-charged political issue in recent years. The Welfare Reform Act, which passed into law in 2012, is routinely being described as legislating for the biggest change in the welfare system for more than 60 years. Its main elements, to be implemented over a decade, are designed to limit eligibility for a range of benefits, to incentivise employment for those able to work, and to streamline the system in ways that will achieve a sustainable long-term reduction in levels of welfare spending. There are grounds to expect the views of the public, and those of supporters of the Conservative Party in particular, to be moving in a similar direction. Certainly, an equivalent trend occurred from the late-1990s, when New Labour repositioned itself on issues such as equality and government intervention, and the views of the public in general, and the Party's supporters in particular, subsequently became less pro-welfare (Curtice, 2010). With the coalition government debating and implementing more far-reaching policies to reduce government provision of welfare in Britain, we might expect to see pro-welfare attitudes decline further.

Major reform is, however, being pursued by the coalition government at a time of double-dip recession in the economy, and the highest levels of unemployment seen for almost two decades. British Social Attitudes surveys have demonstrated that, during previous times of economic difficulty, the public has tended to be more sympathetic towards benefit recipients and more supportive of increasing welfare spending (Taylor-Gooby, 2004). Clearly a shift in opinion along those lines would place the public in increasing opposition to a major plank of the Coalition's policy platform, if it were repeated during the current economic downturn. But is that really happening? Are public attitudes to welfare adhering to the cyclical pattern observed in the 1980s and 1990s, or is this recession turning out somehow to be different? And, if so, is this a result of the public's views moving in line with the welfare agenda of the Coalition?

This chapter addresses these questions by exploring the public's views on various aspects of the welfare system. We begin by considering what people think the proper role of government should be in welfare provision and attitudes towards levels of spending on welfare. We then explore attitudes towards benefit recipients and the extent to which they are deemed to deserve help from the state. Next we examine opinions about the way the welfare system operates in practice and how it could be improved. Throughout, we consider attitudes to different types of benefits and benefit recipients, to determine whether the public adopts a holistic stance on welfare or whether attitudes are more nuanced.

Having outlined current trends in attitudes to welfare, we move on to examine whether these are occurring in all sections of the population or whether the views of particular groups are moving in quite different directions. How far do individuals' attitudes match those of the political parties with which they identify? Do those who rely on, or are more likely to rely on, benefits hold different views to those who are more economically advantaged? In addressing these questions, we aim to discover whether the British public is becoming more or less united in its aspirations and expectations for welfare, and whether unsuspected social divisions could impede the government's agenda for reform.

Setting the scene

We begin by outlining the two developments which we might expect to inform public attitudes to welfare in Britain in 2011 and beyond.

In 2011, Britain entered the first double-dip recession since 1975, having experienced the deepest recession since World War II in 2008–2009 as a result of the financial crisis. The impact of the recessions on individuals' lives and employment, examined in the chapter on Work and wellbeing, means that a larger proportion of the public might now have experience of welfare than would be the case in better economic times. This is reflected in the fact that the unemployment rate rose to 8.1 per cent (2.57 million people) in August 2011, the highest level witnessed since 1996, following the early-1990s recession, after which unemployment peaked at 10.4 per cent in 1993.[1] In such circumstances, we might logically expect attitudes towards welfare to become more sympathetic. Individuals would be more likely to recognise the need for welfare support, from media discussion or in their own neighbourhoods or workplaces, require such support themselves or know someone else who does. This expectation is endorsed by the results of British Social Attitudes surveys conducted during previous recessions in the 1980s and early-1990s (Taylor-Gooby, 2004), which have shown that attitudes to the poor and those on welfare benefits have grown more sympathetic in times of recession. Indeed, a review of public attitudes to welfare at the start of the economic crisis revealed the first signs of such a change (Curtice and Park, 2010), with attitudes to those on benefits appearing to become slightly more sympathetic.

However, developments in government policy, as mentioned earlier, might lead us to expect attitudes to welfare to move in the opposite direction. The Welfare Reform Act, which received royal assent on 8 March 2012, legislates for far-reaching changes to the benefits and tax credits system. These, over time, are intended to reduce the underlying demand for welfare support. More immediately, as set out in the March 2012 budget, the government is aiming for welfare cuts of £10 billion by 2016 (HM Treasury, 2012). The Welfare Reform Act sets out a variety of short- and longer-term strategies intended to contribute to spending reductions. Eligibility for a range of benefits is being restricted, alongside reductions in the actual levels of specific benefits being paid, while strategies have been designed to incentivise individuals to move off benefits where possible. For example, Child Benefit will be reduced for households where an individual is earning more than £50,000 and will not be available when an individual is earning more than £60,000, while Housing Benefit entitlement will be limited for social housing tenants whose accommodation is deemed larger than they need. An overall cap has also been introduced, limiting the total amount of benefits that can be claimed to no more than the average earnings of a working family. Among measures designed to make the welfare system more efficient, the introduction of a Universal Credit, from 2013, stands out. This will provide a single streamlined payment for people of working age, aimed at improving work incentives. The government is introducing a range of other changes intended to incentivise employment for those considered capable of work. Around half a million working-age people out of the two million claiming Disability Living Allowance are expected to lose their entitlement after 2013, when it is replaced by a more rigorously tested Personal Independence Payment.

There are reasons to predict that opinion has not followed the pattern of previous recessions, because the public has embraced a more tough-minded view of welfare

How might we expect these changes in policy to impact on the public's attitudes? Existing evidence from British Social Attitudes surveys shows how the supporters of particular political parties, when they have come to trust their party's standpoints, can be expected to adopt and replicate these when asked about their own views (Butler and Stokes, 1974). This tendency was especially noticeable under the 1997 to 2010 Labour government when attitudes among its supporters became markedly less pro-welfare as the party repositioned itself on issues such as equality and government intervention (Curtice, 2010). As a consequence, there are reasons to predict that opinion has not followed the pattern of previous recessions, because the public – under the long-term influence of Labour's stance as well as that of the current coalition – has embraced a more tough-minded view of welfare than it held in the past. We might also suspect that recent political and media debate about the government's welfare reforms – including claims that large numbers of welfare recipients do not really deserve their payments – will have influenced attitudes, inclining people to be less supportive of benefits and those who receive them.

To find out which of these two potential scenarios is closer to the truth – or whether the reality is rather more complex – we begin by considering how far the public endorses the role of the government as the main provider of welfare in Britain.

The role of government

Public attitudes to welfare spending are inevitably framed by people's views about the nature and extent of the government's role in providing welfare. Since the late-1990s, British Social Attitudes has asked respondents whether they think the government, employers or individuals should provide financial support for individuals in different scenarios. Specifically, we ask respondents who should mainly be responsible for …

… paying for the cost of health care when someone is ill?

… ensuring people have enough money to live on in retirement?

… ensuring that people have enough to live on if they become sick for a long time or disabled?

… ensuring people have enough to live on if they become unemployed?

Table 1.1 presents the public's views over time in relation to government responsibility for welfare. It shows how the public discriminates to a considerable degree in its response to the four scenarios. In 2010, the latest year for which data for three of the items is available, almost nine in ten thought the government should be mainly responsible for paying for the cost of health care when someone is ill, while more than eight in ten thought the same about ensuring the long-term sick or disabled have enough to live on. However, when responding to scenarios that do not involve illness or disability, the public is far less certain that government should take the lead. When it comes to ensuring that people who become unemployed have enough to live on, the proportion in 2011 saying government should mainly be responsible declines to six in ten, and, in 2010, to little more than half in the case of ensuring people have enough to live on in retirement. The fact that the public shows the least approval for the government having the main responsibility for providing welfare for those in retirement stands in direct contrast to the hierarchy set out by David Cameron in his speech of 25 June 2012 (Cameron, 2012), when he sought to reassure the public that current welfare provision for the retired would be protected, before outlining how support for the sick, disabled and unemployed would be reduced. This priority given by the Coalition to maintaining the government's role as a provider of support for the retired is clearly at odds with the views of the public.

Table 1.1 Views on government responsibility for providing welfare, 1998–2011

% agree government should be mainly responsible for …	1998	1999	2001	2003	2005	2008	2010	2011
… paying for the cost of healthcare when someone is ill	82	85	87	83	86	86	88	n/a
… ensuring that people have enough to live on if they become sick for a long time or disabled	80	83	84	83	83	84	84	n/a
… ensuring people have enough to live on if they become unemployed	85	87	88	81	n/a	n/a	n/a	59
… ensuring people have enough money to live on in retirement	56	58	62	58	56	58	52	n/a
Weighted base	*3146*	*3143*	*3287*	*3276*	*3210*	*3333*	*3297*	*3311*
Unweighted base	*3146*	*3143*	*3287*	*3272*	*3193*	*3358*	*3297*	*3311*

n/a = not asked

The distinction people make between health-related welfare and support for the unemployed or elderly has become more pronounced

Looking back over time, it is also clear that the distinction people make between health-related welfare and support for the unemployed or elderly has become more pronounced. The relatively high proportions who say government should be mainly responsible for providing welfare when someone is ill or disabled have fluctuated only slightly since the late-1990s. However, the proportion thinking the government should be responsible for providing an adequate retirement income now stands 10 percentage points below its highest point, which was reached in 2001. Agreement that the government should be mainly responsible for ensuring unemployed people have enough to live on has fallen even more sharply – from just over eight in ten in 2003, to less than six in ten now. (Because of the absence of data for the intervening period, we cannot be sure whether endorsement of the government's role declined steadily across the eight years, or whether this change occurred within a more narrowly-defined period.)

If an increasing number of people are disinclined to think that government should take the lead in providing welfare for those who are unemployed or retired, whose responsibility do they think it should be? Replies to our question suggest that the proportions thinking that employers or individuals themselves or their families should be responsible for ensuring sufficient retirement income have increased somewhat over time. More than one in three (35 per cent) say individuals and families should take the main responsibility, while around one in ten (11 per cent) point towards the person's employer. More strikingly, when it comes to support for the unemployed, one in three (33 per cent) think the individual or their family should mainly be responsible, compared with one in ten (10 per cent) who thought this in 1998.

Although these questions were not asked during previous times of recession, we might have expected a greater endorsement for government's role in providing welfare in 2010 and 2011, compared with previous years, given that the need for such support would be more apparent in difficult economic circumstances. Conversely, our findings suggest a growing minority view that it is not the state's role to ensure the unemployed have an adequate income; however, we need to investigate further before interpreting this as a particular endorsement of the government's welfare reforms. The public, after all, remains strong in its view that government should provide for the long-term sick and disabled, whose benefits are also being reassessed. So, having established that the public differentiates between different types of welfare support and its recipients, we next consider how far these distinctions are reflected in attitudes towards government spending on welfare.

Welfare spending

Attitudes to government spending on benefits do not operate within a vacuum. They are likely to be informed by attitudes to government spending and taxation in general, which, rather than remaining static, have been shown to be influenced by comparisons of what the government is perceived currently to be spending with the respondent's 'ideal' level of spending (Wlezien, 1995; Soroka and Wlezien, 2005). Attitudes to spending on welfare may also be influenced by the public's understanding of the current levels of individual benefits and the extent to which these are perceived to be adequate; previous analyses have demonstrated that individuals hold varied and often inaccurate understandings of the value of individual benefits, and express quite different views about their adequacy when asked about the real levels of benefit payments (Hills, 2001). The extent to which the public prioritises spending on welfare will also inevitably be influenced by the priority they ascribe to other areas of government spending. Moreover, an individual might have different attitudes to spending on different types of welfare benefits; as we have seen, there is a far greater endorsement of the government's role as a provider of welfare for the sick and disabled, compared to those who are retired or unemployed, and this might link with greater support for government spending on benefits for these groups.

To start examining people's views in this context, we first look at attitudes to government taxation and spending in general. Since 1983, British Social Attitudes has invited respondents to say which of three options the government should choose:

Reduce taxes and spend less on health, education and social benefits

Keep taxes and spending on these services at the same level as now

Increase taxes and spend more on health, education and social benefits

The responses provided over time are presented in Figure 1.1. This shows that the proportion thinking the government should increase taxes and spend more on health, education and social benefits has declined steadily between 2002 and 2010. Rather than interpret this trend as crude evidence that the public is disenchanted with public spending in those areas, previous reports have emphasised the likelihood that additional spending will appear less necessary in times when public expenditure is known to be increasing rapidly – as it was under the last Labour government, especially on health and education (Curtice, 2010). However, to this we might add that when the government – as now with the Coalition – is embarked on a much-heralded attempt to reduce its budget deficit by cutting overall spending, that too might be expected to convince people that extra spending is either undesirable or just not possible. Certainly in 2010 just three in ten respondents recommended an increase in taxation and spending, which was only half the proportion who did so as recently as 2002. However, we can see in Figure 1.1 that this historical trend may now be reversing, as the proportion who recommend higher taxes and spending has increased by five percentage points in the latest survey, with a comparable decrease in the percentage advocating less taxation and spending. It is too early to lay claim to a new trend, but it is just possible that this shift marks the start of a reaction against the Coalition's spending cuts and a growing acceptance of the claims repeatedly made by Labour that the government has been cutting 'too far and too fast'. However, Figure 1.1 also shows us that currently the most popular option among the three identified in our question is that of keeping taxes and spending on health, education and welfare benefits at the same level as now.

In 2010 just three in ten respondents recommended an increase in taxation and spending; only half the proportion who did so in 2002

Figure 1.1 Attitudes to taxation and spending, 1983–2011

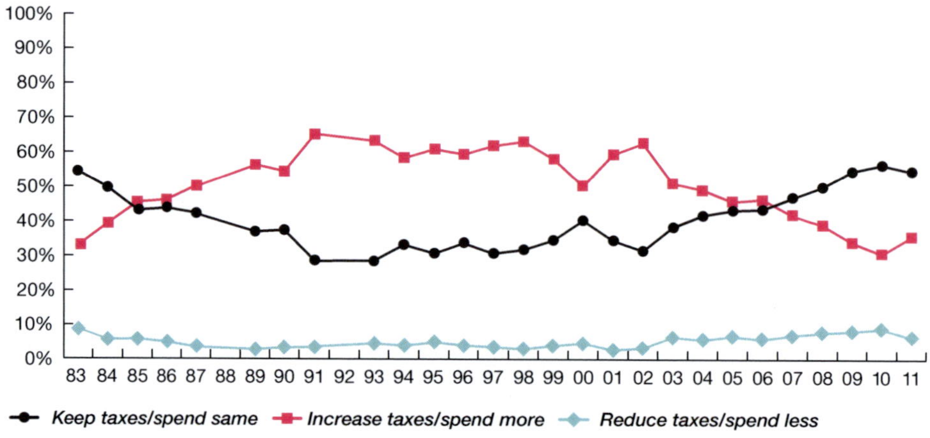

The data on which Figure 1.1 is based can be found in the appendix to this chapter

While it is evident that the majority do not currently favour tax rises and spending increases across the three specified areas, it is useful to know which of the three – health, education or social benefits – is considered the greatest priority by the public. To explore this issue, we can examine responses over time to a question that invites people to identify their top two preferences for (hypothetical) extra government spending. The answers (reported more fully in the chapter on Health) show that, over almost 30 years, people's preferences have remained fairly stable, with health and education consistently identified as the top two priorities by more than half the population. "Social security benefits" not only receives a lower priority but, having been a top choice for 12 per cent of respondents in 1983, in the wake of the early-1980s recession, it is now prioritised by just four per cent.

Another, more specific question routinely asks respondents whether they agree or disagree that:

> ***The government should spend more money on welfare benefits for the poor, even if it leads to higher taxes***[2]

The latest responses suggest that the public is divided on this issue, but with a slight bias towards reducing current benefit spending levels. Almost three in ten (28 per cent) think the government should spend more, while four in ten (39 per cent) disagree with the idea. More than one in three (32 per cent) neither agree nor disagree – demonstrating that it is certainly not the case that most people have a clear view on this issue. In Figure 1.2 we show how the proportion agreeing that the government should spend more on welfare benefits has altered over time, plotted alongside the proportion, discussed previously, who think the government should increase taxes and spend more. For much of the last 25 years, support for these two viewpoints has tended to move in tandem. We also see that levels of support in both cases have declined over most of the last decade, but that the public has generally been more accepting of the case for increased taxation and spending on "health, education and social benefits" in general, than on spending more on "welfare benefits" in particular. It is also interesting that although support for a more general increase in taxation and spending grew a little in the latest survey, support for spending more on welfare benefits did not. Instead, support for extra spending on benefits has gone on declining through the first recent period of negative growth in 2008–2009 and on to the second recessionary 'dip', and remains at an historically low ebb.

Figure 1.2 Attitudes to government spending on welfare benefits and taxation and spending in general, 1987–2011

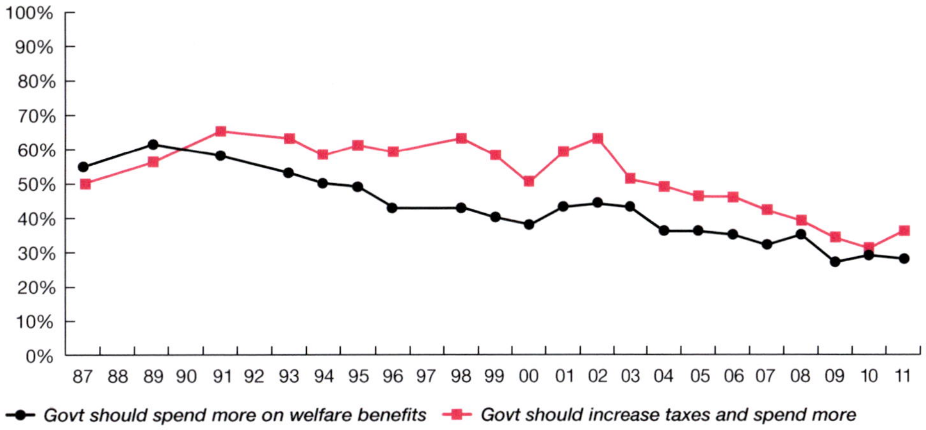

The data on which Figure 1.2 is based can be found in the appendix to this chapter

The next issue we will try to resolve is whether, within the overall welfare budget, there are any particular types of benefit that the public is more prepared to support with extra spending than others. We asked people to say if they would like to see more spending on:

Benefits for unemployed people

Benefits for disabled people who cannot work

Benefits for parents who work on very low incomes

Benefits for single parents

Benefits for retired people

Benefits for people who care for those who are sick and disabled

Their responses and those obtained in previous years are presented in Table 1.2. This shows that public support for extra spending on all types of welfare benefit has declined since the late-1990s – with, in many cases, much of this decline being very recent. Most markedly, support for extra spending on benefits for disabled people who cannot work has fallen by 21 percentage points since 1998 and by 10 percentage points in the last three years. This is perhaps another reflection of the emphasis that Labour, when in government, as well as the Coalition, have placed on reducing the cost of long-term disability benefits, with public announcements that claims have grown faster than any likely increase in the incidence of illness and disability. People's changing views may, therefore, reflect a belief that people are being incorrectly classed as disabled or unable to work, rather than any 'hardline' view that disabled people do not deserve to be helped. Earlier we saw a record level of support for the view that government should be the main provider of welfare for the long-term sick and disabled, something that would seem to support this interpretation.

Support for extra spending on benefits for disabled people who cannot work has fallen by 21 percentage points since 1998

We can also see that support for extra spending on benefits for retired people has fallen markedly over time: by 16 percentage points since 1998. This could be symptomatic of an increasing view, noted previously, that government should not necessarily take the main responsibility for providing financial support for older people in retirement. Public attitudes towards benefits for unemployed people also stand out: partly because there is less support for extra spending here than in other areas – but also because, unlike the other categories, such support as exists has remained broadly level since 2004 at around 15 per cent. Much of the decline in support for extra spending on the other types of benefits has occurred since 2008 when these questions were last fielded. Even in the case of added benefits for those caring for sick and disabled people – consistently the most popular category – there has been a 10 percentage point decline in support since 2008 to 75 per cent.

Table 1.2 Attitudes to government spending on different benefits, 1998–2011

% would like to see more government spending on benefits for ...	1998	1999	2002	2004	2006	2008	2011
... unemployed people	22	25	22	15	16	15	15
... disabled people who cannot work	74	74	72	65	64	63	53
... parents who work on very low incomes	70	71	71	64	68	69	58
... single parents	35	34	40	36	39	38	29
... retired people	73	71	74	74	73	73	57
... people who care for those who are sick or disabled	84	84	84	82	84	85	75
Weighted base	*3146*	*3143*	*3435*	*3199*	*3228*	*3333*	*3311*
Unweighted base	*3146*	*3143*	*3435*	*3199*	*3240*	*3258*	*3311*

The survey evidence reviewed so far does seem to suggest that the current government's policies to reduce spending on benefits and restrict eligibility are either having some impact on public attitudes towards welfare, or – as an overlapping possibility – being driven by them. We have also seen that the prolonged economic downturn has, so far at least, done little to negate this. It is particularly striking that support for extra spending on unemployment benefits remains remarkably low, despite unemployment having reached its highest level since our question was first asked in 1998.

To further understand people's attitudes to the level of unemployment benefits, we asked respondents which of the following statements comes closest to their view:

> *Benefits for unemployed people are too low and cause hardship, or*
>
> *Benefits for unemployed people are too high and discourage them from finding jobs?*

Unemployment stands at its highest point in 15 years, yet this appears to have made no obvious dent on the view that unemployment benefits are too high

Figure 1.3 presents responses over time, alongside the proportion of the UK workforce who were unemployed when each reading was taken. Responses to this question have shifted dramatically over time. Following the recession of the early-1980s, when unemployment stood at 11 per cent, a minority of just over one in three (35 per cent) took the view that benefits for unemployed people were too high and discouraged them from finding jobs. By the early-1990s recession, the proportion expressing this view had declined to a quarter (24 per cent in 1993 – when unemployment stood at more than 10 per cent). But adherence to this view then rose steadily from the late-1990s, to a point where almost two-thirds (62 per cent) of the public takes this view today. Despite some fluctuations, it also appears that the current, prolonged economic downturn has had little discernible impact; unemployment stands at its highest point in 15 years, yet this appears to have made no obvious dent on the view that unemployment benefits are too high. This is not at all the trend we would have expected based on experience of the previous recession. Yet once again we see that public opinion is broadly in line with government policies to restrict welfare.

Figure 1.3 Attitudes to unemployment benefits by unemployment rate, 1983–2011

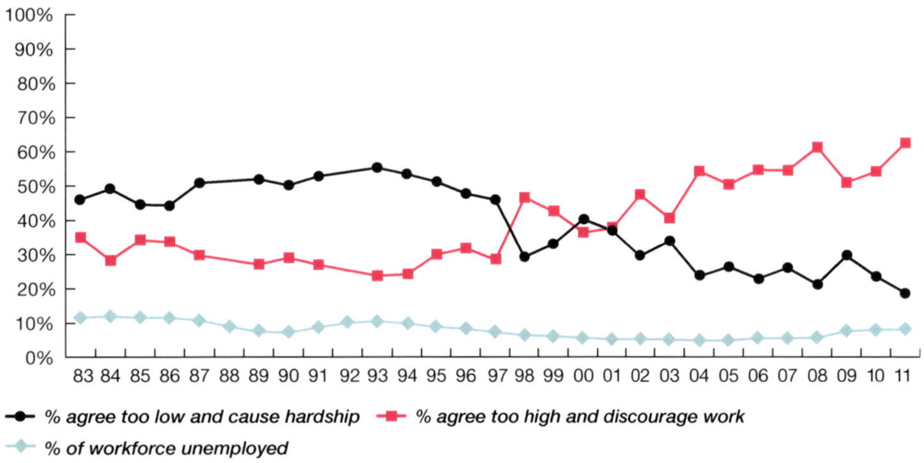

The data on which Figure 1.3 is based can be found in the appendix to this chapter
Source for unemployment data: International Monetary Fund's World Economic Outlook Database, April 2012

The picture we have painted so far is one of a sharp decline in public enthusiasm for increased spending on welfare benefits over the past decade. But is this a reflection of the wider antipathy towards public spending increases noted previously, or is it linked to particular views the public holds about the people receiving benefits and their entitlements? We turn next to consider this possibility.

Attitudes to benefit recipients

Respondents to British Social Attitudes are regularly asked whether they agree or disagree with the following three items, which measure the extent to which benefit recipients are seen as 'deserving' of government support:

> *Many people who get social security don't really deserve any help*
>
> *Around here, most unemployed people could find a job if they really wanted one*
>
> *Most people on the dole are fiddling in one way or another*

37%

of the public believe that most people on the dole are "fiddling"

Looking at the results obtained between 1987 and 2011 for the first two measures, we see that a considerable section of the public clearly do view welfare recipients, and people receiving unemployment benefits in particular, as undeserving. More than a third (35 per cent) currently think that many getting social security "don't really deserve any help" – while the proportion has fluctuated between just above 20 per cent and 40 per cent over time. However, the most pervasive negative view is that "around here, most unemployed people could find a job if they wanted one". Support for this proposition was at its lowest around the time of the early-1990s recession, but rose steadily during much of Labour's time in office until around the start of the current economic downturn. The level of agreement has dropped since then from seven in ten to under six in ten (while only two in ten disagree). Yet this may still be considered a strikingly high level of scepticism given the growth in unemployment. A perception that most people on the dole are "fiddling" is also quite widespread and has more or less tracked the proportion who believe that many people receiving social security "don't really deserve any help"; in 2011, 37 per cent of the public believes that most people on the dole are "fiddling".

Figure 1.4 Attitudes to welfare recipients, 1987–2011

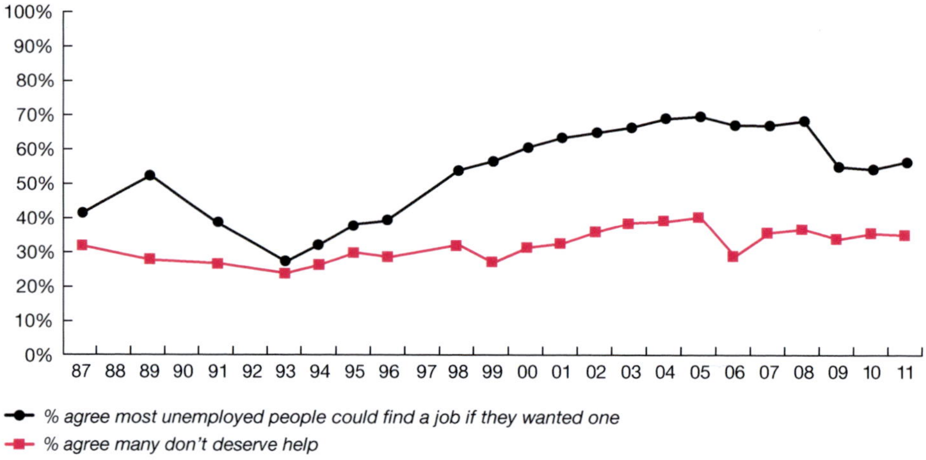

The data on which Figure 1.4 is based can be found in the appendix to this chapter

Negative perceptions of welfare recipients are a pretty constant strand in British public opinion

It would be tempting to conclude from this that declining support for the government's role as a main provider of welfare, and for extra spending on benefits, is a direct consequence of the public's view that many social security recipients are undeserving. However, we have seen how negative perceptions of welfare recipients are a pretty constant strand in British public opinion – and also that, while they are more common than we might have expected in a recession, they have dipped below their peak levels. Could it be that the relatively low support for extra spending on benefits during the current recession reflects popular objections to the concept of welfare and the welfare state itself, as much as a view of benefit recipients as undeserving? This is the issue we next consider.

Attitudes to the welfare state

To find out if attitudes to the welfare state are becoming less supportive we invited people to agree or disagree with these four statements:

> *If welfare benefits weren't so generous, people would learn to stand on their own two feet*
>
> *The welfare state encourages people to stop helping each other*
>
> *Cutting welfare benefits would damage too many people's lives*
>
> *The creation of the welfare state is one of Britain's proudest achievements*

Figure 1.5 presents the proportions of the public, over time, who express a negative view of the welfare state based on these questions. It shows quite clearly that only a little more than one in ten people disagree that the creation of the welfare state is "one of Britain's proudest achievements" (if our chart presented the proportions taking a 'positive' view, it would show that 51 per cent agree with the statement). However, markedly larger proportions agree with the suggestions that welfare encourages dependence and discourages other forms of help. Slightly more than half (54 per cent) believe that people would "stand on their own two feet" if benefits were less generous, while only 20 per cent disagree. This is the reverse of the situation in 1993, when only 25 per cent agreed and 52 per cent disagreed with the statement. It consequently provides a strong indication that this change in perceptions could be an important contributing factor to the public's current lack of support for spending more on welfare benefits. We see that most of the increase occurred during Labour's long period in government. But the view now shared by half the population – that current welfare benefits encourage dependence – clearly also chimes with the rationale claimed by the Coalition for its welfare reforms. The onset of recession and higher unemployment do not appear to have dampened this view.

Figure 1.5 Attitudes to the welfare state, 1983-2011

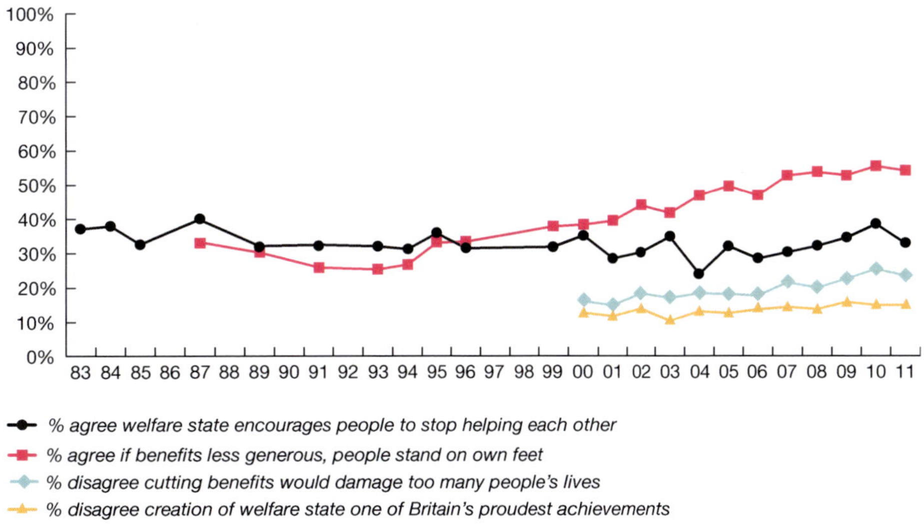

The data on which Figure 1.5 is based can be found in the appendix to this chapter

1 in 3

people agree that the welfare state encourages people "to stop helping each other"

Less strikingly, we see that one in three people (33 per cent) agree that the welfare state encourages people "to stop helping each other" – a proportion broadly in the mid-range of fluctuating levels since 1983. By contrast, although only one in five (23 per cent) nowadays take issue with the view that cutting benefits would "ruin too many people's lives", the proportion is higher than when the question was first asked in 2001 and at any point since, with the exception of 2010. We should, therefore, note that it is the two statements here that ask about "welfare benefits" rather than the "welfare state" that have seen an increase in negative sentiments over time. This may reflect the fact that "welfare state" is often taken to include health and education which – as we have seen – are viewed as greater spending priorities by the public than welfare benefits.

To tap further into people's views about the effectiveness and efficiency of the current benefit system, we also included a number of new questions in the latest British Social Attitudes survey inviting people to agree or disagree that it …

… supports people in low-paid work

… targets benefits only at those who really need them

… is far too complicated

… is slow to respond to changes in circumstances

… effectively encourages recipients to move off benefits

Table 1.3 details the responses obtained, together with an overall assessment for each measure (calculated by subtracting the percentage taking a negative view from those with a positive view and indicating whether the public generally views the welfare system positively or negatively in relation to each issue). Clearly, on most issues, the public's views tend to be negative. A notable exception is the agreement of slightly more than half with the statement that the benefits system "supports people in low-paid work". However, less than a quarter agree that it "targets benefits only at those who really need them", while more than a third disagree. This accords with our earlier finding that a significant minority of the population consider many benefit recipients to be undeserving. Moreover, four in ten people agree that the benefit system is "far too complicated" and that it is "slow to respond to changes in circumstances". More than a third disagree that it is effective in encouraging recipients to move off benefits. Meanwhile, fewer than one in ten give a positive response to any of these three questions.

Table 1.3 Attitudes to the welfare system

Attitudes to the current benefits systems (positive view)		Positive view	Neutral view	Negative view	Overall assess -ment*	*Weighted base*	*Un-weighted base*
It supports people in low-paid work (agree)	%	53	19	13	40	*2841*	*2845*
It targets benefits only at those who really need them (agree)	%	23	21	35	-12	*2841*	*2845*
It is far too complicated (disagree)	%	8	26	39	-31	*2841*	*2845*
It is slow to respond to changes in circumstances (disagree)	%	5	26	43	-38	*2841*	*2845*
It effectively encourages recipients to move off benefits (agree)	%	9	19	36	-27	*2841*	*2845*

**(positive view - negative view)*

It seems the welfare system is widely viewed as inefficient and poorly targeted – both in terms of who receives support and in terms of its ability to prevent long-term dependency. Since these perceptions are broadly in line with the presumptions underpinning the government's Welfare Reform Act, it seems likely that its implementation will, if attitudes persist, enjoy considerable public support.

Further evidence for this impression can be found in the responses to a question asked in the 2010 survey, inviting people to identify their two highest priorities for government to improve the benefits system. In Table 1.4 we see that targeting benefits "only at those who really need them" is the most popular option, picked by one in three respondents as their highest priority and placed among the top two priorities by more than half. We can also see that "providing benefits for those who cannot work" receives a considerably lower priority rating than "rewarding those who work or look for work", "making sure those who are entitled to money claim it", "reducing fraud" or "making sure those who save are not penalised". On this basis, we may reasonably speculate that the tendency in recent years for politicians of all parties to emphasise their support for 'hard-working families' during welfare debates has reflected or influenced the public's view.

Table 1.4 Priorities for improving the benefits system, 2010

Priorities for improving the benefits system	Highest priority	First or second highest priority
	%	%
Targeting benefits only at those who really need them	33	53
Rewarding those who work or look for work	18	37
Making sure those who are entitled to money claim it	14	26
Reducing fraud	13	32
Making sure those who save are not penalised	12	26
Providing benefits for those who cannot work	6	14
Making sure payments are fast and accurate	3	7
Weighted base	*3297*	
Unweighted base	*3297*	

Having found yet more evidence that public attitudes to welfare (and to unemployment benefits in particular) are closer to the thrust of government reforms than might have been expected during a recession, it remains to be considered whether these views are shared by all groups in society, or only some.

How do views vary and whose views have changed?

To assess whether the public is moving towards a shared consensus on welfare or becoming more divided in its views, we focus on three of the measures where we have already identified a striking change in attitudes in recent years. These are:

- whether the government should be mainly responsible for providing welfare support for those who become unemployed;
- whether unemployment benefits are too high and discourage work;
- whether, if benefits were less generous, people would "stand on their own two feet".

Those who are socio-economically more advantaged are least likely to endorse the government's role as the main provider of welfare

The fall in the proportion of the population who think the government should be mainly responsible for providing support for the unemployed is one of the most dramatic changes we have observed, from around eight people in ten in 2003 to under six in ten now. However, by re-analysing the results to examine the views held by different social groups we find this is not an opinion held equally strongly by all sections of society and that the decline in support has not affected all groups to a similar extent. It is immediately apparent from Table 1.5 that those who are socio-economically more advantaged – who would tend to depend least on government support if they became unemployed – are least likely to endorse the government's role as the main provider of welfare. Thus, little more than half of respondents in a professional occupational group agree that the government should have the main role in providing support for the unemployed, compared with two in three of those in a routine occupational group. (On a similar note, 70 per cent of those in the lowest quartile of household incomes in 2011 think the government should mainly be responsible, compared with just 49 per cent of those in the highest income quartile). Less marked differences, though still significant, can be found between people who receive state benefits themselves or whose spouses do so, and non-recipients, with the latter group being less likely to favour the government being the main provider of support for the unemployed. Political affiliations also make a difference. While only half of those who identify with the Conservative Party agree that the government should be the main provider of welfare for the unemployed, the same is true of two-thirds of those who identify with Labour.

No less interestingly, Table 1.5 shows us that public opinion has become more divided on this issue in recent years. In 2003 something approaching a consensus existed across occupational groups and among supporters of the main political parties. For instance, around eight in ten supporters of the Conservatives, Labour and the Liberal Democrats agreed that providing support for the unemployed was mainly a job for government. Overall support for that proposition has fallen by 22 percentage points. However, it has fallen almost twice as steeply among people in professional or intermediate occupational groups, compared with those in routine occupations. And among Conservative supporters, it is down by 29 percentage points, compared with 17 percentage points among those who identify with Labour.

Table 1.5 Agreement that government should be the main provider of support to the unemployed, by demographic characteristics, 2003 and 2011[3]

% agree government should be main provider of support to the unemployed	2003	2011	Change since 2003
Party affiliation			
Conservative	80	51	-29
Labour	83	66	-17
Liberal Democrat	82	56	-26
Occupational class			
Professional	81	53	-27
Intermediate	82	57	-24
Routine	81	67	-14
Receipt of benefits			
Respondent or spouse in receipt of benefits	82	62	-20
Neither in receipt of benefits	79	55	-25
All	81	59	-22

As the question considered previously was not asked between 2003 and 2011, it is not possible to determine whether the views of different groups became more divided with the onset of recession or whether these differences developed in earlier years. However, such analysis is possible for the next two items we consider.

Turning to opinions about whether unemployment benefits are too high and discourage work, Table 1.6 shows that in 2003 around four in ten people in most sectors of society adhered to this view, with those affiliating with the Conservative Party being substantially more likely to do so. While this difference by party identification persists in 2011, the views of groups defined by occupational class and benefit receipt also appear to have become more divided. As in the previous analysis, we see that a negative view of welfare has grown fastest among people in higher occupational groups and among those not in receipt of any state benefits. The proportion of people in receipt of benefits who agree that unemployment benefits are too high and discourage work increased by 19 percentage points between 2003 and 2011, among those not in receipt of such benefits it increased by 27 percentage points. More markedly, between 2007 and 2011, a period marked by the onset of recession, the belief that unemployment benefits are too high and discourage work increased more than three times as much among those not in receipt of any state benefits as among those receiving them. And, among occupational groups, negative views have risen most among those in professional occupations and least among those in routine occupations – though there is little evidence of greater differentiation in views following the onset of recession.

Table 1.6 Agreement unemployment benefits are too high and discourage work, by demographic characteristics, 2003, 2007 and 2011[4]

% agree unemployment benefits are too high and discourage work	2003	2007	2011	Change since 2003	Change since 2007
Party affiliation					
Conservative	56	67	77	+21	+10
Labour	36	49	55	+19	+6
Liberal Democrat	36	51	55	+20	+5
Occupational class					
Professional	40	55	65	+25	+10
Intermediate	44	57	66	+23	+9
Routine	38	50	58	+20	+8
Receipt of benefits					
Respondent or spouse in receipt of benefits	40	55	59	+19	+4
Neither in receipt of benefits	41	54	68	+27	+14
All	40	54	62	+22	+8

When we look at the way different social groups have responded over time to the proposition that less generous benefits would encourage people to "stand on their own two feet", similar trends are evident. As shown in Table 1.7, there was no great consensus between Conservative and Labour supporters in 2003, but support for this view increased by comparable proportions in each of the two groups between 2003 and 2007, and between 2007 and today. However, for groups defined by socio-economic characteristics we see that the level of agreement has increased by markedly different degrees. Again, we can see a possible impact of the recession among those in a routine occupational group; their agreement with the idea people would "stand on their own two feet" if benefits were less generous has declined by three percentage points since 2007 – while agreement among those in a professional occupational group has risen by a similar amount. And, as before, while agreement has risen across society, regardless of benefit receipt, the rise has been greatest among those not in receipt of any benefits.

Table 1.7 Agreement with view that if benefits were less generous, people would stand on their own two feet, by demographic characteristics, 2003, 2007 and 2011[5]

% agree if benefits were less generous, people would stand on their own two feet	2003	2007	2011	Change 2003-2007	Change since 2007	Change 2003-2011
Party affiliation						
Conservative	56	67	69	+11	+2	+13
Labour	36	46	48	+10	+2	+12
Liberal Democrat	27	42	40	+15	-2	+13
Occupational class						
Professional	37	49	54	+12	+4	+16
Intermediate	47	59	59	+12	-1	+12
Routine	44	57	54	+12	-3	+9
Receipt of benefits						
Respondent or spouse in receipt of benefits	43	53	53	+10	+0	+10
Neither in receipt of benefits	42	55	58	+13	+3	+15
All	43	54	55	+11	+1	+12

The increase in negative attitudes towards welfare during the past decade affected certain groups more than others

Clearly, the increase in negative attitudes towards welfare during the past decade, while occurring in all sections of society, has affected certain groups more than others. While supporters of the main political parties are no more divided in their attitudes to welfare than they were a decade ago, the same is not true of groups defined by occupational class and benefit receipt. The growth of anti-welfare views among the least advantaged groups and those likely to rely most on benefits has been slower than among more advantaged groups, and there is some evidence that the speed of change has slowed, stopped or reversed since the onset of recession. Equally clearly, the support we have seen for elements and assumptions of the Coalition's reform programme is not simply about party politics; on two out of three measures, we have seen negative views about benefits increase among Labour and Conservative supporters at a similar rate. So, while the direction of government policy goes some way to explaining movement in attitudes to welfare among the public as a whole, the recession does also appear to have had its expected impact – but only for those groups in society most likely to need to rely upon the welfare state as a result.

Conclusions

In recent years public attitudes to welfare in Britain have appeared to stand at a crossroads. On the one hand, looking at the direction taken by policies under successive governments – both Labour and the Coalition – we might expect opinion to be growing less sympathetic to benefit recipients and less supportive of the government's continued role in funding welfare. On the other, acknowledging the prolonged economic crisis and trends during previous recessions, we might expect attitudes to have grown more sympathetic to welfare and benefit recipients as unemployment increased.

What our data clearly show is that, while attitudes to different aspects of welfare are behaving in a far from uniform way, they are generally moving in line with the current direction of government policy, rather than responding as they have previously to the onset of recession. We see that the public is becoming less supportive of the government taking a leading role in providing welfare to the unemployed, and even to the elderly in retirement. There is less enthusiasm about public spending on all types of benefits and an increasing belief that the welfare system encourages dependence.

As the economic crisis continues to run its course, we may yet see a polarisation of opinion that places real obstacles in the way of government

We have argued that this shift of opinion was nurtured by a tougher stance towards welfare under the previous Labour government. It can also be read as evidence that the coalition government's radical Welfare Reform Act is in tune with public opinion, chiming as it does with so many changing attitudes and assumptions. However, we have also seen how public attitudes to welfare are not moving in the same direction or at the same rate in all demographic groups. Indeed, the fact that these divisions run along socio-economic lines should strike a warning note. Advantaged groups who seem best-placed to weather the recession, and are least likely to rely on welfare if they do fall on hard times, are becoming markedly less supportive of welfare in principle and in practice. So while public opinion overall is moving in the same direction as the current welfare reforms and their underpinning assumptions, there is by no means a consensus – with views on some issues being more divided than they were a decade ago. As the economic crisis continues to run its course, we may yet see a polarisation of opinion that places real obstacles in the way of government, as it pursues the prolonged task of implementing its reforms.

Notes

1. Data on the percentages of the UK labour force who were unemployed, using the harmonised ILO definition, were accessed using the International Monetary Fund's World Economic Outlook Database, April 2012, available at: www.imf.org/external/pubs/ft/weo/2012/01/weodata/index.aspx

2. This question is one of eight items that contribute to the British Social Attitudes 'welfarism' scale, used to derive an overall measure of support for welfare. Further details about the welfare scale can be found in Technical details.

3. Bases for Table 1.5 are as follows:

	2003		2011	
	Weighted base	*Unweighted base*	*Weighted base*	*Unweighted base*
Party affiliation				
Conservative	*814*	*806*	*881*	*926*
Labour	*1200*	*1203*	*1062*	*1039*
Liberal Democrat	*365*	*368*	*247*	*253*
Occupational class				
Professional	*1115*	*1093*	*1155*	*1177*
Intermediate	*1066*	*1062*	*1014*	*1028*
Routine	*985*	*1012*	*963*	*955*
Receipt of benefits				
Respondent or spouse in receipt of benefits	*1968*	*2122*	*1954*	*2128*
Neither in receipt of benefits	*1283*	*1126*	*1315*	*1140*
All	*3276*	*3272*	*3311*	*3311*

4. Bases for Table 1.6 are as follows:

	2003		2007		2011	
	Weighted base	*Unweighted base*	*Weighted base*	*Unweighted base*	*Weighted base*	*Unweighted base*
Party affiliation						
Conservative	*814*	*806*	*773*	*819*	*881*	*926*
Labour	*1200*	*1203*	*1052*	*1058*	*1062*	*1039*
Liberal Democrat	*365*	*368*	*282*	*293*	*247*	*253*
Occupational class						
Professional	*1115*	*1093*	*1101*	*1120*	*1155*	*1177*
Intermediate	*1066*	*1062*	*1007*	*1001*	*1014*	*1028*
Routine	*985*	*1012*	*866*	*881*	*963*	*955*
Receipt of benefits						
Respondent or spouse in receipt of benefits	*1968*	*2122*	*1860*	*2043*	*1954*	*2128*
Neither in receipt of benefits	*1283*	*1126*	*1212*	*1040*	*1315*	*1140*
All	*3276*	*3272*	*3082*	*3094*	*3311*	*3311*

5. Bases for Table 1.7 are as follows:

	2003		2007		2011	
	Weighted base	*Unweighted base*	*Weighted base*	*Unweighted base*	*Weighted base*	*Unweighted base*
Party affiliation						
Conservative	*230*	*223*	*678*	*720*	*773*	*811*
Labour	*320*	*309*	*886*	*882*	*873*	*860*
Liberal Democrat	*96*	*99*	*237*	*251*	*223*	*226*
Occupational class						
Professional	*318*	*304*	*975*	*989*	*1027*	*1049*
Intermediate	*273*	*272*	*845*	*845*	*852*	*864*
Routine	*244*	*254*	*687*	*693*	*802*	*787*
Receipt of benefits						
Respondent or spouse in receipt of benefits	*502*	*540*	*1549*	*1704*	*1666*	*1811*
Neither in receipt of benefits	*353*	*304*	*1036*	*884*	*1113*	*972*
All	*858*	*847*	*2590*	*2593*	*2792*	*2796*

References

Butler, D. and Stokes, D. (1974), *Political Change in Britain*, Basingstoke: Macmillan

Cameron, D. (2012), 'Welfare speech', 25 June, London: Prime Minister's Office, available at: www.number10.gov.uk/news/welfare-speech/

Curtice. J. and Park, A. (2010), 'A tale of two crises: banks, MPs' expenses and public opinion' in Park, A., Curtice, J., Clery, E. and Bryson, C. (eds.), *British Social Attitudes: the 27th Report – Exploring Labour's Legacy*, London: Sage

Curtice, J. (2010), 'Thermostat or weathervane? Public reactions to spending and redistribution under New Labour', in Park, A., Curtice, J., Thomson, K., Phillips, M., Clery, E. and Butt, S. (eds.), *British Social Attitudes: the 26th Report*, London: Sage

Hills, J. (2001), 'Poverty and social security: What rights? Whose responsibilities?', in Park, A., Curtice, J., Thomson, K., Jarvis, L. and Bromley, C. (eds.), *British Social Attitudes: the 18th Report – Public Policy, Social Ties*, London: Sage

HM Treasury, *Budget 2012*, available at: cdn.hm-treasury.gov.uk/budget2012_complete.pdf

Soroka, S. and Wlezien, C. (2005), 'Opinion-Policy Dynamics: Public Preferences and Public Expenditure in the United Kingdom', *British Journal of Political Science*, **35**: 665–689

Taylor-Gooby, P. (2004), 'The work-centred welfare state', in Park, A., Curtice, J., Thomson, K., Bromley, C. and Phillips, M. (eds.), *British Social Attitudes: the 21st Report*, London: Sage

Wlezien, C. (1995), 'The Public as Thermostat: Dynamics of Preferences for Spending', *American Journal of Political Science*, **39**: 981–1000

Acknowledgements

NatCen Social Research is grateful to the Department for Work and Pensions for their generous financial support, which enabled us to ask the questions reported in this chapter. The views expressed are those of the author alone.

Appendix

The data for Figures 1.1, 1.2, 1.3, 1.4 and 1.5 are shown below:

Table A.1 Attitudes to taxation and spending 1983–2011

	1983	1984	1985	1986	1987	1989	1990	1991	1993
	%	%	%	%	%	%	%	%	%
Reduce taxes and spend less	9	5	6	5	3	3	3	3	4
Keep taxes and spending the same	54	50	43	44	42	37	37	29	28
Increase taxes and spend more	32	39	45	46	50	56	54	65	63
Weighted base	*1761*	*1645*	*1769*	*3066*	*2766*	*2930*	*2698*	*2836*	*2945*
Unweighted base	*1719*	*1675*	*1804*	*3100*	*2847*	*3029*	*2797*	*2918*	*2945*

	1994	1995	1996	1997	1998	1999	2000	2001	2002
	%	%	%	%	%	%	%	%	%
Reduce taxes and spend less	4	5	4	3	3	4	5	3	3
Keep taxes and spending the same	33	31	34	31	32	34	40	34	31
Increase taxes and spend more	58	61	59	62	63	58	50	59	63
Weighted base	*3469*	*3633*	*3620*	*1355*	*3146*	*3143*	*2302*	*3287*	*3435*
Unweighted base	*3469*	*3633*	*3620*	*1355*	*3146*	*3143*	*2292*	*3287*	*3435*

	2003	2004	2005	2006	2007	2008	2009	2010	2011
	%	%	%	%	%	%	%	%	%
Reduce taxes and spend less	6	6	7	6	7	8	8	9	6
Keep taxes and spending the same	38	42	43	43	47	50	55	56	55
Increase taxes and spend more	51	49	46	46	42	39	34	31	36
Weighted base	*3276*	*2130*	*2167*	*3228*	*3082*	*2184*	*1134*	*3297*	*3311*
Unweighted base	*3272*	*2146*	*2166*	*3240*	*3094*	*2229*	*1139*	*3297*	*3311*

Table A.2 Attitudes to government spending on welfare benefits and taxation and spending in general, 1987-2011

	1987	1989	1991	1993	1994	1995	1996
% agree government should spend more on welfare benefits	55	61	58	53	50	49	43
Weighted base	*1243*	*2529*	*2428*	*2595*	*2957*	*3145*	*3103*
Unweighted base	*1281*	*2604*	*2481*	*2567*	*2929*	*3135*	*3085*
% agree government should increase taxes and spend more	50	56	65	63	58	61	59
Weighted base	*2766*	*2930*	*2836*	*2945*	*3469*	*3633*	*3620*
Unweighted base	*2847*	*3029*	*2918*	*2945*	*3469*	*3633*	*3620*

	1998	1999	2000	2001	2002	2003	2004
% agree government should spend more on welfare benefits	43	40	38	43	44	43	36
Weighted base	*2546*	*2478*	*2991*	*2821*	*2929*	*873*	*2610*
Unweighted base	*2531*	*2450*	*2980*	*2795*	*2900*	*881*	*2609*
% agree government should increase taxes and spend more	63	58	50	59	63	51	49
Weighted base	*3146*	*3143*	*2302*	*3287*	*3435*	*3276*	*2130*
Unweighted base	*3146*	*3143*	*2292*	*3287*	*3435*	*3272*	*2146*

	2005	2006	2007	2008	2009	2010	2011
% agree government should spend more on welfare benefits	36	35	32	35	27	29	28
Weighted base	*2697*	*2813*	*2663*	*2956*	*963*	*2810*	*2841*
Unweighted base	*2699*	*2822*	*2672*	*3000*	*967*	*2791*	*2845*
% agree government should increase taxes and spend more	46	46	42	39	34	31	36
Weighted base	*2167*	*3228*	*3082*	*2184*	*1134*	*3297*	*3311*
Unweighted base	*2166*	*3240*	*3094*	*2229*	*1139*	*3297*	*3311*

Table A.3 Attitudes to unemployment benefits by unemployment rate, 1983–2011

	1983	1984	1985	1986	1987	1988	1989	1990	1991	1992
% agree too low and cause hardship	46	49	44	44	51	n/a	52	50	53	n/a
% agree too high and discourage work	35	28	34	33	29	n/a	27	29	27	n/a
% unemployed in UK	11	12	11	11	11	9	7	7	9	10
Weighted base	*1761*	*1645*	*1769*	*3066*	*2766*	*n/a*	*2930*	*2698*	*2836*	*n/a*
Unweighted base	*1719*	*1675*	*1804*	*3100*	*2847*	*n/a*	*3029*	*2797*	*2918*	*n/a*

	1993	1994	1995	1996	1997	1998	1999	2000	2001	2002
% agree too low and cause hardship	55	53	51	48	46	29	33	40	37	29
% agree too high and discourage work	24	24	30	32	28	46	42	36	37	47
% unemployed in UK	10	10	9	8	7	6	6	6	5	5
Weighted base	*2945*	*3469*	*1199*	*3620*	*1355*	*3146*	*3143*	*3426*	*3287*	*3435*
Unweighted base	*2945*	*3469*	*1234*	*3620*	*1355*	*3146*	*3143*	*3426*	*3287*	*3435*

	2003	2004	2005	2006	2007	2008	2009	2010	2011
% agree too low and cause hardship	34	23	26	23	26	21	29	23	19
% agree too high and discourage work	40	54	50	54	54	61	51	54	62
% unemployed in UK	5	5	5	5	5	6	7	8	8
Weighted base	*3272*	*3199*	*3210*	*3228*	*3082*	*3333*	*1134*	*3297*	*3311*
Unweighted base	*3276*	*3199*	*3139*	*3240*	*3094*	*3258*	*1139*	*3297*	*3311*

n/a = not asked
Source for unemployment data: International Monetary Fund's World Economic Outlook Database, April 2012

Table A.4 Attitudes to welfare recipients, 1987-2011

	1987	1989	1991	1993	1994	1995	1996
% agree many don't deserve help	31	28	26	24	26	30	28
% agree most unemployed people could find a job if they wanted one	41	52	38	27	32	38	39
Weighted base	*1243*	*2529*	*2428*	*2595*	*2957*	*3145*	*3085*
Unweighted base	*1281*	*2604*	*2481*	*2567*	*2929*	*3135*	*3103*

	1998	1999	2000	2001	2002	2003	2004
% agree many don't deserve help	32	27	31	32	36	38	39
% agree most unemployed people could find a job if they wanted one	54	56	60	63	65	66	69
Weighted base	*2956*	*2478*	*2991*	*2821*	*2929*	*881*	*2610*
Unweighted base	*3000*	*2450*	*2980*	*2795*	*2900*	*873*	*2609*

	2005	2006	2007	2008	2009	2010	2011
% agree many don't deserve help	40	29	36	37	34	35	35
% agree most unemployed people could find a job if they wanted one	69	67	67	68	55	54	56
Weighted base	*2697*	*2813*	*2663*	*2956*	*963*	*2810*	*2841*
Unweighted base	*2699*	*2822*	*2672*	*3000*	*967*	*2791*	*2845*

Table A.5 Attitudes to the welfare state, 1983–2011

	1983	1984	1985	1987	1989	1991	1993	1994
% agree welfare state encourages people to stop helping each other	37	38	32	40	32	27	32	31
% agree if benefits less generous, people stand on own feet	n/a	n/a	n/a	33	30	26	25	27
% disagree cutting benefits would damage too many people's lives	n/a	n/a	n/a	n/a	n/a	n/a	n/a	n/a
% agree creation of welfare state one of Britain's proudest achievements	n/a	n/a	n/a	n/a	n/a	n/a	n/a	n/a
Weighted base	*1610*	*1522*	*1502*	*1243*	*2529*	*2428*	*2595*	*2957*
Unweighted base	*1650*	*1562*	*1530*	*1281*	*2604*	*2481*	*2567*	*2929*

	1995	1996	1999	2000	2001	2002	2003	2004
% agree welfare state encourages people to stop helping each other	36	31	32	35	28	30	35	24
% agree if benefits less generous, people stand on own feet	33	33	38	38	39	44	42	47
% disagree cutting benefits would damage too many people's lives	n/a	n/a	n/a	16	15	18	17	18
% agree creation of welfare state one of Britain's proudest achievements	n/a	n/a	n/a	13	12	14	10	13
Weighted base	*3145*	*3085*	*2478*	*2991*	*2821*	*2929*	*881*	*2610*
Unweighted base	*3135*	*3103*	*2450*	*2980*	*2795*	*2900*	*873*	*2609*

	2005	2006	2007	2008	2009	2010	2011
% agree welfare state encourages people to stop helping each other	32	28	30	32	34	38	33
% agree if benefits less generous, people stand on own feet	49	47	52	54	53	55	54
% disagree cutting benefits would damage too many people's lives	18	18	21	20	22	25	23
% agree creation of welfare state one of Britain's proudest achievements	12	14	14	14	16	15	15
Weighted base	*2697*	*2813*	*2663*	*2956*	*963*	*2810*	*2841*
Unweighted base	*2699*	*2822*	*2672*	*3000*	*967*	*2791*	*2845*

n/a = not asked

Immigration
"Fewer but better"? Public views about immigration

The period since the late-1990s has seen the largest inflow of immigrants to Britain in history. How has the public reacted to this? Does it support the Coalition's approach in wanting to see immigration reduced and how does it think immigration has affected British society? Do attitudes to different types of migrants vary?

Scale and impact

Demands for a reduction in overall immigration have increased while views about the impact of migration have grown more negative.

Three out of four (75%) respondents advocate a **reduction in immigration** overall, a rise from 63% since 1995. 51% want a large reduction.

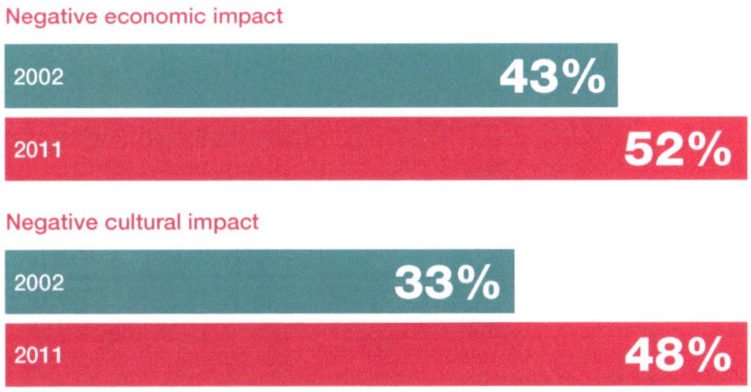

The proportion who view the economic **impact of migrants** negatively increased by nine percentage points between 2002 and 2011, from 43% to 52%. Negative judgements about the cultural impact of migration increased by 15 percentage points during the same period, from 33% to 48%.

Migrant characteristics

The characteristics of different types of migrants are strongly linked to people's attitudes towards them. Migrants' qualifications are paramount in predicting attitudes, regardless of countries of origin.

More than 50% of respondents regard **professional migration** as a good thing, regardless of whether it is from Eastern Europe or Pakistan, but less than 20% feel positively about **unskilled labour migration** from these regions.

Around two-thirds of respondents are neutral or positive about the **migration of students** from any of four regions in the world into Britain if they have good grades, but less than one third feel the same way about students with bad grades.

Authors

Robert Ford, Gareth Morrell and Anthony Heath
Robert Ford is Lecturer in Politics at the University of Manchester. Gareth Morrell is a Senior Research Director in the Society and Social Change Team at NatCen Social Research. Anthony Heath is Professor of Sociology at the University of Manchester and Emeritus Professor of Sociology at the University of Oxford

Introduction

Immigration has reshaped British society in the post-war era, and in recent years has consistently been at the top of the political agenda. As an island nation with a global imperial legacy, the question of who we let into our country and why has a unique resonance in Britain. Attitudes towards immigration say something about our understanding of the fundamental relationship between citizens and the state, fairness and human rights.

Ever since social surveys and opinion polls began to ask questions on the topic in the 1960s, the British public has always favoured a reduction in the numbers of immigrants, even during periods when immigrant inflows have been low (Blinder, 2011b). However, the history of British immigration is one characterised by a gap between public attitudes and public policy (Hansen, 2000), with government's ability or willingness to reduce net migration often constrained. During the last century, a desire to extend and equalise subjecthood during the British Empire, a business need for cheap, unskilled labour and regional institutions and international laws all played a part in shaping policy in this area. Following large-scale immigration from Commonwealth countries in the 1950s, a more restrictive policy gradually evolved through a series of legislative reforms starting with the 1962 Commonwealth Immigrants Act and ending with the 1981 British Nationality Act. Migration flows were tempered rather than halted or reversed; while primary migration more or less ceased, family reunion inflows continued. A shift in emphasis was marked by the 1993 Asylum and Immigration Appeals Act and the incorporation of the European Convention for Human Rights (ECHR) in 1998, representing a new, more open approach driven by the election of New Labour and the realities of globalisation (Somerville, 2007). Labour migration controls were relaxed and tools to restrict asylum were initially limited during this period. Yet a backlash was just around the corner. The number of people seeking asylum in the UK increased threefold from 1996 to around 85,000 in 2002 (Blinder, 2011b). The institutions set up to deal with this particular inflow of migrants were unable to cope and the press and public felt the system was open to abuse and had lost its integrity. The political salience of the issue was not lost on the government or the press.[1]

In 2003, data collected by the British Social Attitudes survey on public attitudes towards immigration reflected the negativity surrounding the issue, with public opposition increasing sharply from the already high levels recorded in 1995. On the heels of the collection of these data, Britain experienced a large wave of immigration from Eastern Europe following the accession of eight countries (the A8 countries) to the EU in 2004 – which contributed to net migration peaking in that year at 245,000. The extent of this migration was not foreseen by the British government. Around 13,000 arrivals were anticipated (Dustmann et al., 2003), yet in 2004, 54,000 arrived as long-term migrants. While the nature of A8 migration is varied and often temporary, the population of A8 citizens in the UK is now estimated by the Annual Population Survey to be 872,000 (Vargas-Silva, 2012).

Coalition policy has been focused around an attempt to cap the overall level of net migration

Since then, there has been a strong shift towards greater restriction in both policy discourse and policy implementation, which began under Labour and has continued under the Coalition. Coalition policy has been focused around an attempt to cap the overall level of net migration and a move to systems that aim to increase government control over migration flows to achieve this goal. Debate continues over the economic impact and fairness of this approach. Firstly, a points system is now in place for economic migrants, which distinguishes between migrants in terms of age, earnings, qualifications and employment to determine entry. According to the Migration Advisory Committee, students will be equally affected. The stated aim here is to attract the 'brightest and the best' despite concerns over the broader economic impact of this policy (Ruhs, 2011; Cavanagh and Glennie, 2012).

Secondly, extra-territorial measures have been adopted to reduce the number of asylum seekers arriving in the UK; and increased containment once in the UK aims to increase the number of asylum seekers that can be removed when their claims fail (Blinder, 2011a). Proposals to limit the numbers of immigrants arriving in the UK through family reunification have also been introduced.[2] The stated aim here is to put a stop to abuses of the system, although concerns remain over potential violations of human rights.

So how have these policies fared? As Figure 2.1 shows, since 2004 both total and net long-term migration have remained broadly steady. Net migration is more volatile, falling to 163,000 in 2008 but then returning to 2004 levels of over 240,000 in 2010, while the total migration inflow remains almost unchanged at just under 600,000 every year. Recent shifts in net migration, the statistic which attracts the most media and policy maker attention, therefore reflect volatility in the number of people leaving the UK, not the number entering.[3] It is clear that institutional and political realities continue to make sharply reducing immigration difficult: having opted out of initial restrictions on A8 migrants the government cannot formally control immigration from the EU,[4] and as a result poorer Central European members such as Poland have continued to provide the largest source of labour migration. The humanitarian requirements of international law and the requirements of the ECHR make draconian restrictions on asylum or family reunion migration similarly difficult to achieve. While the number of people seeking asylum (17,916 in 2010) is now much lower than its 2002 peak, there is debate over the fairness of the government's approach to influencing this (Asylum Aid, 2010) and the impact of these measures on re-enforcing negative public attitudes (Gibney, 2011).

Figure 2.1 Total and net migration inflow, 1991–2011

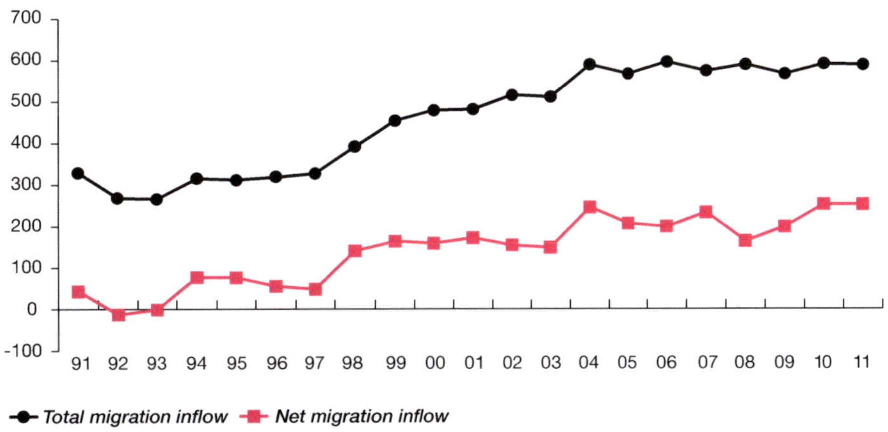

Source: Office for National Statistics, Long Term International Migration Estimates
2011 figure is estimate for year to September
The data on which Figure 2.1 is based can be found in the appendix to this chapter

It is important to gather better and more nuanced information on which migration inflows concern the British public and which do not

So while the shift in policy in the past decade has not yet achieved its stated aims, it does reflect a perception among policy makers that hardening public attitudes towards immigration demand a restrictive policy response. These attitudes are arguably further accentuated by two factors. Firstly, specific incidents – crises or scandals – have highlighted ineffective systems or incompetent personnel who are charged with managing immigration. These incidents may fuel the view that if immigration cannot be managed fairly and for the benefit of Britain, it should be halted completely. Secondly, it is clear that the public perception of contemporary migration flows is very different from that of policy makers. A recent study found that when thinking about immigration, people are far more likely to have in mind asylum seekers, who made up four per cent of immigrants in 2009, and least likely to have in mind students, the largest group in 2009 at 37 per cent (Migration Observatory, 2011). Given the complexity of contemporary migration flows and an intricate and constantly evolving institutional apparatus, it is important to gather better and more nuanced information on which migration inflows concern the British public and which do not, and how these perceptions link with attitudes to immigration per se.

In this context, the data used in this chapter were gathered in part to try to overcome the influence of misinformation, by collecting systematic and unbiased data on the public's views of a contentious and complex issue. They were also collected to try to elicit more nuanced views on immigration among the British public: if there is anti-immigration sentiment, towards which groups is this strongest and among which groups is this most keenly felt? In doing so, the chapter aims to provide an insight into the public response to the government's approach to reducing, or at least better controlling, immigration into Britain.

Views of immigration: inflows and impact

We begin with a review of British attitudes to immigration overall.

The period since the late-1990s has seen the largest inflow of immigrants to Britain in history. There are two ways we can assess how the British public have reacted to this. The first is to examine views of overall migration levels. Do the public want to see immigration reduced, and if so, how steeply? A second is to examine what impacts the public thinks immigration has had on British society. These two kinds of assessment are very different – individuals may favour reductions to immigration even if they feel the impact to date has been limited, because they may worry about future impacts. Conversely, a respondent may concede that migration has had negative impacts, but still support high migration levels, feeling that the benefits outweigh the costs.

The sensitivity of these items to changes in immigration may also vary. Demands for reduction may rise and fall in response to inflows, or alternatively respondents may 'default' to a demand for reductions in migration, irrespective of migration inflows, supporting reduced immigration as a way of expressing their view that any migration is socially damaging. Views about the impacts of immigration may shift in response to changes in settlement levels, often with a time lag as the overall effects of migration may take time to manifest, or respondents may treat the question as a backward-looking judgement on social effects going back over a long time period, in which case responses may not be sensitive to recent events. In short, there are many reasons for treating views about levels and impacts as distinct from each other, and worthy of separate analysis.

75%

of respondents advocate a reduction in immigration overall

To explore the public's views about levels of migration, we asked respondents:

Do you think the number of immigrants to Britain nowadays should be increased a lot, increased a little, remain the same as it is, reduced a little or reduced a lot?

Table 2.1 presents the answers provided in 2011 and on the three occasions that this question has been asked previously. It highlights a sustained increase in demands for lower overall immigration since the question was first asked. The proportion of respondents favouring some reduction in migration rose from 63 per cent in 1995 to 72 per cent in 2003 and 78 per cent in 2008, just before the onset of the economic crisis. Since then, there has been a small decline, with 75 per cent of respondents in 2011 advocating a reduction in immigration overall and 51 per cent wanting a large reduction. Most of the increase in demand for reduction thus dates to the late-1990s/early-2000s, and the balance of public concern has remained broadly stable since 2003. However, the overall balance of opinion remains strongly in favour of the Coalition's stated policy aim of lowering immigration levels. It is worth noting, however, that nearly 40 per cent of respondents also supported large cuts in migration in 1995, when net migration inflows were very low. Part of this overall demand for reduction therefore seems to be insensitive to present migration levels – and may perhaps instead reflect a 'default preference' for reduced migration in all circumstances.

Table 2.1 Views of immigration levels, 1995–2011

	1995	2003	2008	2011	Change 1995–2011	Change 2003–2011
The number of immigrants to Britain should ...	%	%	%	%		
... increase a lot/a little	4	5	4	3	-1	-1
... remain the same	27	16	17	18	-9	+2
... reduce a little	24	23	23	24	0	+1
... reduce a lot	39	49	55	51	+12	+2
Weighted base	*987*	*873*	*2236*	*3311*		
Unweighted base	*1078*	*881*	*2239*	*3311*		

Turning to impacts, we consider two broad spheres in which these can occur: culture and economics. The perceived cultural impacts of immigration have become more salient as concerns over Muslim integration and Islamic extremism have grown, following riots in Muslim areas in 2001 and terror attacks in 2005 and 2007 (although, in practice, these were committed by British-born extremists). Meanwhile economic concerns have grown with reports arguing that migrants were outcompeting native Britons for scarce jobs, an anxiety which can only be magnified in the harsh economic climate following the recession of 2008–2009.

To explore public perceptions of the impacts of migration, we asked respondents:

On a scale of 0 to 10, where 0 is extremely bad and 10 is extremely good, would you say it is generally bad or good for Britain's economy that migrants come to Britain from other countries?

[0 Extremely bad for economy, 5 Neither, 10 Extremely good for economy]

And on a scale of 0 to 10, would you say that Britain's cultural life is generally undermined or enriched by migrants coming to live here from other countries?

[0 Cultural life undermined, 5 Neither, 10 Cultural life enriched]

Table 2.2 presents the answers provided in 2011, compared with data from the 2002 European Social Survey, which asked almost identical questions.[5] Although the British in the early-2000s strongly favoured reductions in migration levels, their views about migration impacts are more evenly divided: the net rating of the economic impact of migration was modestly negative (-17), while the net rating of the cultural impact was positive (+11). Much of the demand for reduction seen in 2003 may have reflected concern about the likely future effects of continued high migration rather than a perception that immigrants had already had significant negative effects.

A decade of high migration levels, and prominent political debates about the effects of immigration, have not been well-received by the British public

In 2011, the public's verdict on impacts was more downbeat. The net rating of economic impacts fell five points to -22, while the net rating of cultural impacts swung more sharply, falling 25 points to -14. The largest increases in both cases were in the share judging migration's effects as very negative (i.e. "extremely bad for the economy" or "cultural life undermined"). A decade of high migration levels, and prominent political debates about the effects of immigration, have not been well-received by the British public. Despite the hard economic times, it also seems that it is concerns about culture which have risen the most over the decade. However, despite this negative shift, nearly half of respondents (48 per cent) perceive the economic impact of migration to be neutral or positive and slightly more than half (51 per cent) feel the same way about the cultural impact. Even after the largest and most sustained inflow of migration in British history, the public remain much more evenly divided when they think about the effects of the migrants who have already settled than when they are asked about whether more migrants should be allowed into the country.

Table 2.2 Views of the economic and cultural impact of immigration, 2002 and 2011[6]

Views of immigration impacts	2002	2011	Change 2002–2011
Economic impact	%	%	
Very good	2	5	+3
Good	24	25	+1
Neither good nor bad	28	18	-10
Bad	32	31	-1
Very bad	11	21	+10
Net rating (good–bad)	**-17**	**-22**	**-5**
Cultural impact	%	%	
Very good	6	8	+2
Good	38	26	-12
Neither good nor bad	22	17	-5
Bad	24	27	+3
Very bad	9	21	+12
Net rating (good–bad)	**+11**	**-14**	**-25**
Weighted base	*1995*	*3311*	
Unweighted base	*2052*	*3311*	

Source for 2002: European Social Survey

Having looked at views about inflows and impacts separately, we now move to consider the relationship between the two. Table 2.3 examines whether overall views about immigration's effects and demands for reduced inflows are more closely related to judgements about economic effects or about cultural effects. Views about immigration's effects were summarised using responses to the following question included on the 2011 survey:

Using this card, please tell me on a scale of 0 to 10 how good or bad you think the settlement of migrants in the last ten years has been for Britain?

[0 Extremely bad, 5 Neither, 10 Extremely good]

Overall opinion of the settlement of migrants is negative, with 60 per cent of respondents rating the impact negatively, and only 24 per cent holding a positive view (a net negative rating of -36). Interestingly, this overall rating is more negative than ratings of either the economic or cultural impacts of migration, so many respondents were negative about migration overall despite being positive about its economic or cultural effects.

60%

rate the settlement of migrants as bad for Britain

Table 2.3 shows that both areas of concern clearly have a strong relationship with overall judgements about migration impacts and demands for reduction: more than eight in ten of those who are negative about the economic or the cultural impact of immigration also view immigration negatively overall, and want it reduced. However, we also see more evidence of a 'default' demand for reduction in immigration levels: over half of those rating the economic and cultural impacts of immigration as "good" still want to see inflows reduced, and more than three in ten of those who rate the impacts as "very good" feel likewise. This finding demonstrates how different the issues of immigration levels and its cultural impacts are in the public mind.

Table 2.3 Overall assessments of immigration and immigration levels, by perceptions of economic and cultural impact[6]

	% with negative assessments of immigration overall	% wanting immigration reduced	*Weighted base*	*Unweighed base*
Economic impact				
Very good	12	35	*148*	*130*
Good	21	54	*819*	*752*
Neither good nor bad	43	74	*498*	*610*
Bad	85	90	*1029*	*1040*
Very bad	94	93	*687*	*745*
Cultural impact				
Very good	15	31	*252*	*211*
Good	33	64	*871*	*821*
Neither good nor bad	52	74	*571*	*604*
Bad	77	89	*888*	*893*
Very bad	95	93	*682*	*736*

How have perceptions of the impacts of immigration changed across the public as a whole? One possibility is that anxieties have become more widespread, spreading from social groups who were already concerned about migration impacts to other groups who were previously sanguine about its effects. Another is that immigration attitudes have become more socially polarised, with groups who were already negative about migrants becoming more anxious while those who were unconcerned remain so. A third possibility is that concern about migration has become more socially differentiated, with different groups expressing different anxieties. Citizens who are in economically marginal positions may worry more about economic impacts, while those in more secure employment may focus on cultural impacts.

As the recession has taken hold, the experiences of more economically marginal groups may have diverged from the more secure groups in society

We explore the links between economic and cultural anxieties and judgements about immigration impacts by comparing the attitudes of groups who are more or less likely to feel culturally and economically threatened by immigration. It has been assumed that those with lower or less secure incomes, and those in jobs exposed to immigrant competition, will be more economically threatened by migrants, while cultural threat will be concentrated among those with more negative views of diversity, such as the racially prejudiced, those with low education levels and those with no close social contact with migrants from different cultures.

Table 2.4 presents the results of this analysis. Several key messages emerge. Firstly, even in 2002 there were significant social divisions in judgements about immigration. More economically threatened groups, such as poorer and working class Britons, gave more negative assessments of both the economic and cultural impacts of migration than economically secure groups. For example, less than four in ten of those from a professional occupational group saw immigration as having negative economic impacts, compared with more than five in ten of those from a routine occupational group. The same is true of groups more likely to perceive cultural threat from immigration, such as those with low education levels or admitting to some racial prejudice: such groups are 15 to 25 percentage points more negative about both forms of impact than more cosmopolitan groups such as those with degrees or those with some migrant heritage.

Secondly, attitudes have socially polarised over the decade: in nearly every case, the negative shift in assessments of immigration impacts is much larger for the groups that were already threatened more by migration. The proportion of those with a degree who think immigration has a negative effect culturally has risen by seven percentage points between 2002 and 2011, compared with a 20-point rise for those with no educational qualifications in the same period, who already held more negative views. The British in 2011 are thus much more internally divided about immigration than they were in 2002. Majorities of the more threatened groups are consistently negative about immigration impacts, while among more secure groups most remain positive or neutral.

Finally, this polarisation is more evident on views about the economic impact of immigration. Economically comfortable and culturally more cosmopolitan groups show little change in their assessments of economic impacts, but economically and socially insecure groups have become dramatically more hostile. By contrast, all groups have become at least somewhat more negative about the cultural effects of migration, although this change has been more marked for those groups likely to feel more culturally threatened by immigration. This may reflect the dual impact of both immigration and recession on the more economically marginal groups in society. As the recession has taken hold, the experiences of more economically marginal groups such as those with low or insecure incomes may have diverged from the more secure groups in society, as both their general economic anxiety and their specific concerns about immigration have risen.

Table 2.4 Negative views of immigration impacts, by economic and cultural characteristics, 2002 and 2011[7]

% negative assessments of immigration (0–4)	Economic impact 2002	Economic impact 2011	Economic impact Change 2002–2011	Cultural impact 2002	Cultural impact 2011	Cultural impact Change 2002–2011
Economic characteristics						
Class						
Professionals	36	40	+4	26	37	+11
Routine	51	62	+11	40	56	+16
Income						
Top quartile	39	39	0	24	37	+13
Bottom quartile	47	61	+14	40	54	+14
Subjective income						
Comfortable	40	48	+8	30	44	+14
Struggling	47	62	+15	33	58	+25
Cultural characteristics						
Education						
Degree or higher	26	30	+4	17	24	+7
No qualifications	51	66	+15	42	62	+20
Migrant heritage						
1st or 2nd generation migrant	30	29	-1	18	26	+8
British born, British parents	46	58	+12	36	53	+17
Racial prejudice						
None[8]	36	42	+6	26	35	+9
Some or a lot	59	71	+12	48	68	+20

Source for 2002: European Social Survey

Less migration or more selective migration?

Given the strength of public feeling about migration, it is no surprise that the Coalition has prioritised reduction and control. But a focus solely on aggregate attitudes can be misleading – does the public want all forms of migration reduced, or are they more accepting of migrants they perceive as having more to offer? The government emphasises both ideas in its migration policy, pressing for an overall cap on numbers but also pushing for stricter regulation of migrant qualifications through reforms such as tightening the points system and imposing English language criteria. In this section we focus on answering two questions. Firstly, how responsive is the public to differences in the characteristics and region of origin of migrants? Secondly, how do anxieties about the economic and cultural impacts of immigration affect the patterns of selection? For example, do those who worry about economic impacts place greater stress on economic selection criteria, while those who worry about cultural impacts stress selection by origin region?

To test the effect of these influences, we conducted a series of survey experiments. Respondents were given brief descriptions of three migrant groups and, in each case, asked whether they regarded settlement of migrants like this as good or bad for Britain. What respondents did not know was that each group description they saw was randomly varied. Each respondent was asked one question about labour migrants, one about students and one about family reunion migration. Respondents were read the introduction below and were then asked three different questions, with the characteristics in brackets being randomly allocated:

> ***I would now like to ask you about some of the groups of migrants who come to settle in Britain. For each group, I would like you to indicate whether you think accepting these migrants is a bad thing or a good thing for Britain.***
>
> ***[Highly qualified professionals/Unskilled labourers] from [East European countries like Poland/Muslim countries like Pakistan] [who have been recruited to fill jobs where there are labour shortages/who have come to Britain to search for work].***
>
> ***Students with [good grades/poor grades) from [West European countries like Germany/East European countries like Poland/Muslim countries like Pakistan[9]/East Asian countries like China].***
>
> ***Migrants from [West European countries like Germany/East European countries like Poland/Muslim countries like Pakistan/African countries like Nigeria] bringing over their wife and children after living in Britain for [3 years/10 years].***
>
> ***[0 Extremely bad, 5 Neither, 10 Extremely good]***

Because respondents were randomly assigned to different group descriptions, when we compare their responses we can be confident that any statistically significant difference is the product of having been asked about different groups.

Despite being negative about migration overall, Britons are in fact supporters of professional migrants

The results of the first such experiment, focusing on labour migration, are shown in Table 2.5. Here we varied three characteristics of the migrant group – their qualifications (professionals or unskilled labourers), their region of origin (Eastern Europe or Muslim countries such as Pakistan) and their reason for migration (to fill jobs or to search for work). All three of these factors have substantial effects on attitudes, and the very large differences in reactions to different kinds of migrants demonstrate how misleading it is to speak of public views about "immigrants" as a homogenous group. The largest impact comes from migrant qualifications: in every condition where the migrant group is described as "professionals" supporters outweigh opponents by 20 points or more. For example, net support for professional migrants from Eastern Europe is +39 when they come to fill jobs, and +33 when they come searching for work. When migrants are described as unskilled labourers, opponents outweigh supporters by even greater margins. For example, net support for unskilled labourers coming from Eastern Europe to search for work is -51; for similar migrants coming from Pakistan the figure is even lower: -69. Respondents take migrants' qualifications very seriously: despite being negative about migration overall, Britons are in fact net supporters of professional migrants, regardless of their circumstances or origins, but are strongly opposed to unskilled labour migration, again regardless of circumstances or origins.

Table 2.5 Views of labour migrants, by migrant characteristics[6]

	Migrants from Eastern Europe				Migrants from Muslim countries like Pakistan			
	Professionals		Unskilled labourers		Professionals		Unskilled labourers	
	Filling jobs	Searching for work	Filling jobs	Searching for work	Filling jobs	Searching for work	Filling jobs	Searching for work
Settlement of these migrants is …	%	%	%	%	%	%	%	%
… very good for Britain	17	14	2	2	13	12	2	2
… good for Britain	46	45	27	17	48	40	15	8
… neither good nor bad for Britain	12	14	13	10	15	17	11	11
… bad for Britain	16	17	32	39	15	17	39	36
… very bad for Britain	8	9	24	31	7	13	32	43
Net support (good–bad)	**+39**	**+33**	**-27**	**-51**	**+39**	**+22**	**-54**	**-69**
Weighted base	*437*	*449*	*390*	*391*	*381*	*442*	*414*	*407*
Unweighted base	*422*	*447*	*397*	*405*	*372*	*436*	*420*	*412*

Region of origin and motive for migration also have robust, albeit smaller, effects on how migrants are perceived. Net support for migrants coming from Muslim countries such as Pakistan is on average lower than identically-described migrants coming from Eastern Europe, suggesting that concerns about cultural difference significantly reduce support for migrants. However, this effect is smaller for professionals searching for work, and not observed at all for professionals coming in to fill jobs. This is an important nuance that public debate has completely failed to recognise, and it suggests that a positive economic profile can override cultural concerns (or possibly that cultural concerns are weaker in relation to professionals – perhaps because they are seen to be 'more like us'). The reason for migration has a similar effect, with support for migration consistently lower when migrants are described as searching for work rather than filling jobs where there are labour shortages. For example, net support for Muslim professional migrants is +39 when they come to fill jobs, but falls to +22 when they come to search for work. The gap is once again larger for unskilled labourers than for professionals, and is larger still for unskilled labourers from Eastern Europe: net support falls from -27 for those filling jobs to -51 for East Europeans coming to search for work. This suggests particular public sensitivity about the inflow of labourers from the A8 countries, the principal source of unskilled labour migration in recent years.

Table 2.6 shows us how the differences discussed above appear to reflect individual views about the general economic and cultural impact of migration. Those who are more negative about immigration's economic impact discriminate more strongly in favour of professional migrants and those with jobs, as we might expect. Specifically, those who think the economic impact of migration is negative have a net preference for professionals over labourers of 45 percentage points, while for those who are positive about the economic effects of migration the figure is 10 points lower at +35. They are less likely, however, to discriminate in favour of East Europeans over Muslims. Those with stronger cultural concerns about immigration are also more likely to favour professional migrants over labourers, perhaps because they perceive highly educated professionals as more able to integrate. However, despite widely documented anxieties about the integration of British Muslims, respondents who are more negative about the cultural effects of migration do not discriminate more strongly against Muslim migrants than those who are positive about the cultural impact of migration.

Table 2.6 Patterns of preference for different migrant groups, by views of the economic and cultural impact of migration

	Net preference for professionals over labourers	Net preference for those with jobs over searching	Net preference for East Europeans over Muslims	*Weighted base*	*Unweighted base*
Respondents who think economic impact is positive	+35	+7	+15	*966*	*882*
Respondents who think economic impact is negative	+45	+11	+5	*1714*	*1785*
Difference in net preference (positive–negative responses)	**-10**	**-4**	**+10**		
Respondents who think cultural impact is positive	+37	+8	+6	*1122*	*1032*
Respondents who think cultural impact is negative	+47	+8	+8	*1567*	*1629*
Difference in net preference (positive–negative responses)	**-10**	**0**	**-2**		

Net preference is defined as the difference in net support between the more preferred and less preferred groups

The evidence from our first experiment shows the public take distinctions between labour market migrants seriously, and respond to them regardless of how they feel about the economic and cultural impacts of immigration. We next turn to our final two experiments, to explore whether the same is true of student migration and family reunion migration.

Our experiment suggests the British favour admitting students from all quarters of the world, as long as they are strong performers

As noted previously, the largest group of migrants in the past few years has been students coming to learn in British colleges and universities. Yet there is little evidence on how the public regard such migrants. In our survey experiment, as shown earlier, we varied two characteristics: their grades (good or bad) and their region of origin (Western Europe, Eastern Europe, East Asia or Muslim countries). The results are presented in Table 2.7. Two findings are apparent. First, qualifications are a central factor driving reactions to student migrants. Supporters of students with good grades consistently outnumber opponents, regardless of region of origin, while opposition to the entry of students with bad grades is very strong, again regardless of where they come from. For example, net support for students from East Asia is +24 when they have good grades but -63 when they have poor grades. Our experiment thus suggests the British favour admitting students from all quarters of the world, as long as they are strong performers.

It is also clear that region of origin matters little: it has no impact in the "bad grades" condition and only Muslim students are regarded differently in the "good grades" condition, with net support lower by about 10 points, though it remains positive. This suggests concerns about cultural difference and integration do not have a strong impact on public reactions to student migrants, although there are clearly some reservations about Muslim students. We cannot say for sure why this is, but it seems likely that the more transitory nature of student migrants[10] and the higher levels of education and English language skills students must have in order to study in Britain, contribute to a perception that most students do not pose serious integration problems, though media stories about extremism on university campuses may have increased concerns about Muslim students. However, although those with positive grades are positively regarded, student migrants are on balance slightly less popular than professional workers.

Table 2.7 Views of student migrants, by migrant characteristics[6]

	Student migrants with good grades				Student migrants with bad grades			
	From West Europe	From East Europe	From Muslim coun-tries	From East Asia	From West Europe	From East Europe	From Muslim coun-tries	From East Asia
Settlement of these migrants is …	%	%	%	%	%	%	%	%
… very good for Britain	9	7	8	7	2	1	1	1
… good for Britain	41	43	35	44	9	9	9	9
… neither good nor bad for Britain	20	17	22	19	17	14	13	15
… bad for Britain	18	21	20	20	42	45	44	44
… very bad for Britain	10	12	13	7	29	30	30	29
Net support (good–bad)	**+22**	**+17**	**+10**	**+24**	**-60**	**-65**	**-64**	**-63**
Weighted base	*414*	*415*	*379*	*421*	*419*	*410*	*396*	*457*
Unweighted base	*412*	*414*	*396*	*421*	*426*	*400*	*394*	*448*

Our third survey experiment examined public views about family reunion migration. We varied two characteristics – how long the primary migrant had been in the country (three years or 10 years), and which region they came from (Western Europe, Eastern Europe, Africa or Muslim countries). Table 2.8 shows that three stories emerge from the results. Firstly, respondents are consistently negative about family reunion migration. Regardless of where the relatives are migrating from, or how long the primary migrant has been in the country, the balance of opinion is negative. Note that our question focuses on whether the settlement of family is "good or bad for Britain" so it is possible that many respondents would support admitting family members on other grounds – compassion or human rights, for example – while still regarding their admission as negative for Britain. Nonetheless, the public clearly do perceive more problems with family reunion migrants than they do with economic or student migrants. This may relate to a perception that the family reunion migration system is more open to abuse,[11] that family reunion migrants impose more economic costs or that the migration of relatives poses more problems for integration.

It is also clear that region of origin has a larger impact on reactions to family reunion migrants than it did in the previous two experiments. Net support for settled migrants from the least favoured regions – Africa and the Muslim world – bringing over their relatives is around 30 points lower than it is for migrants bringing relatives from Western Europe, the most favoured region. Eastern Europe falls half-way between these two extremes. Perhaps this is because family members from such regions are regarded as less likely to speak English or to work. They may therefore be regarded as more culturally different, posing greater integration problems, than family members settling from elsewhere within Europe. Further work is needed to probe the nature of these concerns and examine which policy options, if any, would assuage them.

Respondents also recognise, and respond to, the length of time a migrant has been settled in the country. Net reactions to migrants settled for 10 years bringing over family members are between 13 and 17 points less negative than when the primary migrant has been in Britain for three years. This is not because respondents feel obliged to express a more favourable view of the longer-settled migrant – each respondent answers only one question on family migrants, so the difference is purely the result of whether they were randomly assigned to answer about a long-settled or more recently-settled migrant. While further work is needed to understand the reasoning being applied here, respondents clearly recognise and respond to a longer period of settlement in the country. This may reflect a commitment to reciprocity – rewarding longer commitment to Britain with more favourable treatment – or it may reflect a perception that the families of migrants with longer residence in Britain are less likely to pose integration problems or economic costs. Finally, it may reflect a perception that longer-settled migrants are less likely to abuse the family reunion migration system.

The more favourable reactions to longer-term residents do not result in more equitable treatment of migrants from different regions, however. The 'ethnic hierarchy' in reactions to the different regions remains precisely the same, with West Europeans regarded most favourably, followed by East Europeans with net support around 15 points lower, with Africans and Muslim migrants a further 12–20 points behind. White Europeans are consistently preferred to non-white Africans and Muslims, and richer West Europeans preferred to poorer East Europeans. Culture, race and economics may all play a role here. Finally, given the heated public debate about Muslim integration in Britain, it is noteworthy that reactions to migrants explicitly labelled as "Muslim" are no more negative than those to "African" migrants. Although many migrants from the latter group are Muslim, respondents did not show extra hostility to a group explicitly labelled as "Muslim" than to a non-white migrant group whose religious affiliation is not highlighted.

Table 2.8 Views of family reunion migration, by migrant characteristics[6]

	Migrants bringing over their family after living in Britain for three years				Migrants bringing over their family after living in Britain for 10 years			
	From West Europe	From East Europe	From Africa	From Muslim countries	From West Europe	From East Europe	From Africa	From Muslim countries
Settlement of these migrants is …	%	%	%	%	%	%	%	%
… very good for Britain	3	1	2	1	4	3	2	5
… good for Britain	22	19	11	13	30	26	17	17
… neither good nor bad for Britain	24	18	16	14	25	18	17	19
… bad for Britain	33	31	38	33	22	31	35	26
… very bad for Britain	16	29	31	38	18	21	27	31
Net support (good–bad)	**-24**	**-40**	**-56**	**-57**	**-6**	**-23**	**-43**	**-35**
Weighted base	*460*	*386*	*389*	*412*	*399*	*392*	*407*	*466*
Unweighted base	*459*	*389*	*392*	*414*	*407*	*399*	*403*	*448*

Conclusions

The flow of migrants into Britain over the past 15 years has been the largest in British history. The public has reacted to this with strengthened demands for a reduction in migration and increasingly negative views about the cultural and economic impact of migrants on Britain. But even more strikingly, there has been a polarisation between different social groups in their concerns about immigration. While all groups have become more concerned, the trend has been greater among the less qualified and among less-skilled workers.

Britons are not opposed to migration across the board, but strongly favour migrants they perceive as being socially beneficial and easy to integrate

We have also sought here to move beyond aggregate views about immigration inflows and impacts to gain a more nuanced understanding of reactions to more specific groups of migrants. In three experiments, we looked at how migrants' characteristics were linked to public reactions. What emerges is a broadly pragmatic response: Britons are not opposed to migration across the board, but strongly favour migrants they perceive as being socially beneficial and easy to integrate. It is also clear that, despite the widespread concerns about cultural impact, qualifications trump origins. So professionals and high-quality students are regarded positively, regardless of where they come from, while unskilled labourers and poor-quality students are opposed, regardless of where they come from. Culture comes to the fore in the case of family reunion migration, where the economic case is less clear-cut and where difficulties of integration might be perceived as greater.

The Coalition's goal with immigration policy has been clear from the outset: less immigration overall, and a more selective policy on who is allowed to enter. Immigration minister Damian Green has spoken of a need to end an "addiction to foreign workers" and to focus on toughening selection criteria so Britain has "fewer and better" migrants.[12] Among the criteria that have been debated are more stringent skills criteria for economic migrants, tougher English tests for family reunion migrants and stricter qualification requirements for students and accreditation tests for the institutions admitting them. Our evidence suggests that the broad outlines of this approach are in line with public opinion – more than anything, what sways British voters in favour of migration is the perception that migrants are highly-qualified.

While the current policy framework broadly chimes with public demands for less and more selective migration, it remains poorly-designed to address more specific public concerns about different migrant groups. Limits are imposed on groups of migrants who do not concern the public, such as students and professionals, but are not imposed on other groups who generate concerns, such as East European labourers or family reunion migrants from more culturally-different regions of origin. Partly this reflects the constraints the current government must operate within, in terms of EU treaties and international law. However, it also reflects a tension produced by the desire to deliver a sharp overall reduction to migration inflows when many inflows cannot be controlled. The consequence is a need to impose sharp cuts to migration inflows regarded positively (again, students, professionals) simply because other, less popular, migrant flows cannot be controlled (e.g. East European workers). Given this tension, more targeted measures and limits focused on the groups which actually generate public concern might be preferable. Our evidence suggests the British public perhaps take a more sophisticated and nuanced view of the issues than politicians seem to recognise at present, and, setting aside the current constraint, Britain would benefit from a policy response which reflected this nuance.

Our evidence suggests the British public perhaps take a more sophisticated and nuanced view of the issues than politicians seem to recognise at present

Notes

1. More meetings were called by Prime Minister Tony Blair in relation to asylum between 2001 and 2004 than any other issue apart from Iraq (Spencer, 2009: 359).

2. Speech by immigration minister Damian Green, 15th September 2011, available at www.homeoffice.gov.uk/media-centre/speeches/family-migration

3. In particular, the sharp fall in net migration in 2008 reflects a major exodus that year following a dramatic deterioration in economic conditions.

4. Though controls are applied to the 'A2' – Romania and Bulgaria – and were recently extended.

5. Respondents to the 2002 European Social Survey were asked the following questions:

   Would you say it is generally bad or good for Britain's economy that people come to live here from other countries? Please use this card. [0 Bad for the economy, 10 Good for the economy]

   ***And, using this card, would you say that Britain's cultural life is generally undermined or enriched by people coming to live here from other countries?
   [0 Cultural life undermined, 10 Cultural life enriched]***

6. This table is a transformation of the original data, which asked respondents to rate the impacts of migration on a 0–10 scale. We have coded scores of 0–1 as "very bad", 2–4 as "bad", 5 as "neither good nor bad", 6–8 as "good" and 9–10 as "very good".

7. Bases for Table 2.4 are as follows:

	Weighted base		Unweighted base	
	2002	**2011**	**2002**	**2011**
Economic factors				
Class				
Professionals	*799*	*1155*	*802*	*1177*
Routine	*459*	*963*	*463*	*955*
Income				
Top quartile	*716*	*641*	*630*	*799*
Bottom quartile	*306*	*657*	*397*	*579*
Subjective income				
Comfortable	*850*	*493*	*818*	*481*
Struggling	*240*	*236*	*262*	*240*
Cultural factors				
Education				
Degree	*523*	*473*	*524*	*435*
No qualifications	*1065*	*636*	*1107*	*743*
Migrant heritage				
1st or 2nd generation migrant	*330*	*681*	*325*	*600*
British born, British parents	*1722*	*2629*	*1727*	*2711*
Racial prejudice				
None	*1304*	*1338*	*1288*	*1328*
Some or a lot	*746*	*820*	*766*	*831*

8. Racial prejudice is measured slightly differently in the two surveys. On the European Social Survey this refers to levels of discomfort about a relative marrying an immigrant from a different ethnic group. On British Social Attitudes respondents were asked to rate their level of racial prejudice, with three categories: "a lot", "a little" or "none". The cut points in the European Social Survey data are chosen to reflect the same general distribution as these categories.

9. In our experiments, we repeatedly use "Muslim countries" as a comparison region, usually using Pakistan and Bangladesh as examples. This is for two reasons. Firstly, Muslim countries have been a large source of migrants to Britain for several decades. Secondly, Muslims and Muslim migrants have featured very heavily in recent debates over migration and integration, so much so that some authors have argued they have become singled out as a 'pariah' group (Saggar, 2010). We therefore wanted to test if public concerns about immigrants who are clearly labelled as Muslims were stronger than those about immigrants from other regions.

10. A 2010 Home Office report suggested 79 per cent of 2004 student migrants had left the UK by 2010 (Achato et al., 2010).

11. Searches of the websites of Britain's two largest populist 'tabloid' newspapers – The Sun and The Daily Mail – reveal many stories about abuse of the family migration system, focusing in particular on fraudulent 'sham marriages' and on the problem of 'forced' or 'arranged' marriages. These stories also tend to focus on migrants from poorer non-white regions such as Africa and the Muslim countries of the Indian sub-continent, which may explain why support for migrants from these regions is particularly low.

12. Speech by Immigration minister Damian Green, 2nd February 2012, available at: www.homeoffice.gov.uk/media-centre/speeches/making-immigration-work?version=1

References

Achato, L., Eaton, M. and Jones, C. (2010), 'The Migrant Journey', *Home Office Research Report 43,* London: Home Office

Asylum Aid (2010), 'Unsustainable: the quality of initial decision-making in women's asylum claims', *Women's Asylum News*, **97**: 1-4

Blinder, S. (2011a), 'Migration to the UK: Asylum', *Migration Observatory Briefing Paper*, available at: www.migrationobservatory.ox.ac.uk/briefings/migration-uk-asylum

Blinder, S. (2011b), 'UK public opinion toward immigration: Overall attitudes and level of concern' *Migration Observatory Briefing Paper*, available at: www.migrationobservatory.ox.ac.uk/briefings/uk-public-opinion-toward-immigration-overall-attitudes-and-level-concern

Cavanagh, M. and Glennie, A. (2012), *International students and net migration in the UK*, Institute for Public Policy Research, available at: www.ippr.org/images/media/files/publication/2012/04/international-students-net-migrationApr20128997.pdf

Costello, C. (2011), 'UK migration policy and EU law', *Migration Observatory Policy Primer*, available at: www.migrationobservatory.ox.ac.uk/policy-primers/uk-migration-policy-and-eu-law

Dustmann, C., Casanova, M., Fertig, M., Preston, I. and Schmidt, C.M. (2003), *The impact of EU enlargement on migration flows*, Research Development and Statistics Directorate, London: Home Office

Gibney, M. (2011), 'Asylum Policy', *Migration Observatory Policy Primer*, available at: www.migrobs.vm.bytemark.co.uk/policy-primers/asylum-policy

Hansen, R. (2000), *Citizenship and Immigration in Post-War Britain*, Oxford: Oxford University Press

Migration Observatory (2011), *Thinking behind the numbers: Understanding public opinion on immigration in Britain*, Oxford: Migration Observatory, available at: www.migrobs.vm.bytemark.co.uk/sites/files/migobs/Report%20-%20Public%20Opinion.pdf

Ruhs, M. (2011), 'Responding to employers: labour shortages and immigration policy', *Migration Observatory Policy Primer*, available at: www.migrationobservatory.ox.ac.uk/policy-primers/responding-employers-labour-shortages-and-immigration-policy

Somerville, W. (2007), *Immigration under New Labour*, Bristol: The Policy Press

Spencer, S. (2009), 'Immigration', in Seldon, A. (eds.), *Blair's Britain 1997–2007*, Cambridge: Cambridge University Press

Vargas-Silva, C. (2012), 'Migration Flows of A8 and other EU Migrants', *Migration Observatory Briefing Paper*, available at: www.migrationobservatory.ox.ac.uk/briefings/migration-flows-a8-and-other-eu-migrants-and-uk

Acknowledgements

NatCen Social Research is grateful to Unbound Philanthropy, the Trust for London, the Joseph Rowntree Foundation, the Joseph Rowntree Charitable Trust, the Paul Hamlyn Foundation and the Diana, Princess of Wales Memorial Fund for their generous financial support which enabled us to ask the questions reported in this chapter. We are also grateful to Will Somerville, Heaven Crawley, Ian Preston, Lauren McLaren, Zrinka Bralo, Kirsteen Tait, Shamit Saggar, Chris Attwood, Jon Simmons, Ayesha Sara, Eleanor Taylor, Alison Park and the late, and much missed, Roger Jowell for their advice and assistance in developing the immigration question module. The views expressed are those of the authors alone.

Appendix

Table A.1 Total and net migration inflow, 1991-2011

	Migration inflow	
Year	Total migration	Net migration
1991	329,000	44,000
1992	268,000	-13,000
1993	266,000	-1,000
1994	315,000	77,000
1995	312,000	76,000
1996	318,000	55,000
1997	327,000	48,000
1998	391,000	140,000
1999	454,000	163,000
2000	479,000	158,000
2001	481,000	171,000
2002	516,000	153,000
2003	511,000	148,000
2004	589,000	245,000
2005	567,000	206,000
2006	596,000	198,000
2007	574,000	233,000
2008	590,000	163,000
2009	567,000	198,000
2010	591,000	252,000
2011	589,000	252,000

Source: Office for National Statistics, Long Term International Migration Estimates
2011 figure is estimate for year to September

Constitutional reform

Constitutional reform: a recipe for restoring faith in our democracy?

The first coalition since the Second World War is itself an innovation at Westminster. But it also came to power committed to an ambitious programme of constitutional reform – including fixed-term parliaments, directly elected mayors and local police commissioners, and the wider use of referendums. Could any of these changes reverse the long-term decline in public trust in government?

Attitudes to politicians

Despite some increase in levels of trust since the MPs' expenses scandal, people express considerable scepticism about politicians and government. Meanwhile, the proportion who would prefer Britain to be governed by a coalition rather than a single party has fallen to the lowest level ever recorded.

Fewer than one in ten (9%) **trust British politicians** "a great deal" or "quite a lot", compared with 58% who say they trust the police.

The proportion **favouring a coalition** has fallen from 40% in 2010 to 28% in 2011, while support for single-party government has risen from 48% to 63%.

Popular reforms

Most people, including those with least trust in politicians and governments, favour the wider use of referendums on a range of issues and ballots on 'recalling' MPs guilty of wrongdoing. They are more ambivalent about new forms of representative democracy, including elected mayors and local police commissioners.

88% support the Coalition's proposal that voters should have the right to force MPs who have "broken the rules" to resign and fight a by-election. However, as many as 58% would like to go further and be able to **recall an MP** who is "not doing a very good job".

65% think **elected police commissioners** would ensure the police focus on crimes that are of greatest public concern. However, 38% think that police commissioners would bring about too much political interference, while only 29% disagree.

Authors

John Curtice and Ben Seyd
John Curtice is Professor of Politics at the University of Strathclyde and Research Consultant at NatCen Social Research. Ben Seyd is Lecturer in Politics at the University of Kent

Introduction

The last Labour government came to power in 1997 acutely concerned about an apparently widespread lack of regard for and trust in politics and politicians. Tony Blair had argued in opposition that "so low is popular esteem for politicians and the system we operate that there is now little authority for us to use unless and until we first succeed in regaining it" (Blair, 1996). The Party's 1997 manifesto promised to "rebuild this bond of trust between government and the people" (Labour Party, 1997). Central to fulfilling Labour's ambition was a wide-ranging programme of constitutional reform. Voters in some parts of the country – notably Scotland, Wales, Northern Ireland and London – were given control over new, devolved tiers of government. The representation of hereditary peers in the Lords was curtailed. In addition, however, there was also a striking emphasis on transparency and regulation (Curtice, 2011). Government was made more open and transparent by introducing new freedom of information rules, while political funding was exposed to greater public scrutiny and regulated more tightly. Transparency was seen as an antidote both to the perception and the occurrence of political misbehaviour.

Yet after 12 years in power, Labour – along with other political parties – was caught in a wide-ranging scandal over MPs' expenses. Many a politician was accused of having sought to maximise their ability to benefit from the financial support that MPs could claim for running two homes. A few were eventually found guilty of false accounting. Labour's hopes of restoring trust and confidence were dealt a body blow through revelations that, ironically, came to light through the passage of its own freedom of information legislation.

Unsurprisingly, the scandal generated renewed interest in ways of rekindling citizens' trust in their elected representatives. In 2010 history repeated itself and a new administration, a coalition between the Conservatives and the Liberal Democrats, came to power committed to restoring the public's trust in government through constitutional reforms. The Conservatives' election manifesto talked of citizens being "detached from the political process, devoid of trust in the political classes, and disillusioned with our system of government" and promised to "restore trust in our political system" (Conservative Party, 2010: 65, ix). Their partners in government, the Liberal Democrats, described the political system as "rotten" (Liberal Democrat Party, 2010: 87), while the Party's leader, Nick Clegg, called for a wholesale "revamp" of the political system (Clegg, 2009), declaring that his aim was to persuade people "to put your faith in politics once again" (Clegg, 2010).

However, the new government's proposed reform programme had a somewhat different character from that of its predecessor. Although, like Labour, the Coalition contemplated changing the system of representative, party-based politics, its proposals, which included a referendum on the Commons voting system and a wholly or partly elected House of Lords, focused more on politics at Westminster than on the governance of the devolved territories. At the local level radical changes to the nature of the electoral process were envisaged with the promotion and extension of 'presidential' style local political offices, in the form of directly elected mayors and police commissioners, whose elections were expected to be about personality as much as party politics. Most strikingly, however, the government proposed to depart from the norms of representative democracy by giving voters a direct say in certain decisions. A variety of referendums were to be held at both national and local level, while voters were to be given the ability to 'recall' their MP. Instead of simply opening up politics to public scrutiny as Labour had done, it was now to be subjected as well to the discipline of greater public involvement.

But in so far as it is implemented, is the Coalition's proposed approach to reform any more likely to succeed in restoring public trust? For that to have any prospect of happening, we suggest that two important conditions would need to be satisfied. Firstly, the reforms should be popular with the public at large. Secondly, the changes would need to have particular appeal for those whose trust in the existing system was particularly low.

Existing research offers reason to be hopeful on the second count at least. Those with low levels of trust have been found to be particularly keen on the idea of direct democracy (Bromley et al., 2001; Dalton et al., 2001; Bowler et al., 2007). It has been argued, too, that levels of trust and confidence tend to be higher in states in the US where electors can insist that policy propositions are put to a popular vote (Bowler and Donovan, 2002; Smith and Tolbert, 2004; though see also Dyck, 2009; Dyck and Lascher, 2009). So perhaps the coalition government's reform programme really is better suited than that of its predecessor to the task of addressing public scepticism (see also Bogdanor, 2009).

This chapter uses data collected by the 2011 British Social Attitudes survey to consider whether this is, indeed, the case. We begin by looking at levels of trust in the political system and assess whether the Coalition is correct in its assessment that they are all very low. Thereafter we consider how popular the government's proposed reforms are among the public in general, bearing in mind that the formation of a coalition government was itself an innovation for the post-war period. Finally, we examine the appeal the reforms have for those who have the lowest levels of trust in the current political system in particular.

How sceptical are people in Britain?

Politicians are often accused of misrepresenting reality in order to sell their policy wares. Yet their perceptions of a lack of trust in the political system can hardly be viewed as a distortion of the way British citizens think about their government. Since 1986, the British Social Attitudes survey has regularly asked:

> *How much do you trust British governments of any party to place the needs of the nation above the interests of their own political party?*

Levels of trust have improved a little since the MPs' expenses scandal

As shown in Table 3.1, the responses reveal a sharp decline over time in levels of trust. The proportion saying they trust governments "just about always" or "most of the time" fell from 40 per cent in 1986 to just 16 per cent in 2009, following the MPs' expenses scandal. Over the same period, the proportion saying they "almost never" trust government rose from 12 per cent to 40 per cent. The decline has not been straightforwardly linear. In particular, trust is consistently higher just after an election, perhaps because casting a ballot gives voters the feeling they do have some influence over their politicians. Even so, the degree of trust recorded in 2010 was much lower than after the 1987 election. Meanwhile, levels of trust have actually improved a little since the nadir in 2009 and are much the same now as in 2006. It appears that despite the furore it evoked at the time, the MPs' expenses scandal has not contributed to any significant, further long-term erosion of trust. Even so, it is evident that Labour did not achieve its aspiration to reverse the decline in trust that had become marked during John Major's 1992–97 administration. If anything levels of trust fell away even more during its time in office.

Table 3.1 Levels of political trust, 1986–2011

	86	87 (1)	87+ (2)	91	94	96	97 (1)	97+ (2)	98
Trust British governments of any party	%	%	%	%	%	%	%	%	%
Just about always/most of the time	40	37	47	33	24	22	26	33	28
Only some of the time	48	46	43	50	53	53	48	52	52
Almost never	12	11	9	14	21	23	23	12	17
Weighted base	*1548*	*1375*	*3413*	*1422*	*1140*	*1171*	*1355*	*2906*	*2067*
Unweighted base	*1548*	*1410*	*3414*	*1445*	*1137*	*1180*	*1355*	*4214**	*2071*

	00	01	02	03	05	06	07	09	10	11
Trust British governments of any party	%	%	%	%	%	%	%	%	%	%
Just about always/most of the time	16	28	26	18	26	19	29	16	20	22
Only some of the time	58	50	47	49	47	46	45	42	45	45
Almost never	24	20	24	31	26	34	23	40	33	31
Weighted base	*2293*	*1108*	*2285*	*3305*	*3161*	*1077*	*993*	*1141*	*1083*	*2198*
Unweighted base	*2293*	*1099*	*2287*	*3299*	*3167*	*1077*	*992*	*1143*	*1081*	*2215*

+Source: British Election Study

Readings that are shaded were taken shortly after an election had been held; (1) = just before general election, (2) = just after general election

**The unweighted base is much higher than the weighted base because in this year the British Election Study oversampled people from an ethnic minority and people living in Scotland*

However, previous studies have shown that people's expressed levels of trust are sensitive to the way survey questions on the subject are worded and the particular aspects of trust that respondents are asked to evaluate (e.g. Citrin and Muste, 1999). We can check whether the picture of low levels of trust we derive from our regular question on the subject is, in fact, a valid one, by examining responses to a new set of questions asked for the first time in 2011. These questions asked respondents how much trust they had in the Westminster parliament, British politicians, British governments and – as a non-political point of reference – the police.

As seen in Table 3.2, the results confirm the picture painted by the original measure. Only around one in six people trust either British governments or the Westminster parliament "a great deal" or "quite a lot", while less than one in ten trust British politicians. By contrast, almost six in ten (59 per cent) indicate "a great deal" or "quite a lot" of trust in the police.[1] Equally, whereas 57 per cent do not trust politicians "very much" or "at all", just 11 per cent say the same of the police.

Table 3.2 Trust in political institutions and the police

	British governments in general	Parliament at Westminster	British politicians in general	The police
	%	%	%	%
A great deal	1	1	1	10
Quite a lot	16	14	8	48
Some	39	36	33	29
Not very much	33	35	42	9
Not at all	10	12	15	2
Weighted base	*2198*	*2198*	*2198*	*2198*
Unweighted base	*2215*	*2215*	*2215*	*2215*

We have, thus, found solid evidence of public scepticism towards politicians and governments. Levels of trust have fallen over the past 25 years and, despite some recovery since the MPs' expenses scandal, remain at a relatively low ebb. So how likely is it that the Coalition's constitutional reforms will succeed in reversing this trend?

Views on the government's reforms

As previously noted, the constitutional reforms originally agreed by the Coalition can be divided into three types. Firstly, there are reforms that represent changes to the party-based representative model of democracy at Westminster. These include reform of the Commons electoral system, changes to the composition of the House of Lords and a move to fixed parliamentary terms. Secondly, there are reforms that represent a bigger challenge to a party-based model of representative democracy, since they potentially weaken the role of political parties. These include efforts to increase the number of directly elected mayors, the introduction of directly elected police and crime commissioners throughout England and Wales, and changes to the way political parties choose their election candidates. Thirdly, there is a cluster of reform proposals that represent potentially the biggest challenge of all to representative democracy, by providing for direct citizen involvement in decision-making. These include the wider use of referendums and granting voters the power to 'recall' errant MPs.

Parliamentary democracy

As we have already noted, the formation of a coalition after the 2010 election itself represented something of a constitutional innovation. This would, thus, seem a good place to start our examination of attitudes towards the government's proposed reforms of the system of parliamentary democracy at Westminster. During the course of the last 30 years British Social Attitudes has regularly asked respondents whether they prefer single party or coalition government:

> ***Which do you think would generally be better for Britain nowadays ...***
>
> ***... to have a government at Westminster formed by one political party on its own,***
>
> ***or, to have a government at Westminster formed by two political parties together – in coalition?***

28%

prefer coalition to single party government, lower than ever before

Figure 3.1 shows that on most occasions since 1983 single party government has proved to be the more popular. Initially the formation of the Coalition did little to disturb this picture; in 2010 just under half (48 per cent) said they preferred single party government, while two-fifths (40 per cent) favoured a coalition. Early experience of the reality of a governing coalition appeared neither to have won hearts and minds for the idea nor generated a strong adverse reaction.

This, though, is no longer the case. The proportion preferring a coalition has fallen away to just 28 per cent and is now lower than ever before. It might be thought this change is simply the consequence of an adverse partisan reaction among opposition Labour Party supporters. Indeed, those who identify with Labour are now particularly opposed to coalitions, by a margin of 71 per cent to 23 per cent. Moreover, support for single party government among this group is now 10 percentage points higher than a year ago. However, this increase is almost matched by an eight point rise (from 53 per cent to 61 per cent) among Conservative identifiers and even a six point increase (from 32 per cent to 38 per cent) among Liberal Democrat identifiers. Disenchantment with the idea of coalition has evidently spread well beyond the ranks of opposition supporters.

Figure 3.1 Attitudes to single party versus coalition government, 1983–2011[2]

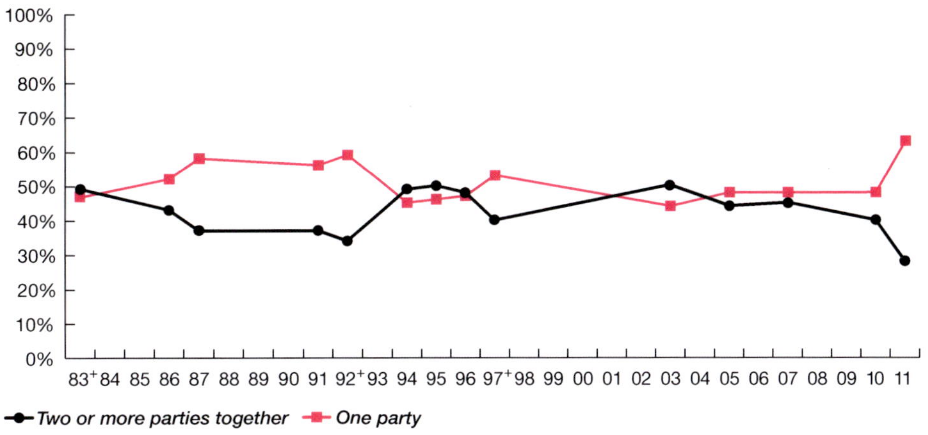

The full data on which Figure 3.1 is based can be found in the appendix to this chapter
+Source: British Election Study

A key issue in the negotiations that led to the formation of the Coalition was how elections to the House of Commons should be conducted in future. The Liberal Democrats preferred proportional representation, while the Conservatives wished to keep 'first-past-the-post'. In the event, the two parties bridged the gap between them by promising a referendum on a relatively minimal reform, the Alternative Vote. Although the Alternative Vote is far from being a proportional system, one argument put forward by opponents is that its introduction would make 'hung' parliaments – and thus coalition administrations – a more likely (and undesirable) outcome of elections. Given the resounding 'no' vote (68 per cent) when the referendum was held in May 2011, perhaps this argument resonated particularly strongly with the public, thereby accounting for the decline in support for coalitions?

The referendum certainly coincided with a sharp decline in support for electoral reform. For more than a quarter of a century British Social Attitudes has regularly asked the following question:

> ***Some people say we should change the voting system for general elections to the UK House of Commons to allow smaller political parties to get a fairer share of MPs. Others say that we should keep the voting system for the House of Commons as it is to produce effective government. Which view comes closer to your own ...***
>
> ***... that we should change the voting system for the House of Commons,***
>
> ***or, keep it as it is?***

Unlike some differently worded questions (Curtice et al., 2007), this question has typically found no more than between a third and two-fifths in favour of change (see Figure 3.2). However, in the immediate wake of the indeterminate outcome produced by the 2010 election, support passed the 40 per cent mark on this measure for the first time. But then between 2010 and 2011 it slumped to an all time low of just 27 per cent.

Figure 3.2 Attitudes to electoral reform, 1983–2011[2]

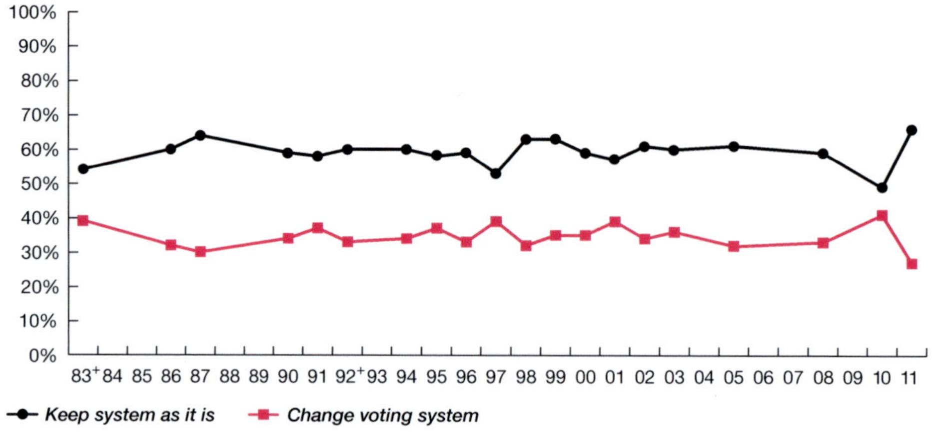

The full data on which Figure 3.2 is based can be found in the appendix to this chapter
+Source: British Election Study

Support for coalitions has dropped since 2010

It is, however, less clear that the historically low level of support for electoral reform is directly linked to the fall in support for coalition government. For example, in 2010 only 49 per cent of those in favour of electoral reform also said they preferred coalition government, a figure not markedly higher than the 38 per cent level of support for coalitions among those who preferred to keep the existing voting system. On these figures any decline in support for electoral reform would have only a minimal impact on support for coalition government. What in practice has happened is that support for coalitions has dropped since 2010 among both those in favour of electoral reform (down to 41 per cent) and those who are opposed (to 23 per cent). Evidently, many people have changed their mind about the merits of coalition government irrespective of their views on the merits of electoral reform. All in all, it is hard to escape the conclusion that the current administration at Westminster has come to be regarded as a poor advertisement for coalition government irrespective of its particular partisan composition or the debate about the merits of electoral reform.

While the outcome of the referendum has ensured that the electoral system used in elections to the House of Commons will not be changed for the foreseeable future, the coalition government has made a significant change to the timing of general elections. In future, they will take place at fixed, five-yearly intervals, rather than at the Prime Minister's discretion. This move is strongly backed by the British public. We asked:

> ***Which of the statements on this card comes closest to your view ...***
>
> ***... General elections should be held on a fixed date every four or five years,***
>
> ***or, the Prime Minister should be able to hold a general election whenever he or she decides?***

More than four times as many people prefer fixed legislative terms (79 per cent) to flexible ones (16 per cent). However, this is to overstate the popularity of the government's particular reform. For when asked how often elections should be held, only 28 per cent back the five-year parliamentary terms adopted by the Coalition. No less than 43 per cent feel that elections should occur every four years, while 28 per cent say that three-year terms are long enough. There is evidently considerable scepticism about allowing politicians the luxury of long periods in office without having to face the electorate.

The Coalition's reform programme originally extended to the House of Lords, settling on proposals, since withdrawn, for replacing its almost wholly appointed membership with a largely but not wholly elected second chamber (Cabinet Office, 2011; UK Parliament, 2012). We sought to ascertain where the public stood on this debate by asking respondents what balance of elected and appointed members should sit in the Upper House:

> *Some people say that having appointed members brings valuable expertise to the House of Lords. Other people argue that members of the House of Lords should be elected for it to be democratic. Which comes closest to your view?*
>
> ***All** members of the House of Lords should be **appointed***
>
> ***Most** members of the House of Lords should be **appointed***
>
> *Roughly **equal** numbers should be **appointed and elected***
>
> ***Most** members of the House of Lords should be **elected***
>
> ***All** members of the House of Lords should be **elected***

The principle of an elected chamber is widely supported, although not necessarily to the exclusion of some appointed members. More than one in four (27 per cent) believe that all members of the Lords should be elected, while another 16 per cent would like to see most members elected. By contrast, just 16 per cent favour the appointment of most or all members of the Lords, although a further 29 per cent would prefer equal numbers of elected and appointed members. Thus, while there is relatively little support for a wholly appointed house, as exists at present, there is no public consensus about what the alternative should be.

55%

agree the House of Lords should consist of independent experts, not party politicians

One argument put forward for retaining at least some appointed members in the Lords is that it would help ensure the House retained the professional expertise required to scrutinise legislation effectively. There appears to be widespread public sympathy for this argument. As many as 55 per cent support the proposition that "the House of Lords should consist of independent experts, not party politicians", while only seven per cent disagree. However, the public does not necessarily regard this as an argument in favour of an appointed House. Rather, those who favour a chamber composed of independent experts are actually more likely (34 per cent) to support a wholly elected Lords than are those who disagree (24 per cent). Perhaps there is some scepticism that appointment would enhance the inclusion of experts rather than party politicians in the Upper House.

In summary, none of the reforms advanced by the Coalition for changing the practice of representative government at Westminster appears to strike a resounding chord with the public. The principle of fixed-term parliaments is widely supported, but people would prefer that elections were held every four, rather than five, years. The principle of electing members to the House of Lords is widely endorsed, but there is no consensus about how far the principle should apply. Meanwhile, following the defeat of proposals for Alternative Vote elections to the House of Commons, public support for electoral reform has never been lower. Even the idea of political parties governing in coalition has never had so few friends. All in all it seems unlikely that the Coalition's Westminster reforms can contribute much to restoring public trust and confidence in the political system.

'Presidential' reforms at local level

Another striking feature of the Coalition's various constitutional initiatives has been an enthusiasm to invest executive authority at local level in a single directly elected individual. The first steps towards the introduction of such 'presidential-style' offices were taken by the previous Labour government, which introduced a directly elected mayor for a new London-wide authority, while inviting local authorities and their electorates in other areas of England and Wales to initiate a referendum on creating such a post in their area. However, of 37 local referendums on adopting elected mayors held while Labour was in office, just 12 produced a majority in favour. Moreover, voters in one of these localities – Stoke-on-Trent – subsequently chose to abolish their mayor (Hope and Wanduragala, 2010). Nevertheless, the model was revived by the coalition government, which decided that referendums should be held on introducing the system in 12 of the largest English cities. More controversially, the government legislated to create the new office of elected police and crime commissioner. Each of the 41 police authorities in England and Wales outside London (where the position is held by the directly elected mayor) is to be headed by a police commissioner, who will set the strategic direction for local policing while being accountable to local citizens through the ballot box.

The concept of directly elected mayors receives a mixed response from the public

For their supporters, one of the virtues of directly elected mayors and police commissioners is that they open the way for politically independent figures to win elected office. Indeed, in 30 mayoral elections held up to and including May 2012, 11 were won by a figure not aligned at the time to a political party.[3] However, the concept of directly elected mayors receives a mixed response from the public across Britain as a whole. The idea that mayors can act as advocates for their locality secures widespread assent. Six in ten (58 per cent) agree that directly elected mayors mean "there is someone who can speak up for the whole area", while only 15 per cent disagree. However, faced with a commonly-heard criticism that having a mayor "gives too much power to one person", more people agree (35 per cent) than disagree (27 per cent). Many people, too, remain unconvinced that an elected mayor "makes it easier to get things done". While those who agree (37 per cent) outnumber those who disagree (21 per cent), another 38 per cent say they neither agree nor disagree.[4] All in all, perhaps it should not have come as too much of a surprise that when, in May 2012, referendums on introducing a directly elected mayor were held at the Coalition's behest in 10 of the largest English cities, only one – Bristol – voted in favour.[5]

The public exhibits a similar lack of clear or consistent support for the idea of directly elected police and crime commissioners. Our questions, fielded for the first time in the latest survey, ran as follows:

> *It has been suggested that every police force should be headed by a commissioner who is elected by all the people in the area and who would be responsible for setting priorities for how the area is policed. Please say how much you agree or disagree that having locally elected police commissioners would ...*
>
> *... ensure the police concentrated on tackling those crimes that most concern ordinary people?*
>
> *... result in too much political interference in the way the police do their job?*

38%

agree elected police commissioners will bring about too much political interference

There is widespread assent that elected police commissioners will ensure the police focus on crimes that are of greatest public concern. Indeed, 65 per cent agree that they will deliver this benefit, while just 17 per cent disagree. Yet one of the key doubts expressed about the new arrangements – not least by the police themselves – that they will result in undue political interference, receives an echo too. More people (38 per cent) agree that directly elected commissioners will bring about too much political interference than disagree (29 per cent), while another 28 per cent neither agree nor disagree.

There is, then, no consistent support for the Coalition's proposals to extend direct candidate-centred elections for local leaders. True, people seem to believe that elected mayors and police commissioners can provide stronger local advocacy and responsiveness. But alongside this run concerns that these elected posts might give undue political power to individuals and compromise the independence of the police service.

If undue political interference is a concern for some people, how much appetite is there for opening up political parties themselves to greater popular involvement by giving the public a greater say in whom they nominate in the first place? Before the 2010 general election, the Conservative Party held 'open' primary elections in a number of constituencies. Ordinary citizens as well as party members and officials could vote in a ballot to determine who should be the party's local parliamentary candidate. The coalition agreement between the Conservatives and the Liberal Democrats (Cabinet Office, 2010) pledged to extend such primaries to 200 constituencies in advance of the next general election, although the commitment has yet to be implemented. To assess support for this idea we asked:

> ***Before each general election, each of the political parties has to choose someone as their candidate to be the local MP. Who do you think should have a say in deciding who stands as a party's candidate? Should it be …***
>
> ***… only those who are paid-up members of the party locally,***
>
> ***all those locally who usually vote for the party,***
>
> ***or, everyone in the constituency, whether they usually vote for the party or not?***

The idea of giving citizens some say in the selection of party candidates is popular in principle but, as we saw with elections to the House of Lords, there is no consensus on how far it should extend. While 30 per cent think all voters should be able to take part in such primaries, another 28 per cent want participation limited to those who usually vote for the party. Meanwhile, 23 per cent are happy to leave the decision to party members, while a further 19 per cent could not decide between these options.

Direct democracy

Thus, as in the case of reform of party-based representative government at Westminster, measures that focus greater attention on the merits of individual candidates rather than just their parties largely receive no more than lukewarm, and certainly far from uncritical, support. But is this also true of reforms that give the public a more direct say in decision making? How, in particular, do people view the increased use of referendums and the coalition government's plans for the recall of Members of Parliament?

Since coming to power, the Coalition has both held and made provision for a variety of referendums. We have already referred to the referendum in May 2011 that rejected the Alternative Vote for elections to the House of Commons, and the referendums held in May 2012 in some English cities on whether or not to introduce directly elected mayors. In addition, voters in Wales were invited in March 2011 to decide whether or not their National Assembly should assume full legislative powers in its devolved areas of responsibility. The Coalition has, meanwhile, legislated for a referendum to be held before any further significant transfer of powers to the European Union can take place. It has also required any local council in England wishing to increase the council tax by more than a government-recommended maximum to secure the assent of its voters in a referendum. At one stage, the Coalition also proposed to enable voters in any local authority to initiate an advisory referendum vote on an issue of local concern. However, this proposal was dropped following opposition in the House of Lords, not least because of the expense of holding such ballots (Lords HC Deb 10 October 2011, cols.1406–1413).

All of the Coalition's referendum proposals are popular

All these referendum proposals are popular. For example, 67 per cent agree that "a council that wants to increase the council tax by more than inflation should have to get a majority vote in favour through a local referendum", while just 13 per cent disagree.[6] People appear equally keen on being able to initiate a local referendum on issues where there is "a lot of local concern"; two-thirds (67 per cent) are in favour while only 16 per cent object. Again, 67 per cent say voters rather than MPs should decide in a referendum "whether or not Britain should agree to giving more powers to the European Union". Meanwhile, as many as 69 per cent reckon voters should directly determine the electoral system used in House of Commons elections, while no less than 76 per cent support holding a referendum to decide "whether or not a town or city should have a directly elected mayor".

One Coalition reform whose origins lie directly in the MPs' expenses scandal is the proposal that voters should be able to 'recall' their MP in the event of 'serious wrongdoing'. If an MP received a custodial sentence[7] or was adjudged guilty of wrongdoing in a vote of the whole House of Commons, a by-election would be called in their constituency provided that more than 10 per cent of the local electorate signed a petition demanding one. No less than 88 per cent feel voters should be able to compel an MP who has "broken the rules" to resign and fight a by-election.[8] However, public support for this approach goes well beyond what the government envisages; six out of ten people (58 per cent) feel that MPs should also be subject to recall in cases where no rules have been broken but where voters think the MP is "not doing a very good job".[9]

In contrast to the rather muted response to the coalition government's proposals for reforming representative democracy, those reforms that offer an element of direct democracy are generally favourably received. The public gives solid backing to reforms that give them the right to vote to decide certain local and national issues, as well as to require errant MPs to face the judgement of the ballot box. What, however, is less clear is whether the government's direct democracy reforms go far enough to satisfy the public mood. Most people support more powerful recall measures for MPs than the Coalition is proposing, as well as local policy referendums of a kind that the government has now dropped. We might note, too, that 61 per cent believe that any decision to reintroduce the death penalty should be decided by a referendum as well. Nevertheless, of all the constitutional reforms so far enacted or announced by the government, it seems that its direct democracy measures are the ones best placed to help restore the public's trust in politics. We still need, however, to apply the second of two key tests we identified at the start of this chapter, that is to assess whether the government's reforms appeal particularly to those who are currently most sceptical about government and politics.

Do the government's reforms appeal to the less trusting?

In Table 3.3 we compare the level of support for the various elements of the Coalition's reform programme among those with low and high levels of trust. The measure of trust we employ is a scale based on the combined answers to three questions introduced earlier on how much people trust the Westminster parliament, politicians and governments.[10] Those deemed to have 'low trust' comprise the one fifth or so with the lowest levels of trust on this scale, while those with 'high trust' are the one fifth with the highest levels. The difference between the two groups in their levels of support for each reform is shown in the third column of the table; positive scores indicate that the reform in question is more popular among those with low levels of trust.

Many of the Coalition's reforms are particularly appealing to those with low levels of trust in government and politics

Many of the Coalition's reforms are particularly appealing to those with low levels of trust in government and politics. Such voters are, for example, relatively keen on an elected second chamber (albeit a fully elected one) and on allowing the public to choose a party's candidate in a primary election (so long as all voters can participate). However, in neither case does the measure command majority support among those with low levels of trust. Meanwhile, the idea of fixed-term parliaments with elections every five years appears no more popular among those with low levels of trust than those with high levels, while the pattern is actually reversed when it comes to directly elected mayors. People with low levels of trust apparently do not regard having more visible and powerful local politicians as the solution to Britain's political ills.

The one type of reform that is consistently both absolutely and relatively popular among the sceptical is that which gives citizens a direct say in decisions. This is especially true of citizen-initiated local referendums and referendums on transferring powers to the European Union. Also of particular appeal to those with low levels of trust is the proposal to allow voters to recall their MP, though this difference is more pronounced when it comes to recalling MPs who have not necessarily broken any rules but are simply seen as doing a poor job.

Table 3.3 Attitudes to constitutional reform by level of political trust

	Low trust	High trust	Difference Low trust - High trust
% saying should be decided by referendum			
Fixed-term parliaments	79	78	+2
Elections every five years‡	29	31	-2
Fully elected House of Lords	37	19	+18
% saying			
Elected mayors …			
… speak up for area	49	71	-22
… easier to get things done	28	47	-19
… power to one person*	25	38	-13
Police commissioners …			
… concentrate on crimes	71	60	+11
… political interference*	32	25	+7
Party candidates decided by everyone‡	36	21	+15
% saying should be decided by referendum			
Council tax increase‡	70	60	+10
Elected mayors‡	77	69	+8
Issues of local concern‡	76	59	+17
Electoral system‡	71	66	+5
Powers to EU‡	74	57	+17
% saying recall MPs …			
… who break the rules	93	81	+12
… who are not doing good job	71	47	+24

* *Figures show the percentage who disagree with this item*

Except for the items marked‡, the unweighted base for those with low trust is 401 and for those with high trust, 384; the weighted bases are 357 and 415 respectively

In the case of the items marked‡, the unweighted base for those with low trust is 339 and for those with high trust, 336; the weighted bases are 300 and 354

In the case of nearly all reforms distrust is positively related to support for reform

It seems that people who are already sceptical of politicians and governments are particularly receptive to constitutional changes that reallocate decision-making power away from elected representatives towards ordinary citizens. Moreover, these links are not artefacts, concealing more important relationships between the attributes of individuals and their support for constitutional change. Further statistical analysis summarised in the appendix to this chapter shows that even when we take into account a variety of other possible reasons as to why people might support or oppose constitutional reform, the patterns illustrated in the difference column of Table 3.3 are largely still evident. In only two cases – the concern that elected police commissioners will introduce political interference into policing and the introduction of fixed five-year parliamentary terms – are people's reactions largely unrelated to their existing levels of trust. Meanwhile, as we would expect from Table 3.3, there is a negative relationship between distrust and people's views on the merits or otherwise of directly elected mayors (people who are sceptical of politicians are less, not more, likely to favour elected mayors). But in the case of all other reforms, distrust is positively related to support for reform, indicating that support for constitutional change is more likely to be found among the ranks of the sceptical than among those who are more trusting of politicians. However, this relationship is particularly strong in respect of all of the various measures of direct democracy, namely, giving voters the power to recall MPs and holding referendums on both local and national issues.

Conclusions

No informed commentator would sensibly argue that an assortment of constitutional reforms is, in itself, sufficient to persuade a hitherto sceptical population that their political leaders and institutions are now worthy of their trust. But the chances that reform will assist that endeavour are likely to be greater if the particular measures both command a high degree of popular support in general and appeal, in particular, to those who are especially sceptical of politicians.

We have found that many of the coalition government's original package of reforms, not all of which are in any event being pursued, lack either one or both of these qualities. For example, in the case of elections for members of the House of Lords, local mayors and police commissioners, we discover that public support for the changes is accompanied by residual concerns about concentration of power or undue political influence. Moreover, in the case of directly elected mayors, the idea appeals most to those who are already least sceptical about politics and politicians. Yet it is also evident that some of the government's reforms pass both our tests, most notably reforms such as referendums and the recall of MPs that give voters a greater direct say in the political process.

But here our results pose an additional dilemma for policy makers. For they suggest there are further reforms that the Coalition has not pursued – such as giving voters the ability to initiate referendums and recall MPs thought to be incompetent – which attract substantial public support, particularly among the sceptical. However, politicians who have acquired power through the representative mechanisms of political parties and elections unsurprisingly are often reluctant to transfer that power back to citizens. Yet it is precisely such direct democratic reforms that particularly appeal to sceptics. If the current government, or a future administration, wishes to use institutional reform as a recipe to restore public faith in British politicians, then the mix of ingredients may need to become even more radical.

Notes

1. This picture of low trust in politicians relative to other professional actors, such as the police, is confirmed by data from other polling organisations, such as MORI's 'Trust in Professions' surveys (Ipsos-MORI, 2011).

2. Readings are indicated by data marker; the line indicates an overall pattern but where there is no data marker the line cannot be taken as a reading for that year.

3. These figures have been collated from various House of Commons Library papers supplemented by data from the New Local Government Network.

4. Nor have attitudes to elected mayors improved since their introduction in 2000. The same questions about speaking up for the area, getting things done and giving too much power to a single person were also asked on British Social Attitudes in 1998 and 2000. The proportions agreeing that mayors speak up for the area and help gets things done were no higher in 2011 than in 1998, while the proportion agreeing that mayors give too much power to a single person fell by only 10 percentage points, from 45 per cent in 1998 to 35 per cent in 2011.

5. Two other of England's largest cities, Leicester and Liverpool, had previously decided to introduce a directly elected mayor without holding a referendum. In four other referendums on directly elected mayors held since the 2010 general election, the proposal was approved in two cases (Salford and Tower Hamlets) and rejected in a third (Great Yarmouth). Doncaster voted in May 2012 to keep its elected mayor.

6. The Coalition's proposal is that a referendum should be held when a council wishes to increase the level of council tax by more than a limit specified by the government. To simplify matters, we couched this as referring to an above inflation increase. Note though that voters are not necessarily keen that decisions about the council tax should routinely be referred to them. Only 43 per cent say that decisions about the council tax should be made by voters in a referendum, while 52 per cent would prefer the decisions to be made by their elected council. It would appear that, while voters are happy to have a referendum as a potential bulwark against a particularly large increase in council tax, they are not sure they trust their fellow citizens to make decisions about the tax on a regular basis.

7. Strictly speaking this provision would apply to custodial sentences of 12 months or less, as longer sentences already result in automatic disqualification from membership of the Commons.

8. The full question wording was:

   It has been suggested that sometimes voters should be able to force their local MP to resign and fight a by-election. First of all, say that the MP has broken the rules. How much do you agree or disagree that in those circumstances voters should be able to force their MP to resign?

   Respondents were invited to answer using a five point scale ranging from "strongly agree" to "strongly disagree".

9. The full question wording was:

   And what if the MP had not broken any rules, but voters thought he or she was not doing a very good job? Should voters be able to force their MP to resign?

   Again respondents were invited to answer using a five point scale.

10. The scale was created by adding the scores (ranging from 1 to 4) across the three items and dividing the resulting total by three. Multi-item measures of complex concepts like trust are usually held to be more reliable and valid than single item measures (Zeller and Carmines, 1980: 48-52; Heath and Martin, 1997). Cronbach's alpha for this particular scale is 0.90.

References

Blair, A. (1996), 'Democracy's Second Age', *The Economist*, 14 September: 33–35

Bogdanor, V. (2009), *The New British Constitution*, Oxford: Hart

Bowler, S. and Donovan, T. (2002), 'Democracy, Institutions and Attitudes about Citizen Influence on Government', *British Journal of Political Science*, **32**: 371–390

Bowler, S., Donovan, T. and Karp, J. (2007), 'Enraged or Engaged? Preferences for Direct Citizen Participation in Affluent Democracies', *Political Research Quarterly*, **60**: 351–362

Bromley, C., Curtice, J. and Seyd, B. (2001), 'Political engagement, trust and constitutional reform', in *British Social Attitudes: the 18th Report*, London: Sage

Cabinet Office (2010), *The Coalition: our programme for government*, London: Cabinet Office

Cabinet Office (2011), *House of Lords Reform Draft Bill*, Cm 8077, London: The Stationery Office

Citrin, J. and Muste, C. (1999), 'Trust in Government', in Robinson, J., Shaver, P. and Wrightsman, L. (eds.), *Measures of Political Attitudes*, Vol 2, San Diego: Academic Press

Clegg, N. (2009), 'Voters' trust in democracy is shattered: we must restore it', *The Observer*, 17 May, available at: www.guardian.co.uk/politics/2009/may/17/nickclegg

Clegg, N. (2010), 'Deputy PM's first speech on constitutional reform', 19 May, London: Cabinet Office, available at: www.dpm.cabinetoffice.gov.uk/news/deputy-pms-first-speech-constitutional-reform

Conservative Party (2010), *Invitation to Join the Government of Britain*, London: Conservative Party

Curtice, J. (2011), 'Rebuilding the Bonds of Trust and Confidence?', in Diamond, P. and Kenny, M. (eds.), *Reassessing New Labour: Market, States and Society under Blair and Brown*, London: Wiley-Blackwell

Curtice, J. and Jowell, R. (1998), 'Is there really a demand for constitutional change?', *Scottish Affairs*, Special Issue on Constitutional Change: 61–93

Curtice, J., Fisher, S. and Lessard-Phillips, L. (2007), 'Proportional representation and the disappearing voter', in *British Social Attitudes: the 23rd Report*, London: Sage

Dalton, R., Bürklin, W. and Drummond, A. (2001), 'Public Opinion and Direct Democracy', *Journal of Democracy*, **12**: 141–153

Dyck, J. (2009), 'Initiated Distrust: Direct Democracy and Trust in Government', *American Politics Research*, **37**: 539–568

Dyck, J. and Lascher, E. (2009), 'Direct Democracy and Political Efficacy Reconsidered', *Political Behavior*, **31**: 401–427

Heath, A. and Martin, J. (1997), 'Why Are There so Few Formal Measuring Instruments in Social and Political Research?', in Lyberg, L., Biemer, P., Collins, M., De Leeuw, E., Dippo, C., Schwarz, N. and Trewin, D. (eds.), *Survey Measurement and Process Quality*, London: John Wiley and Sons

Hope, N. and Wanduragala, N. (2010), *New Model Mayors: Democracy, Devolution and Direction*, London: New Local Government Network

Ipsos-MORI (2011), *Trust in Professions 2011*, available at: www.ipsos-mori.com/research publications/researcharchive/2818/Doctors-are-most-trusted-profession-politicians-least-trusted.aspx

Labour Party (1997), *New Labour Because Britain Deserves Better*, London: Labour Party

Liberal Democrat Party (2010), *Liberal Democrat Manifesto 2010*, London: Liberal Democrats

Smith, D. and Tolbert, C. (2004), *Educated by Initiative: The Effects of Direct Democracy on Citizens and Political Organizations in the American States*, Ann Arbor: University of Michigan Press

UK Parliament (2012), *Government Response to the Report of the Joint Committee on the Draft House of Lords Reform Bill*, Cm 8391, London: The Stationery Office

Zeller, R. and Carmines, E. (1980), *Measurement in the Social Sciences: The Link Between Theory and Data*, New York: Cambridge University Press

Acknowledgements

NatCen Social Research is grateful to the Nuffield Foundation for the financial support that enabled us to ask the questions reported in this chapter. The views expressed are those of the authors alone.

Appendix

The data on which Figure 3.1 is based are shown below.

Table A.1 Attitudes to single party versus coalition government, 1983–2011

	83+	86	87	91	92+	94	95
Form of government generally better for Britain	%	%	%	%	%	%	%
One party	47	52	58	56	59	45	46
Two or more parties together	49	43	37	37	34	49	50
Weighted base	*3855*	*1548*	*1375*	*1422*	*2855*	*1140*	*1253*
Unweighted base	*3855*	*1548*	*1410*	*1445*	*3534**	*1137*	*1227*

	96	97+	03	05	07	10	11
Form of government generally better for Britain	%	%	%	%	%	%	%
One party	47	53	44	48	48	48	63
Two or more parties together	48	40	50	44	45	40	28
Weighted base	*1171*	*2906*	*1157*	*1058*	*993*	*1083*	*2198*
Unweighted base	*1180*	*4214**	*1160*	*1075*	*992*	*1081*	*2215*

+*Source: British Election Study*

**The unweighted base is much higher than the weighted base in 1992 because the British Election Study oversampled people from an ethnic minority and people living in Scotland. In 1997 the unweighted base is higher because an oversample was taken of people living in Scotland*

The data on which Figure 3.2 is based are shown below.

Table A.2 Attitudes to electoral reform, 1983–2011

	83+	86	87	90	91	92+	94	95	96	97
	%	%	%	%	%	%	%	%	%	%
Change voting system	39	32	30	34	37	33	34	37	33	39
Keep system as it is	54	60	64	59	58	60	60	58	59	53
Weighted base	*3955*	*1548*	*1375*	*1353*	*1422*	*2855*	*1140*	*1253*	*1171*	*1355*
Unweighted base	*3955*	*1548*	*1410*	*1397*	*1445*	*3534**	*1137*	*1227*	*1196*	*1355*

	98	99	00	01	02	03	05	08	10	11
	%	%	%	%	%	%	%	%	%	%
Change voting system	32	35	35	39	34	36	32	33	41	27
Keep system as it is	63	63	59	57	61	60	61	59	49	66
Weighted base	*1026*	*1066*	*2293*	*1108*	*2285*	*1157*	*1058*	*1153*	*1083*	*2198*
Unweighted base	*1035*	*1060*	*2293*	*1099*	*2287*	*1160*	*1075*	*1128*	*1081*	*2215*

+*Source: British Election Study*

**The unweighted base is much higher than the weighted base because in this year the British Election Study oversampled people from an ethnic minority and people living in Scotland*

Multivariate analysis

The following table summarises the results of multivariate regression modelling of attitudes towards each of the Coalition's proposed reforms. Its purpose was to identify whether or not the statistical relationship between political trust and attitudes towards particular measures of constitutional reform remains significant after taking account of other potentially relevant variables. The additional factors included in our models were a respondent's age (recognising that younger voters might be more willing to contemplate change), their level of education (those with a degree have previously been shown to take a distinctive view on constitutional reform; Curtice and Jowell, 1998), their degree of political interest (acknowledging that support for reform could be primarily a concern of those with an interest in politics) and their party identity. The table summarises the statistically significant differences in outlook identified among these additional factors and reports the coefficient for respondent's score on our political trust/distrust scale. A positive coefficient indicates that those who are more distrusting are more likely to agree with the relevant proposition.

Table A.3 Summary of results of logistic regressions of attitudes towards constitutional reform

	Age	Education	Party identification	Political interest	Political distrust
Fixed-term parliaments	18–44 support	CSE against	Con/Lab/Lib Dem identifiers support		0.15*
Elections every five years	18–54 against				ns
Fully elected House of Lords	18–24 against	Degree/ higher education/ A level/O level against	Con identifiers against	Interested people support	0.32**
Elected mayors …					
… easier to get things done	18–34 agree	A level/O level/CSE disagree			-0.28**
… speak up for area	18–34 agree				-0.42**
… power to one person†		A level disagree			0.22**
Police commissioners …					
… concentrate on crime	18–44 agree	Degree/ Higher education disagree			0.13*
… political interference†	35–44 disagree	Degree/ CSE agree			ns
Party candidates decided by everyone	18–34 agree	Degree/ A level disagree			0.28**

Table A.3 Summary of results of logistic regressions of attitudes towards constitutional reform (continued)

	Age	Education	Party identification	Political interest	Political distrust
Referendum on ...					
... council tax increase	18–24 disagree	Degree disagree			0.21**
... elected mayors	45–54 disagree	CSE agree			0.40**
... issues of local concern	18–24, 35–54 disagree	Degree disagree	Other party identifiers agree		0.36**
... electoral system	55–64 agree				0.24**
... powers to EU		CSE agree			0.40**
Recall MPs ...					
... who break the rules			Con identifiers agree	Interested people agree	0.56**
... who are not doing good job	35–44 agree	O level disagree			0.35**

†This item was worded in a negative direction, and thus a group that was more likely to agree with this proposition is less supportive of reform.

** = significant at 95% level; ** = significant at 99% level; ns = not significant*

In the regressions, age, education and party identification were entered as categorical variables with those aged 65 plus, those with no qualifications and non-identifiers as the reference category. Thus in the case of these three variables the groups identified are ones that were either significantly more supportive or more opposed than those in the relevant reference group. Political interest was entered as an interval level variable and thus the table indicates the overall direction of the relationship between trust and support for the reform where it is statistically significant.

Full results of the regression models are available at:
http://bsa-29.natcen.ac.uk/read-the-report/constitutional-reform/additional-tables.aspx

Transport
How far will people go to tackle climate change?

One important way the public can help to reduce global warming is by changing their travel behaviour. Yet people seem increasingly sceptical about climate change and its causes. How far do they believe in man-made climate change – and are they willing to cut car or plane use to tackle it?

Beliefs about climate change

Most people believe that climate change is real, however public concern about the environmental impact of climate change has declined.

Three in four people believe **climate change** is happening and that humans are, at least partly, responsible. A minority (16%) believe that climate change exists but is not man-made. Only 7% do not believe in climate change.

Two in three say they are concerned about **the effect of transport** on climate change – compared with 80% seven years ago. The proportion agreeing that motoring and air travel have a serious impact on climate change has also declined.

Air travel and car use

Although most people believe in climate change, they are less certain about action to restrict air travel or car use.

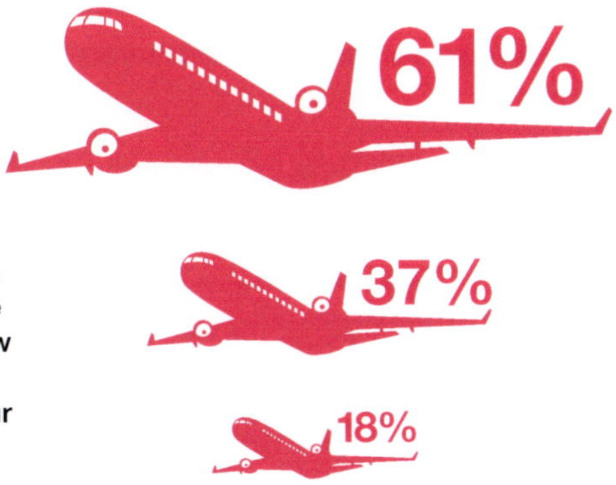

61% think people should be able to **travel by plane** as much as they like. 37% say air travel should be unrestricted even if new terminals or runways are needed. 18% favour unrestricted air travel even if it harms the environment.

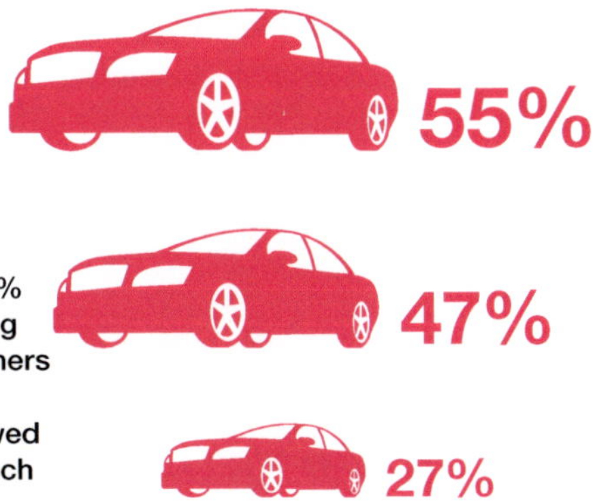

55% think everyone should **reduce their car use** for the sake of the environment. 47% see no point in reducing their car use unless others do the same. 27% say people should be allowed to use their cars as much as they like, even if it damages the environment.

Authors

Alun Humphrey and Andrew Scott
Alun Humphrey is a Senior Research Director, Andrew Scott is a Researcher, both at NatCen Social Research

Introduction

As we saw in last year's British Social Attitudes report, the recent past has seen growing public scepticism about climate change (Taylor, 2011a). The climate change debate itself is well-rehearsed. On one side, the overwhelming majority of climate scientists and the world's leading scientific bodies stand in agreement that climate change is a significant threat to the planet and our way of life. While the causes are many and varied, 'greenhouse' gases (GHG) – especially carbon dioxide emissions from the combustion of fossil fuels – have been identified as the chief contributing factor. On the other side stand dissenting scientists, doubtful politicians and sceptical commentators. Their influence has been increased by controversies such as 'climategate'; even though the British climate scientists accused of manipulating and suppressing data were comprehensively cleared. The 'sceptics' have variously argued that man-made climate change is scientifically unproven, that the threat posed is exaggerated, or that there is little we can do to avert its predicted consequences.

The British public, while experiencing the most prolonged period of economic uncertainty since the 1930s, has had to contend with conflicting assertions about the veracity of climate change theory. In this context, last year's British Social Attitudes report found a 10-year increase from a quarter to more than a third in the proportion of people agreeing that many claims made about environmental threats have been exaggerated (Taylor, 2011a). While identifying significant concern for the impact of transport on climate change, the report also found a distinct lack of support for financial penalties to reduce vehicle use, such as road pricing (Taylor, 2011b).

Politically, each of the main Westminster parties maintain that tackling climate change is a priority. Recent Coalition policy initiatives have included the establishment of a Green Investment Bank, energy efficiency measures for housing and reform of the energy market. Though often criticised for not going far enough, this package of measures is intended to have the dual benefit of encouraging growth in the UK economy and helping to reduce the UK's GHG emissions. Tensions have, nevertheless, been observed inside the Coalition. For example, a party conference speech in 2011 by the Chancellor, George Osborne, was accompanied by media reports that he is critical of the 'green agenda', regarding environmental regulation as an unacceptable burden on British industry.

Achieving a significant transformation will require strong action to 'decarbonise' transport, but progress will also depend heavily on public opinion

Legislation passed by the previous Labour government commits the UK to a 34 per cent reduction in GHG emissions from their 1990 levels by 2020, and an 80 per cent reduction by 2050. It is estimated that transport is responsible for roughly a quarter of UK carbon dioxide emissions, making it the second biggest contributor to GHG in the UK after energy production (Department of Energy and Climate Change, 2012). So if these challenging targets are to be met, it is clear that the transport sector will need to play a major part. Although GHG emissions from the sector peaked in 2007, and have since returned to roughly their 1990 levels, there is still a long way to go. Achieving a significant transformation will require strong action to 'decarbonise' transport, including the further development of emission-reducing technologies. But progress will also depend heavily on public opinion and whether the British people can be persuaded to make transport and travel choices that are less environmentally damaging.

In examining the public's views about climate change and transport, this chapter pursues two main themes. Firstly, it investigates how far people accept the theory of climate change caused by humans and how their beliefs influence concerns about the effects of transport on the environment. It then explores the extent to which the public might be willing to change its transport and travel behaviour in 'greener' ways.

Belief in man-made climate change

For the first time, the 2011 British Social Attitudes survey included a question about belief in climate change. We asked respondents which of the following statements came closest to their view:

> ***I don't believe that climate change is taking place***
>
> ***I believe that climate change is taking place but not as a result of human actions***
>
> ***I believe that climate change is taking place and is, at least partly, a result of human actions***

3 in 4

believe that climate change is happening and that humans are responsible

Given the evidence from previous surveys that concern about the environmental impact of climate change has fallen to historically low levels, the replies to this new question may seem surprising. Three in four people (76 per cent) believe that climate change is happening and that humans are, at least partly, responsible. Another one in six (16 per cent) believe that climate change is taking place, although not as a result of human actions, while just seven per cent do not believe that climate change is taking place at all. In other words, public support for the scientific consensus on climate change is relatively high.

Taylor, in the 28th British Social Attitudes report (2011a), noted how 'concern' about the dangers of climate change to the environment varied by demographic group. Specifically, expressed levels of concern were lowest among older respondents, people without qualifications, those in lower income groups and Conservative Party sympathisers. 'Belief' is, of course, a different concept to 'concern'. It is possible, for example, to believe that climate change is occurring due to human actions but still be unconcerned about how it affects the environment. But do the beliefs about climate change voiced by people in different demographic subgroups vary in a similar way to their expressions of concern?

Table 4.1 shows that they do. People aged 65 and older (66 per cent) are less likely than others to believe that climate change is caused by human actions, while those under 65 (78–80 per cent of 18–64 year olds) are more likely to believe so. Likewise graduates (86 per cent) and people in the top quarter of the income distribution (82 per cent) are more likely to believe in man-made climate change than people without educational qualifications (63 per cent) or those in the lowest income quartile (73 per cent). Distinctions also emerge between supporters of the three main political parties at Westminster. Although the Prime Minister David Cameron has declared that he wants to lead "the greenest government ever",[1] people who identify with his Conservative Party are less likely (71 per cent) to believe that climate change is caused by human actions than those who sympathise with Labour (78 per cent) or his coalition partners the Liberal Democrats (89 per cent).

Table 4.1 Belief that climate change is caused by humans, by demographic group

	% believe climate change is caused by humans	*Weighted base*	*Unweighted base*
Age			
18–34	79	*752*	*948*
35–54	80	*1159*	*1171*
55–64	78	*541*	*496*
65+	66	*856*	*693*
Educational attainment			
Degree or higher	86	*624*	*673*
Below degree level	78	*1635*	*1722*
No qualifications	63	*743*	*636*
Household income (quartiles)			
Highest quartile	82	*799*	*641*
2nd highest quartile	83	*591*	*571*
2nd lowest quartile	75	*594*	*620*
Lowest quartile	73	*579*	*657*
Party identification			
Conservative	71	*926*	*881*
Labour	78	*1039*	*1062*
Liberal Democrat	89	*253*	*247*
All	76	*3311*	*3311*

The effect of transport on climate change

Turning more specifically to the effect of transport on climate change, we examine to what extent people are concerned about pollution from motor vehicles and its consequences for the environment. Each year since the middle of the last decade, we have asked:

Although most people are worried about exhaust pollution and the effect of transport on climate change, the level of concern has decreased since 2005

How concerned are you about exhaust fumes from traffic?

How concerned are you about the effect of transport on climate change?[2]

[Very concerned, fairly concerned, not very concerned, not at all concerned]

Table 4.2 shows that, although most people are worried about exhaust pollution and the effect of transport on climate change, the level of concern has decreased since 2005. In both cases, the proportions expressing concern have declined from around 80 per cent to about 65 per cent. This downward trend was highlighted by Taylor (2011b) a year ago, and the latest data show it has continued.

Table 4.2 Concern about exhaust pollution and the effect of transport on climate change, 2005–2011

	2005	2006	2007	2008	2009	2010	2011
% concerned about exhaust fumes	81	82	79	74	76	70	67
% concerned about the effect of transport on climate change	80	82	76	74	75	68	65
Weighted base	*1107*	*3228*	*3082*	*3392*	*3421*	*3297*	*3311*
Unweighted base	*1101*	*3220*	*3094*	*3393*	*3421*	*3297*	*3311*

We have already noted how people's belief in climate change caused by humans follows a similar pattern among demographic groups to concerns about the consequences of climate change for the environment. In Table 4.3 we see, in addition, that concern about exhaust fumes and the effect of transport on climate change is highest among those who believe that human actions are at least partly to blame for climate change (74 per cent on both measures). Interestingly, almost four in ten people who do not believe in climate change nevertheless express concern about exhaust pollution. This seems likely to reflect the fact that exhaust fumes can be considered detrimental to personal health as well as the environment.

Table 4.3 Concerns about exhaust pollution and the effect of transport on climate change, by belief about climate change

	Belief about climate change		
	Do not believe in climate change	Climate change is not man-made	Climate change is man-made
% concerned about exhaust fumes	38	52	74
% concerned about the effect of transport on climate change	26	42	74
Weighted base	*240*	*517*	*2492*
Unweighted base	*222*	*515*	*2523*

64%

agree that the current level of air travel has a serious effect on climate change

Different modes of transport

We have so far established that three in four members of the British public believe that climate change is both real and caused by humans, and that most of these 'believers' are also concerned about the impact of transport on climate change. Our next step is to consider how the public perceives the impact of specific modes of transport.

British Social Attitudes regularly asks respondents to what extent they agree or disagree that:

The current level of car use has a serious effect on climate change
The current level of air travel has a serious effect on climate change

Table 4.4 shows how the proportions of those agreeing with these two statements have changed between 2005 and 2011. Two key points emerge. Firstly, after peaking in 2006, concern about the impact of both modes of transport has declined considerably: by 14 percentage points for cars and 10 percentage points for air travel. Particularly large falls were seen between 2009 and 2010. Second, the downward trend in concern about car use appears to have stabilised, posting a modest one percentage point increase on last year, while the decline in concern about air travel has slowed. Even so, the proportion of those agreeing that air travel has a serious effect on climate change (64 per cent) is at the same level as when we first asked the question – the lowest in the time series.

Table 4.4 Perceived impact of car use and air travel on climate change, 2005–2011

	2005	2006	2007	2008	2009	2010	2011
% agree the current level of car use has a serious effect on climate change	77	80	72	73	73	65	66
% agree the current level of air travel has a serious effect on climate change	64	74	71	72	72	66	64
Weighted base	*1107*	*3228*	*3082*	*3393*	*3421*	*3297*	*3311*
Unweighted base	*1101*	*3220*	*3094*	*3364*	*3421*	*3297*	*3311*

Freedom to travel?

Although levels of concern are lower than in previous years, we have seen that around two out of three people continue to worry about the impact of transport on climate change. Does this concern translate into a view that people should travel less?

Air travel

Since 2003, British Social Attitudes has asked whether people agree or disagree that:

> ***People should be able to travel by plane as much as they like***
>
> ***People should be able to travel by plane as much as they like, even if new terminals or runways are needed to meet the demand***
>
> ***People should be able to travel as much as they like, even if this harms the environment***

Reporting the responses to these questions in 2009, Shaw and Butt wondered if declining levels of agreement that people should be free to fly as much they liked was "evidence of the beginnings of a shift towards more consistently environmentally-friendly attitudes towards air travel" (p.138). This year, Table 4.5 shows that 62 per cent of Britons agree, the lowest level – a 17 percentage point decline – since we first asked this question.

37%

say people should be allowed to travel by air as much as they like even if this means new terminals or runways are needed

When asked, more conditionally, if people should be allowed to travel by air as much as they like even if new terminals or runways are needed, 37 per cent believe they should. This is a rather lower proportion than in the middle of the last decade. Views on this issue, however, are not clear cut: three out of ten (28 per cent) disagree while another three out of ten (28 per cent) neither agree nor disagree. Opponents and proponents of increased airport capacity in Britain will need to persuade this latter group if they want to win public support for their stance.

There has been little change since 2003 in the minority of the population – around one in five – who agree that people should be able to travel by plane as much as they like even if this harms the environment. Approaching half (45 per cent) disagree, with the remainder taking a neutral view. Since we also know that around a quarter of the population do not believe in man-made climate change (as discussed earlier), the scope for a further reduction in agreement on this measure may prove limited.

Table 4.5 Support for unlimited air travel, 2003–2011

	2003	2004	2005	2006	2007	2008	2009	2010	2011
% agree people should be able to travel by plane …									
… as much as they like	79	77	70	69	63	66	64	64	62
… as much as they like, even if new terminals or runways are needed	52	43	43	44	40	42	42	36	37
… as much as they like, even if this harms the environment	19	15	18	19	19	18	20	18	18
Weighted base	*967*	*889*	*911*	*932*	*851*	*1007*	*965*	*934*	*951*
Unweighted base	*972*	*872*	*913*	*930*	*847*	*990*	*958*	*928*	*936*

To understand how these views translate into support for air fare pricing that reflects the environmental impact of flying, British Social Attitudes also invites respondents to agree or disagree with the following statement:

> *The price of a plane ticket should reflect the environmental damage that flying causes, even if it makes air travel more expensive*

Public agreement that the price of a plane ticket should reflect its environmental impact peaked in 2007 at around half of respondents (49 per cent) (Table 4.6). It has declined since then to around four in ten (41 per cent), though this is still higher than when we first asked the question in 2004. Continuing economic uncertainties seem likely to explain this change as well as the growing burden of Air Passenger Duty. Air Passenger Duty, payable by passengers on flights leaving and arriving in the UK, has increased steadily since it was introduced in 1994. In 2011, it ranged from £12 for short-haul flights up to £85 for the longest distances.

4 in 10

agree that the price of a plane ticket should reflect its environmental impact

Table 4.6 Pricing plane tickets to reflect the environmental costs of flying, 2004–2011

	2004	2005	2006	2007	2008	2009	2010	2011
The price of a plane ticket should reflect the environmental damage caused	%	%	%	%	%	%	%	%
Agree	36	42	48	49	46	45	42	41
Neither	25	29	22	17	23	25	22	25
Disagree	34	24	24	28	26	25	30	27
Weighted base	*889*	*911*	*932*	*851*	*1007*	*965*	*934*	*951*
Unweighted base	*872*	*913*	*930*	*847*	*990*	*958*	*928*	*936*

Car travel

Most people use their cars much more than they travel by air. But does that make them more or less reluctant to accept that car use should be curtailed for environmental reasons? We asked respondents whether they agreed or disagreed that:

> *People should be allowed to use their cars as much as they like, even if it causes damage to the environment*
>
> *For the sake of the environment everyone should reduce how much they use their cars*
>
> *There is no point in reducing my car use to help the environment unless others do the same*

Table 4.7 shows more than half accepting the principle that everyone should reduce their use of cars for the sake of the environment, while only one in seven disagree. However, when it comes to whether people should be allowed to use their cars as much as they like, regardless of environmental damage, there is almost an even split between those who take a 'green' stance by disagreeing with the proposal, those who agree and those who are neutral. Responses to our third question add a further layer of ambivalence: almost half the public believes there is no point reducing the amount they use their cars unless others do too. Only one in four actively disagree.

Table 4.7 Car use and environmental protection

Reduce car use for the sake of the environment	**%**
Agree	55
Neither agree nor disagree	25
Disagree	15
No restrictions on using cars, even if it damages the environment	**%**
Agree	28
Neither agree nor disagree	33
Disagree	33
No point in reducing car use unless others do the same	**%**
Agree	47
Neither agree nor disagree	21
Disagree	25
Weighted base	*951*
Unweighted base	*936*

While more than half the public accepts the principle that everyone should reduce their car use to help the environment, we see that nearly as many people would be reluctant to cut their car use in practice unless they knew that others were doing the same. This suggests that policy makers need to tread warily if they want to reduce the environmental impact of car use in ways that win public acceptance.
We, accordingly, asked respondents whether they agreed or disagreed that:

> *For the sake of the environment, car users should pay higher taxes*
>
> *People who drive cars that are better for the environment should pay less to use the roads than people whose cars are more harmful to the environment*

These two statements represent the 'carrot and stick' of policy instruments. The first implies increases in the cost of Vehicle Excise Duty on all drivers, while the second implies a reduction in Duty for those who drive more environmentally-friendly cars. Perhaps unsurprisingly, our survey finds much greater support for the 'carrot', with around six in ten (58 per cent) agreeing that people driving 'greener' cars should pay less. Just 15 per cent disagree. Conversely, 63 per cent disagree that car users should pay higher taxes, with only 13 per cent taking the opposite view. The responses show non-drivers are more positive towards car tax increases (19 per cent agree) than drivers (10 per cent). But a majority of both groups are opposed.

Britons are more supportive of incentives for environmentally-friendly behaviour through charging less for green choices, and less supportive of measures that will increase the cost of travel for all

Travel behaviour

We have seen that belief in climate change and public concern about the effects of transport on the environment are still both relatively high. In principle (and with caveats) most people support a reduction in the use of cars and air travel "for the sake of the environment". However, when it comes to policy, Britons are more supportive of incentives for environmentally-friendly behaviour through charging less for green choices, and less supportive of measures that will increase the cost of travel for all. With that in mind, we turn to what people say about their own travel behaviour. Does the practice of their travel decisions accord with the views they express in principle? Are those sceptical about climate change less likely to travel in an environmentally-friendly way? If so, might we expect growing scepticism about climate change to result in changes in the ways people choose to travel?

Our survey confirms one unsurprising fact: as a nation we are very reliant on the car. Of those interviewed 69 per cent identify themselves as drivers and – as shown in Figure 4.1 – around half say they travel by car as a driver or passenger "every day or nearly every day". Complementary statistics from the most recent National Travel Survey show that two-thirds (64 per cent) of all journeys undertaken in Britain are made by car (Department for Transport, 2011b). Figure 4.1 also shows how daily use of the car peaked 10 years ago before declining slightly. Since 2006 the proportion seems to have stabilised at around 43 per cent. In an analysis of trends up to 2007, Stradling et al. (2008) hypothesised that the modest adjustment in people's daily travel arrangements might have resulted from rising fuel costs, congestion, the rise of internet communications (reducing the need for travel) or possibly changes in attitudes in response to concern about the environment.

Figure 4.1 Daily transport use, 1993–2011

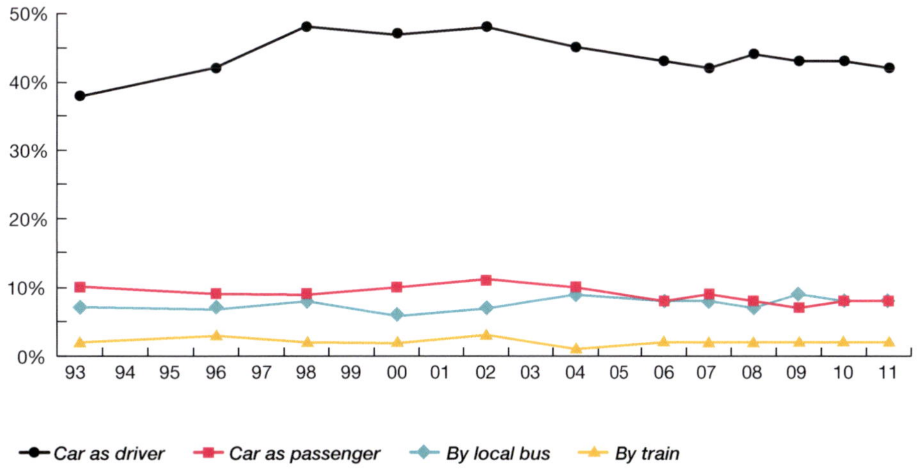

The data on which Figure 4.1 is based can be found in the appendix to this chapter

To investigate this last possibility, we now look at how closely travel behaviour is related to views about climate change and, specifically, whether climate change sceptics make greater use of cars than other people. The latest survey responses suggest this is not the case. Comparing people's frequency of car travel with their views about climate change, we find that 45 per cent of non-believers in climate change report using a car every day (or nearly), as do 46 per cent of those who acknowledge climate change but discount the causal role of humans and 50 per cent of those who accept that climate change is at least partly man-made. However, although three-quarters of the population believe in man-made climate change, they are likely to hold a spectrum of views about the seriousness of the problem and the extent to which transport impacts on climate change. If we compare people's car use against our more specific measure of whether they express concern about the effect of transport on climate change, we find that those who are most concerned make travel choices that are somewhat different from others. Table 4.8 shows that the level of car use (either as a driver or a passenger) among those who say they are "very" concerned about the effect of car use on climate change is noticeably lower (39 per cent) than for those who report being "fairly", "not very" or "not at all" concerned. This is particularly true of frequent car use.

Table 4.8 Frequency of car use, by concern about effect of transport on climate change

	Concern about the effect of transport on climate change			
	Very concerned	**Fairly concerned**	**Not very concerned**	**Not at all concerned**
Frequency of car use	%	%	%	%
Every day or nearly every day	39	51	53	43
At least once a week	44	39	40	42
Less than once a week	16	10	7	14
Weighted base	*649*	*1499*	*847*	*282*
Unweighted base	*645*	*1479*	*846*	*299*

Of course, people's daily travel choices are affected and constrained by a range of factors other than concern about environmental impact, not least the availability of suitable public transport options. This seems likely to explain why the association between concern about climate change and travel behaviour is relatively weak.

48%

of participants in the latest survey have flown in the past year, compared with 56 per cent in 2008

We also looked at air travel. Given the distances involved and a lack of practicable alternatives where most international travel is concerned, people's decisions about whether to fly will often be about whether to make their trip at all. There has been much publicity about the impact of air travel on the environment and the high 'carbon footprint' associated with flying. It is also worth noting that the use people in Britain make of air travel has stagnated in recent years. Since 2003, British Social Attitudes has asked people about the number of air trips they have undertaken by plane in the preceding 12 months. The replies show that 48 per cent of participants in the latest survey have flown in the past year, compared with 56 per cent in 2008. Figures from the Department for Transport also show a decline in air passenger numbers from the UK since 2007, associated with the economic recession. Despite this, air travel is predicted to grow significantly in the future (Department for Transport, 2011c) and the environmental impact of flying is likely to become an even more important issue.

As with car use, we can also investigate whether the amount people fly is linked to their views about climate change. Again, there turns out to be little difference in the frequency of flying between those who do not accept that climate change is occurring and those who do (Table 4.9). While 45 per cent of people who do not believe in climate change report flying in the past year, the same is true of 46 per cent of those who doubt that climate change is man-made and 49 per cent of those who believe it is at least partly caused by humans. Even when looking at our more specific measure of concern about transport and the environment, there turns out to be little difference in frequency of air travel between those who say they are "very" concerned and those who are less so. Indeed, those least concerned about transport and the environment are likely to have flown rather less than others, 63 per cent not having flown in the preceding year compared with around half of others.[3]

Table 4.9 Air travel in the last year, by concern about the effect of transport on climate change

	Concern about the effect of transport on climate change			
	Very concerned	Fairly concerned	Not very concerned	Not at all concerned
Number of trips by air in last year	%	%	%	%
None	51	50	52	63
One	22	22	16	15
Two	12	15	15	9
Three or more	16	14	17	14
Weighted base	*649*	*1499*	*847*	*282*
Unweighted base	*645*	*1479*	*846*	*299*

While there appears to be some relationship, though weak, between car use and concern about climate change, the amount that people travel by air does not appear related to their views or concerns about climate change. What then are the implications for future efforts to reduce emissions of greenhouse gases? Does the difference between public attitudes in principle and people's travel choices in practice mean initiatives to change travel behaviour are doomed to fail? That is the issue we examine in the final part of this chapter.

Willingness to change travel behaviour

Having considered people's current behaviour, we move on to look at how able and willing they are to change the way they travel in order to reduce the impact on climate change. One of the Department for Transport's key environmental impact indicators is the proportion of urban trips under five miles that people take either by walking, cycling or public transport (Department for Transport, 2011a). On a similar theme, British Social Attitudes asks how easy it would be for respondents to make short journeys currently undertaken by car by other means, although the question focuses on journeys of less than two miles. People were asked whether they agreed or disagreed with these statements:

> *Many of the journeys of less than two miles that I now make by car I could just as easily walk*

> *Many of the journeys of less than two miles that I now make by car I could just as easily go by bus*

> *Many of the journeys of less than two miles that I now make by car I could just as easily cycle, if I had a bike*

There is evidence of some willingness to consider change for short journeys. Four out of ten (41 per cent) either agree or agree strongly that they could walk instead of driving, a third (33 per cent) say they could get the bus and another four out of ten (38 per cent) say they could cycle. These proportions have changed little during the decade the question has been asked. However, we must remember that these questions tap into people's ability to alter their travel behaviour as well as their willingness to do so. Their ability to use alternative means of transport even for short journeys may be constrained by health problems or the lack of a suitable bus service. Our results show that 25 per cent disagree or disagree strongly that they could walk instead of driving, and 39 per cent disagree that they could take the bus as an alternative.

We additionally asked the drivers in our survey about other transport choices they might be prepared to make "to help reduce climate change". We asked whether they agree or disagree that:

> ***I am prepared to reduce my speed on the motorway to help reduce my CO_2 emissions***

> ***Next time I buy a car, I would be willing to buy a car with lower CO_2 emissions. This might be an ordinary car with a smaller or more efficient engine, or a vehicle that runs on electric or alternative fuels***

> ***I am willing to reduce the amount I travel by car***

We then asked everyone taking part in the survey whether they agree or disagree that:

> ***I am willing to reduce the amount I travel by plane***

Note that respondents were also able to give a spontaneous response that they already engage in these behaviours.

The responses indicate considerable willingness to change. Seven out of ten drivers (70 per cent) say they would be willing to buy a car with lower carbon dioxide emissions, while a further two per cent say they already do so. Six out of ten (60 per cent) would be willing to reduce their speed on the motorway to help reduce climate change, with one per cent saying that they already do so. This finding compares interestingly with the government's proposal to increase the speed limit on motorways from 70mph to 80mph,[4] rather than reduce it. As might be expected from earlier replies to questions about reducing car and air travel, the response to these possibilities is less positive. Four out of ten drivers (40 per cent) agree they would be willing to reduce their travel by car, but an equal proportion disagree (a further four per cent say they are already travelling less by car in response to climate change). Meanwhile, although one in four (24 per cent) among the wider public say they are prepared to travel less by plane, one in three (32 per cent) disagree. We may also note that five per cent say they are already reducing their air travel to help tackle climate change, while almost one in four (23 per cent) insist they never fly anyway.

Looking at Table 4.10 we can see that there is – not surprisingly – a strong connection between people's willingness to change their travel behaviour to help reduce climate change and their beliefs about its existence and cause. Just 27 per cent of drivers who don't believe climate change is taking place are willing to reduce their speed on the motorway (or already do so), compared with 69 per cent of those (the majority of the population) who believe that climate change exists and is at least partly due to human actions. Likewise, only 34 per cent of drivers who don't believe in climate change would be prepared to buy a car with lower CO_2 emissions (or have already done so), compared with 78 per cent of those who believe in man-made climate change. We see similar patterns in relation to lowering car use and, across the population as a whole, to reducing travel by plane. Logistic regression analysis confirms that willingness to change behaviour in each of these ways is independently associated with belief in climate change (having controlled for sex, age, level of education, income, party identification and urbanicity).[5]

Table 4.10 Willingness to change travel behaviour, by belief about climate change

	Belief about climate change		
	Don't believe climate change taking place	**Believe climate change does not result from human actions**	**Believe climate change at least partly results from human actions**
% saying ...			
... prepared to/already reduce myspeed on the motorway to help reduce my CO_2 emissions	27	42	69
... willing to buy/already bought a car with lower CO_2 emissions	34	60	78
... willing to/already reduce the amount I travel by car	19	34	48
*Weighted base**	*130*	*356*	*1770*
*Unweighted base**	*141*	*351*	*1760*
% saying ...			
... willing to/already reduce the amount I travel by plane	13	22	33
Weighted base	*222*	*515*	*2523*
Unweighted base	*240*	*517*	*2492*

* *Base: all drivers*

Does this mean that increasing scepticism about climate change carries implications for policy efforts to tackle climate change through behaviour change? Potentially yes, given that climate change sceptics are clearly less willing to change. However, while scepticism has increased, it still runs at a relatively low level. Most people believe in climate change caused or partly caused by human behaviour and are concerned about the impact of transport on the environment.

Who is most willing to change?

When we divide individuals who are willing to change their behaviour to help reduce climate change into demographic subgroups, we find that women drivers are more willing to take action than men. Seventy per cent of women motorists agree that they would be prepared to reduce their speed on the motorway to help reduce the impact of climate change (or say they already do so) compared with 56 per cent of men. Women drivers are also rather more willing than men to consider buying a car with lower emissions (75 per cent compared with 70 per cent) and reduce the amount they travel by car (47 per cent compared with 41 per cent).

There is also some evidence that younger people are more willing than older people to make less use of air travel. The proportion agreeing that they would be willing to reduce the amount they travel by plane (or already do so) declines from 34 per cent among 18–24 year olds to 25 per cent among people aged 65 or over. However, older people are much less likely to fly in the first place. There is also a tendency for graduates and others with higher qualification levels to show greater willingness to change their behaviour than those with lower or no qualifications, though again it must be noted that those without qualifications are far less likely to fly in the first place. These differences in relation to age and educational qualifications are what we might expect to see given our earlier findings about the way people's beliefs in climate change vary between groups (see Table 4.1). People in higher income brackets were slightly less willing to reduce the amount they travel by car than those with lower incomes, or to reduce their speed on motorways. In terms of party political affiliation, people who identify themselves with the Conservatives express less willingness to change their transport and travel behaviour than those of Labour or the Liberal Democrats. For example, 36 per cent of Conservative supporters are willing to reduce the amount they travel by car (or do so already) compared with 50 per cent and 46 per cent of Labour and Liberal Democrat supporters respectively. It seems probable that the Conservatives' endorsement of 'green' policies before and after the 2010 General Election may have held less appeal for their own core sympathisers than for supporters of the other main parties.

For the first time, British Social Attitudes asked people directly about their belief in climate change and found that climate sceptics are in the minority in Britain

Conclusions

The findings reported in this chapter could be described as 'a mixed bag' for those concerned about the environment and how best to reduce the adverse impact of transport on the environment. For the first time, British Social Attitudes asked people directly about their belief in climate change and found that climate sceptics are in the minority in Britain. For those accepting the scientific consensus and its implications for reducing emissions of greenhouse gases, the recognition of climate change by the majority is reassuring. While there are demographic variations in this belief, a majority in all the social groups we have examined accept that climate change is real and that it is, at least in part, caused by human activity. Yet it is also clear that a substantial minority – around one quarter – either reject the notion of climate change altogether or believe that it is not man-made.

Since 2006, we have observed a trend of declining public concern about the part that transport plays in climate change. Our latest survey shows that this is continuing, albeit at a slower pace. A year ago, Taylor (2011a) suggested that declining concern may be a result of the economic uncertainties being experienced in Britain. Since both economic uncertainty and decreasing concern have continued into this year, this may well be the case. Only time will tell whether economic recovery can help to reverse the trend.

We have also found only a weak association between the amount people travel and their views about climate change and the environment. There is limited willingness to reduce car and plane use, and low levels of support for policies that make motoring or air travel more expensive. This suggests that policies geared to making transport more sustainable will be met with less resistance than those that try to influence travel choices. As Stradling et al. (2008) acknowledged in the 24th British Social Attitudes report, there are real difficulties facing any government that tries to apply demand-side measures as a way of influencing millions of individual lifestyle choices. In the latest survey it is even more apparent that willingness to change travel behaviour is lower among those who decline to believe that climate change is caused by humans or who are unconcerned by it.

Attempts by government to convince Britons to consider changing their behaviour are a long way from being realised. A significant minority have yet to be convinced about the need to take action in the first place. However, this does not suggest that attempts to bring about a shift should be abandoned. There is evident willingness among many people to consider reducing the amount they travel by car and plane, particularly among those who express concern about pollution and the environment. But the greatest challenge for those wishing to encourage environmentally-friendly travel continues to be that of convincing sceptics that climate change caused by humans is real – and a real threat.

Notes

1. Speech by David Cameron at Department of Energy and Climate Change, www.decc.gov.uk/en/content/cms/news/pn10_059/pn10_059.aspx

2. This question does not ask specifically about car use, but is placed with other questions about road transport.

3. It has previously been noted that those most concerned about the environment can often themselves be the most frequent flyers (Commission for Integrated Transport, 2007).

4. Transport policy in Scotland is devolved so this would only apply in England and Wales.

5. The multivariate analysis technique used was logistic regression – more details of the methods used can be found in the Technical details chapter of this report. Further details of the analysis results are available from the authors on request.

Acknowledgements

NatCen Social Research is grateful to the Department for Transport for their financial support which enabled us to ask the questions reported in this chapter. The views expressed are those of the authors alone.

References

Commission for Integrated Transport (2007), *Attitudes to Aviation and Climate Change*, available at: www.ipsos-mori.com/Assets/Docs/Publications/attitudes-to-climate-change-and-aviation-2007-report.pdf

Department of Energy and Climate Change (2012), *2011 UK Greenhouse Gas Emissions, Provisional Figures and 2010 UK Greenhouse Gas Emissions, Final Figures By Fuel Type And End-User*, available at: www.decc.gov.uk/assets/decc/11/stats/climate-change/4817-2011-uk-greenhouse-gas-emissions-provisional-figur.pdf

Department for Transport (2011a), *Business Plan 2011-2015*, available at: assets.dft.gov.uk/publications/business-plan-2011-2015/DFT-Business-Plan.pdf

Department for Transport (2011b), *National Travel Survey, Statistical Release*, available at: assets.dft.gov.uk/statistics/releases/national-travel-survey-2010/nts2010-01.pdf

Department for Transport (2011c), *UK Aviation Forecasts*, available at: assets.dft.gov.uk/publications/uk-aviation-forecasts-2011/uk-aviation-forecasts.pdf

Stradling, S., Anable, J., Anderson, T. and Cronberg, A. (2008), 'Car use and climate change: do we practise what we preach?', in Park, A., Curtice, J., Thomson, K., Phillips, M., Johnson, M. and Clery, E. (eds.), *British Social Attitudes: the 24th Report*, London: Sage

Shaw, A. and Butt, S. (2009), 'Pay more, fly less? Changing attitudes to air travel', in Park, A., Curtice, J., Thomson, K., Phillips, M. and Clery, E. (eds.) *British Social Attitudes: the 25th Report*, London: Sage

Taylor, E. (2011a), 'Concern about climate change: a paler shade of green?', in Park, A., Clery, E., Curtice, J., Phillips, M. and Utting, D. (eds.) *British Social Attitudes: the 28th Report*, London: Sage, available at: www.natcen.ac.uk/BSA28

Taylor, E. (2011b), 'Congested Britain? Public attitudes to car use', in Park, A., Clery, E., Curtice, J., Phillips, M. and Utting, D. (eds.) *British Social Attitudes: the 28th Report*, London: Sage, available at: www.natcen.ac.uk/BSA28

Appendix

The data for Figure 4.1 are shown below.

Table A.1 Daily transport use, 1993–2011

	1993	1996	1998	2000	2002	2004
% who usually travel every day or nearly every day by ...						
... car as driver	38	42	48	47	48	45
... car as passenger	10	9	9	10	11	10
... local bus	7	7	8	6	7	9
... train	2	3	2	2	3	1
Weighted base	*1451*	*1235*	*1079*	*1133*	*1150*	*1069*
Unweighted base	*1460*	*1219*	*1075*	*1133*	*1148*	*1053*

	2006	2007	2008	2009	2010	2011
% who usually travel every day or nearly every day by ...						
... car as driver	43	42	44	43	43	42
... car as passenger	8	9	8	7	8	8
... local bus	8	8	7	9	8	8
... train	2	2	2	2	2	2
Weighted base	*3228*	*3082*	*3393*	*3241*	*3297*	*3311*
Unweighted base	*3220*	*3094*	*3364*	*3241*	*3297*	*3311*

Health

Health care in Britain: is there a problem and what needs to change?

Health services are subject to a real-terms expenditure freeze and are under unprecedented pressure to improve productivity during a period of sweeping organisational reforms. How satisfied is the public with the NHS and does it share the government's enthusiasm for change?

Satisfaction with the NHS

Public satisfaction with the NHS has fallen sharply since 2010 when it reached a record high, while most people think the standard of health care has improved or stayed the same in the past five years.

70% 2010

58% 2011

Nearly six in ten people are "very" or "quite" **satisfied** with how the NHS runs nowadays, a sharp drop from 2010 when seven in ten were satisfied.

Around a third of people think the **standard of care** in the NHS has been getting better in the last five years, only just higher than the proportion who think it has got worse.

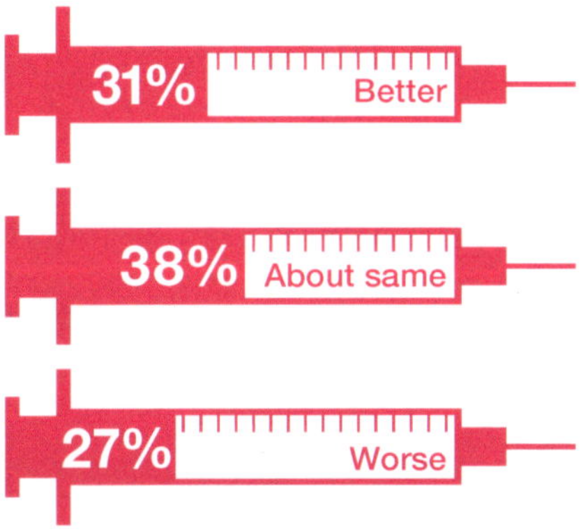

Attitudes to change

People tend to think the health care system needs to change, but there is little appetite for fundamental reform of the NHS. There is some, though not overwhelming, support for the government's policy of giving GPs control over local NHS budgets.

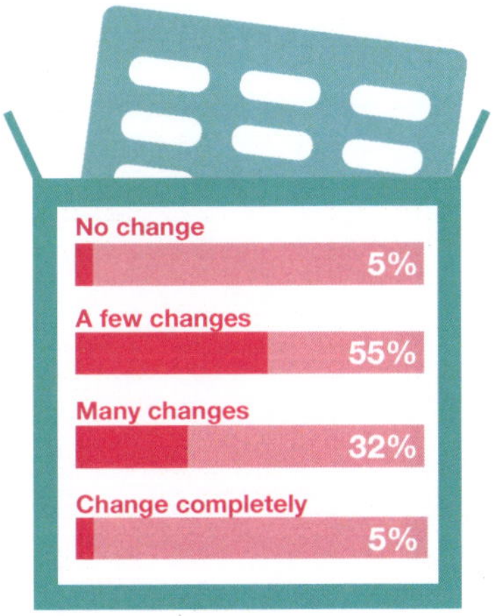

The majority of people (87%) think the health care system in Britain needs some ("a few" or "many") changes.

34% say **family doctors should set local NHS spending priorities**, compared with 30% who say the government, and 17% each saying local people and local councils.

Authors

John Appleby and Lucy Lee
John Appleby is Chief Economist at the King's Fund. Lucy Lee is a Researcher at NatCen Social Research and Co-Director of the British Social Attitudes survey series

The productivity task that the NHS has been set is unprecedented

Introduction

Health care in Britain – and the National Health Service (NHS) in particular – has been affected by significant shifts in the policy and economic landscapes in recent years. In 2011–2012, as the country grappled with the economic standstill and the coalition government's austerity policies started to bite, the NHS began the year with virtually no increase in real funding. After a decade when real spending doubled, the NHS has been allocated little extra funding over and above inflation until April 2015, with the prospect of a continuing freeze for some years beyond that. The productivity task that the NHS has been set in response to this squeeze on its finances is unprecedented. By 2015, a virtually unchanged NHS budget will have to generate an extra 20 per cent more value – the equivalent of around £20 billion of extra funding for the NHS in England alone. Given that there has been little or no improvement in productivity during the past decade and a half (Appleby, 2012a), this represents a huge challenge.

The timing of the latest British Social Attitudes survey was also significant in wider policy terms as interviews took place when the government was pursuing its controversial Health and Social Care Bill through Parliament. Now an Act of Parliament (2012), this provides for what the Chief Executive of the NHS in England has memorably described as reforms so big "they could be seen from space" (Timmins, 2010). At the heart of the changes lies the abolition of Primary Care Trusts and the transfer of the budgets and responsibility for commissioning most NHS services to local clinical commissioning groups (CCGs) led by general practitioners (GPs).

The challenges in terms of both increasing productivity and reforming services rest on an understanding that the NHS is experiencing a 'problem' that needs 'fixing'. Regarding the former, the problem is fairly easy to perceive: how to maintain a quality service with virtually zero real growth in funding and growing needs. However, regarding reform – while acknowledging that performance and organisation in health care can always be improved to some degree – the problem has been less easy to identify. A central criticism of the Coalition's reform plans for the English NHS has been not just that they lack a persuasive narrative about the need for change, but also that they lack evidence that change is necessary on the scale proposed. Indeed, the previous British Social Attitudes survey carried out in 2010 seemed to provide evidence to the contrary by showing that 70 per cent of people were satisfied with the way the NHS runs – the highest level recorded since the survey began in 1983 (Clery, 2011).

How, in the context of an impassioned debate about the future of the NHS, have public attitudes towards the NHS changed since then? This chapter firstly explores the public's views about how the NHS is performing, looking at satisfaction with services and perceptions of change over recent years, and seeks to explain why opinion has shifted. Secondly, in the light of the wider debate about whether the fundamental nature of the NHS will – or should – change in response to the intensifying pressure on funding, the chapter looks to the future, exploring public attitudes to radical changes in the way the NHS is funded and accessed as well as its priorities for spending.

Satisfaction with the NHS and its standards of health care

We begin with an examination of the public's views on how well the NHS is performing. To do so we use people's responses to the latest British Social Attitudes survey including their replies to questions asked as part of the International Social Survey Programme.[1]

In most years since 1983 British Social Attitudes has asked the public:

> *All in all, how satisfied or dissatisfied would you say you are with the way in which the National Health Service runs nowadays?*

In our previous survey, carried out in 2010, the public expressed the highest level of satisfaction yet recorded by the study, with 70 per cent saying they were "very" or "quite" satisfied with the NHS. Our most recent reading (Figure 5.1) shows that satisfaction has fallen since then by 12 percentage points to 58 per cent.

Figure 5.1 Satisfaction with the NHS overall, 1983–2011

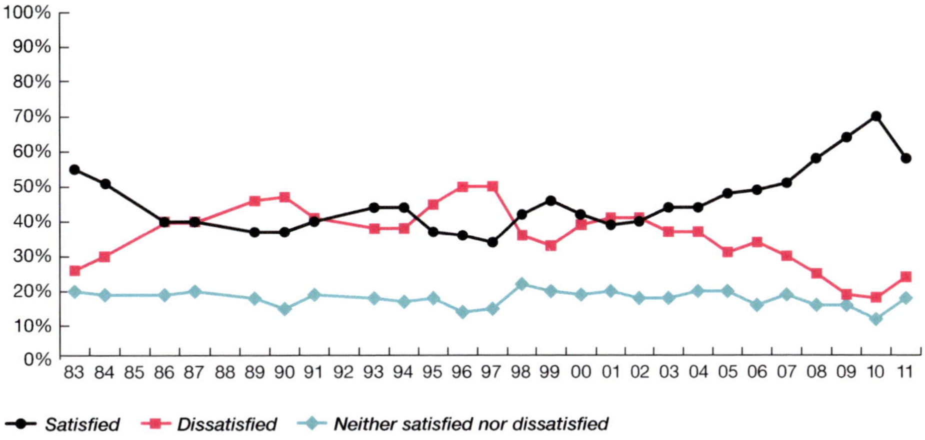

The data on which Figure 5.1 is based can be found in the appendix to this chapter

The decline in satisfaction with the NHS overall is broadly reflected in views about different NHS services with a decline in satisfaction with GPs, Inpatients, Outpatients and Accident and emergency services between 2010 and 2011 (Table 5.1). Conversely, satisfaction with dentistry increased, rising five percentage points to 56 per cent in 2011. This has been attributed to increased funding and efforts to improve access following the Steele review of NHS dental services (Steele, 2009; Appleby, 2012b).

Table 5.1 Satisfaction with NHS services, 2010 and 2011

% satisfied with...	2010	2011	Difference (2010–2011)
... GPs	77	73	-4
... Dentists	50	56	+5
... Inpatients	59	55	-5
... Outpatients	67	61	-6
... Accident and emergency services	61	54	-7
Weighted base	*3297*	*1113*	
Unweighted base	*3297*	*1096*	

How can we explain this decline in overall satisfaction and with many NHS services? Firstly, it may well be that respondents are expressing greater dissatisfaction with the NHS as a proxy for their dissatisfaction with other matters – such as the coalition government itself or its wider policies. Previous surveys have shown us that people who identify with a particular political party tend to voice greater satisfaction with the NHS when that party is in power – and vice versa (Appleby and Alvarez-Rosete, 2003). However, while we see Labour supporters' satisfaction fall by 17 percentage points a year after the 2010 election – reflecting an expected partisanship – we also see Conservative and Liberal Democrat satisfaction fall. So while there is a degree of partisanship apparent, and this can explain some of the decline, the fact that even supporters of the governing parties recorded a decline in satisfaction suggests a more complicated story. There were no significant differences by other demographic indicators – satisfaction levels fell among all age groups, income bands and educational qualifications.

Part of the story could be that expectations of good service from the NHS have increased disproportionately compared with the quality of service being delivered. Public expectations of the quality of the services the NHS provides can be expected to go on increasing over time. But there seems little reason (or evidence) to suppose that rising expectations outstripped NHS performance to the extent that they alone could account for the biggest fall in satisfaction since the survey began in 1983.

Alternatively, falling satisfaction might reflect an actual deterioration of the quality of service people receive. British Social Attitudes asks for people's perceptions of whether the general standard of health care in the NHS has been getting better or worse "over the last five years". Comparing responses to the latest survey with replies obtained in 1995, we see a picture of perceived improvement. Three in ten now say the NHS has got better in the last five years, compared with one in six when the question was first asked (Table 5.2). However, in line with the decline in current satisfaction, we see that there has been a fall of nine percentage points since 2010 in the proportion thinking there have been improvements. The proportion who say that the standard of health care has got worse has, meanwhile, increased by 11 percentage points to 27 per cent.

Table 5.2 Perceptions of change in NHS health care standards over the last five years, 1995–2011

	1995	2001	2008	2009	2010	2011
	%	%	%	%	%	%
Better	18	22	32	40	40	31
About the same	32	37	38	39	41	38
Worse	49	40	27	18	16	27
Weighted base	*2434*	*2179*	*3333*	*3421*	*3297*	*1113*
Unweighted base	*2399*	*2188*	*3358*	*3421*	*3297*	*1096*

Interestingly, other recent surveys (Care Quality Commission, 2012a, 2012b; Department of Health, 2012b) have not recorded a decline in the public's actual experience of the NHS. Key performance data collected on waiting times and health care-related infections have also generally been good (Appleby et al., 2012). Evidently, though, there is now a perception among the general public that improvements made over the last few years are not being sustained.

A further possible explanation for declining satisfaction is that people are responding to negative media coverage of the NHS rather than thinking of their own experiences of health care. To investigate this we compare respondents with experience of hospital services in the last 12 months against those without.[2] While both groups' satisfaction with the NHS is likely to be influenced by media stories, it might be expected that those with recent experience of the NHS will, in addition, take account of their own personal experience. In 2009 those with recent experience of hospital services expressed higher levels of satisfaction with the NHS overall than those with no recent experience (68 per cent and 61 per cent respectively). This remains the case in the latest survey, with 62 per cent recent hospital service users expressing satisfaction, compared with 56 per cent of non-users (though the difference is no longer statistically significant, likely due to the smaller base size). Importantly, however, as satisfaction fell by similar amounts for both groups we are not able unequivocally to conclude that a decline in satisfaction was due either to media influence or actual experience.

Decline in satisfaction might be explained by the ambient effect of an intense political and media debate when the questions were asked

Finally, decline in satisfaction might be explained by the ambient effect of an intense political and media debate about the NHS that was taking place during the summer and autumn of 2011 when the British Social Attitudes questions were asked, and also worries for the future of the NHS arising both from the government's reform plans and well-publicised funding pressures. Not only was there continuing strong criticism of the Health and Social Care Bill from the British Medical Association and other health professionals, but the government was also facing renewed objections in the House of Lords after it had felt obliged to 'pause' the Bill's progress for a month of consultation. The declining satisfaction identified by our survey may, therefore, reflect uncertainty surrounding the future of the NHS and widespread antipathy to the proposed reforms. These may be reinforced by an impression that the NHS is coming under financial pressure (see Appleby, 2012b).

However, if we think that controversy surrounding the Coalition's health reforms is largely responsible for the sharp decline in satisfaction, it is important to remember that the new legislation applies only to England. This makes it potentially surprising that satisfaction levels also fell in Scotland (by 17 percentage points to just 50 per cent) and Wales (by nine percentage points, to 55 per cent), where governments have devolved powers over the NHS. The lower number of interviews in Scotland and Wales means we must interpret our figures with caution. However, we have seen in previous years that attitudes in Scotland tend to parallel those in England (Curtice and Ormston, 2011) and with both Scotland and Wales enduring a tighter squeeze on NHS funding than England, declines in satisfaction are perhaps to be expected.

In order to untangle what factors are affecting people's reported levels of satisfaction with the NHS we ran a logistic regression (full results can be seen in the appendix to this chapter). Through this we can see that, after controlling for a range of respondent characteristics, there are certain attitudes that are strongly linked with satisfaction. For example, as might be expected, those who thought that services had got better in the last five years were more likely to express satisfaction overall. Also, satisfaction with certain services, notably GPs, Inpatients and Outpatients, was linked with satisfaction with the service overall. Further, those who believe the NHS will remain freely accessible in 10 years' time (dealt with later in the chapter) are more likely to express satisfaction with the NHS now.

In summary, it seems likely that a decline in overall satisfaction with the NHS can be explained by several different factors. Of these, anxieties about the government's far-reaching reforms to the organisation of the NHS and – to an extent – worries arising from the slow-down in funding growth are likely to play a prominent role.

Does the NHS need to change and, if so, how?

So far we have seen that overall satisfaction with the NHS, although it remains quite high, has taken a sharp downturn since 2010. The proportion of the population who think the service has improved over the last five years has also declined. We look now at respondents' thoughts on the future of the NHS.

For the first time, the latest survey asked people if they thought the general standard of health care in the NHS would improve or get worse in the next five years. In line with our thesis that current dissatisfaction relates to the level of public uncertainty about NHS reform, more than a third believe that NHS health care will get worse (Table 5.3). They outnumber the roughly one in four who consider it will improve.

Table 5.3 Expectation of changes to the standard of health care on the NHS over the next five years

	%
Better	27
Same	35
Worse	36
Weighted base	*1113*
Unweighted base	*1096*

This pessimistic view chimes with a Department of Health survey of NHS staff, which showed that 53 per cent of those surveyed in the winter of 2011 felt the standard of NHS care to patients would get worse – an increase over the result of the Winter 2010 survey (49 per cent) and the Spring 2009 survey (34 per cent) (Department of Health, 2012c: 21).

We then looked at what enthusiasm, if any, exists for changing the NHS by asking:

> ***In general, would you say that the health care system in Britain needs no changes, needs a few changes, needs many changes, or, needs to be completely changed?***

The replies suggest an appetite for modest, though possibly not radical, reform

The replies suggest an appetite for modest, though possibly not radical, reform. Over half (55 per cent) believe that "a few changes" are needed, and another third (32 per cent) that the NHS requires "many changes". Only five per cent say that no change is necessary – which is also the proportion who maintain that the service "needs to be changed completely". Since this question has not been asked in previous British Social Attitudes surveys we cannot assess how the public's view may have changed over time. Nevertheless, having established that most people favour at least some reform of the NHS, we move on to consider what types of change they are most likely to support.

Tax, public spending and the future of the NHS

Those who feel Britain's health system needs to be improved are faced with a number of choices as to how to do this. Three fundamental ones are what public spending priority to assign to health; what the scope of health services should be; and who should have access to them. We start by examining what spending priority the public assigns to health versus other areas of government spending, and people's personal willingness to pay more to improve health care. We also test people's confidence that a National Health Service funded through general taxation will remain the chosen model for providing health care in future. Since people generally favour reform, might not some believe that it is the NHS's founding ambition to provide a comprehensive, universal health care service that most needs to change?

As reported in the Welfare chapter, support for more taxation to pay for public services has been on the decline since 2002. Having stood at 63 per cent 10 years ago it has now fallen to 36 per cent in the latest survey (though this is up five percentage points from 2010). Correspondingly, there has been an increase in the proportion saying the government should "keep taxes and spending at the same level", from 31 per cent in 2002 to 54 per cent in the latest survey – a trend in part reflecting increases in spending in some key areas (such as the NHS) over this period: as more is spent, a decreasing proportion of the public see the need to spend even more.

68%

of people choose Health as their first or second priority for extra government spending

British Social Attitudes also asks people to choose from a list one area of government spending they would prioritise for extra spending, and then to select an area as their second choice. As seen in Figure 5.2, when first and second choices are added together, health has consistently been the public's top priority, with 68 per cent choosing health in the current survey. Education comes a reliable second, while other areas of government spending such as police and prisons and housing (the third and fourth top priorities in 2011) are given much lower priority. The priority that the public accords to health can, in a sense, be said to accord with the coalition government's spending priorities, which are to hold level the amount of money going to the NHS, while other areas undergo extensive cuts. However, it is interesting to note the general decline in the priority given by the public to the NHS for extra funding since the turn of the century. As with the declining proportion of those who want higher taxes and more spending on public services in general, this is a trend that perhaps mirrors the funding increases the NHS has received since that time; as more money goes in, the public have perceived less need for increased funding. Of interest too is the fact that this decline in the priority accorded to the NHS continues in 2011. This might suggest that worries about funding are not in fact a significant factor explaining the fall in satisfaction with the NHS.

Figure 5.2 First or second priorities for extra government spending, 1983–2011

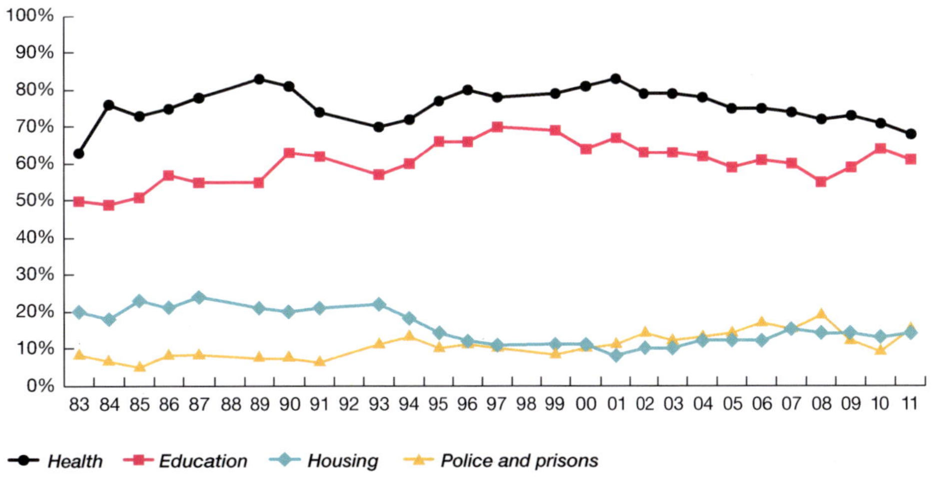

The full data on which Figure 5.2 is based can be found in the appendix to this chapter

Our next question investigates people's own willingness to pay higher taxes in order to improve the level of health care "for all people in Britain". In line with opinions on the question of whether taxation should rise to fund public services, we find that nearly four in ten (38 per cent) say they would be prepared to pay more. Another one in four (26 per cent) say they would be neither willing nor unwilling, while almost one in three (31 per cent) would be unwilling. We find a significant link (at the 90 per cent level) between satisfaction with the NHS and willingness to pay more to support the service. So it could be that steps to ease funding constraints would be a way to arrest the current decline in public satisfaction.

When we compare the answers to this and the previous question by demographic group, we find those who favour raising taxes to pay for public spending in general are outnumbered in most groups by those who would be willing to pay more tax to fund the NHS in particular (Table 5.4). Willingness to pay more tax to fund the NHS is especially strong among people aged 55 to 64, among Labour and Liberal Democrat supporters, and among those with higher academic qualifications. Conservative supporters, although least likely to give a positive answer to either question, are noticeably more likely to express willingness to pay more tax themselves to benefit the NHS than to support tax increases for public services in general.

Table 5.4 Willingness to pay more tax to improve health care, compared with support for raising taxes to increase overall public spending[3]

	% willing to pay more tax for increased health spending to improve health care	% support tax increases to spend more on public services	Difference
All	38	36	+2
Age			
18–34	35	30	+5
35–54	35	37	-2
55–64	47	40	+8
65+	41	37	+3
Political affiliation			
Conservative	35	26	+9
Liberal Democrat	52	40	+12
Labour	47	46	+1
Household income (quartiles)			
Lowest quartile	39	41	-2
2nd lowest quartile	38	35	+3
2nd highest quartile	40	34	+6
Highest quartile	40	35	+5
Educational attainment (highest level)			
Higher education	45	37	+8
A level	37	31	+5
O level / CSE	31	37	-6
No qualifications	41	37	+4

An alternative to 'tax and spend' could be to reduce the scope of what the NHS offers by limiting access. For example, we ask:

> ***It has been suggested that the National Health Service should be available only to those with lower incomes. This would mean that contributions and taxes could be lower and most people would then take out medical insurance or pay for health care. Do you support or oppose this idea?***[4]

The answers (Figure 5.3) show that, for more than 20 years now, the proportion opposing this suggestion "a lot" or "a little" has consistently remained at or above 70 per cent. (The lowest level of opposition – and the highest level of support – was recorded back in 1983 when the then Prime Minister, Margaret Thatcher, was at her most popular.) The latest survey does, however, show a dip in opposition, and an increase in support for a health care system based on medical insurance or direct payment. But the proportion in favour of changing the NHS funding model is still below 30 per cent.

Figure 5.3 Support for and opposition to the NHS being made available only to those on lower incomes, 1983–2011[5]

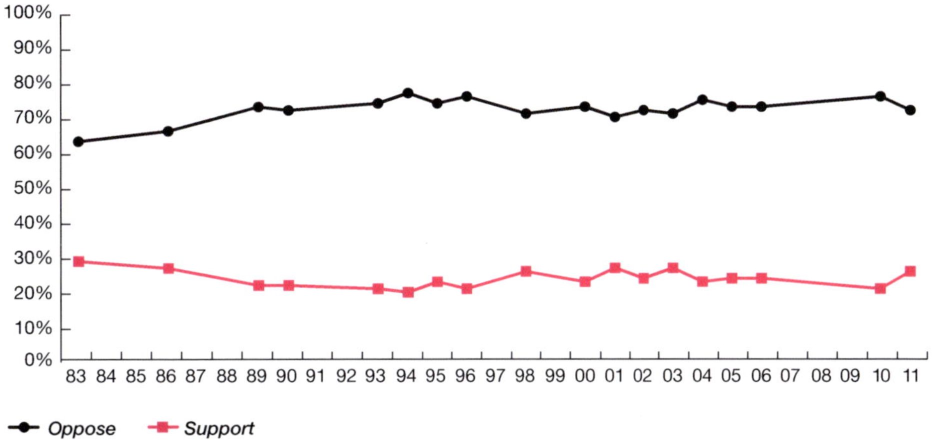

The data on which Figure 5.3 is based can be found in the appendix to this chapter

In a similar vein, but without referring to income, the latest British Social Attitudes survey also asks how much people agree or disagree that "the government should provide only limited health care services". Again, 73 per cent voice opposition to the proposition. However, the level of agreement is much lower than for the previous question at just nine per cent.

We also ask what people believe will happen in reality:

> ***In ten years' time, do you think the NHS will still be paid for by taxes and free to all?***

The public is not overwhelmingly confident that the service's traditional funding model will survive. While just under half (47 per cent) reply "yes", a very similar proportion (44 per cent) say "no". When we look at this against people's reported levels of satisfaction with the NHS overall we see that those who think the NHS will not be free and available to all in 10 years' time are significantly less likely to express satisfaction with the service now (50 per cent, compared with 63 per cent of those who think the NHS will remain freely accessible). Whether a view that the NHS will not be tax-funded and free to all in future causes lower satisfaction now or vice versa is impossible to say. Furthermore, it cannot be assumed that everyone who thinks NHS funding and access will change in future necessarily regards this is a bad thing – although the responses to our previous question on limiting access to the NHS (Figure 5.3) do suggest that most would see this as a negative change.

44%

of people think that in 10 years' time the NHS will not still be paid for by taxes and free to all

While many feel the NHS needs to change to some degree, radical changes to its funding source and the scope of its services are not generally the kind of change they have in mind. Even so, a large minority think this is what will, in fact, happen.

Setting priorities and commissioning local health services

While the coalition government's reforms stop short of any fundamental changes to the NHS as a publicly-funded, universal and comprehensive service, the administrative changes it is implementing are nevertheless far-reaching. As previously noted, the key reform is the creation of local clinical commissioning groups run by GPs, replacing primary care trusts as the purchasers of secondary care. The central argument advanced for this change has been that GPs are better-placed to make decisions about priorities and spending as they are closer to patients. But who do the public think can best decide how NHS money is spent? What sort of service priorities do they think the NHS should pursue and – more broadly – what kind of public health measures do they favour for promoting healthier living?

We asked people who they think "should decide how money is spent on your local NHS" and offered them four options: "the government", "your local GPs", "your local council" and "local people". The responses (Table 5.5) show that there is no majority view. Around one in three say the spending decisions should be taken by local GPs, while just under a third consider that they should be the remit of central government, and around one in six choose "local people" or the "local council" respectively. Broadly then, there is some support – though not overwhelming – for the central plank of the government's reform programme to put GPs in charge of deciding how around 60 per cent of the NHS budget should be spent.

Table 5.5 Who should decide how money is spent on the local NHS

Spending on local NHS should be decided by …	**%**
… your local GPs	34
… the government	30
… your local council	17
… local people	17
Weighted base	*1113*
Unweighted base	*1096*

Regardless of who makes the decisions about health care spending, any NHS service commissioner faces difficult choices about the priorities for that spending. To test public opinion about the types of health spending that should receive priority, given limited resources, we invited respondents to imagine they had charge of an NHS budget, with 40 "beans" or counters to allocate between four specific areas of spending. These were selected broadly to represent community services ("increase community nurses to support people with long term health problems in their own homes"), hospital care ("reduce hospital waiting times for people who need a hip operation"), mental health treatment ("expand access to counselling and 'talking therapies' for mild/moderate depression") and preventive public health services ("give more help for people who need to lose weight").

38%

of the hypothetical budget was allocated by the public to community nursing services

Aggregating the way people allocated their beans across these four areas produces the distribution shown in Table 5.6. We see that respondents collectively earmark 38 per cent of the hypothetical health budget for community nursing services. Public support for this sort of service, helping people with long term conditions at home, chimes with professional efforts over many years to shift care provision towards the community where appropriate, rather than providing it in hospitals. The strength of support for more investment in community services may also reflect a feeling that, notwithstanding the long term shift in policy, such care continues to be underfunded. It is also interesting that despite substantial reductions in the waiting times for operations and other hospital treatments in recent years, the public votes to allocate as much as 30 per cent of its notional health budget to reduce the time that people need to wait for a hip operation.

Support for the mental health option is given less priority, attracting 20 per cent of the notional budget, while the lowest share (12 per cent) is given to support for public health through a weight loss programme. The low priority given to this last choice may, in part, reflect a feeling among some people that helping people who need to lose weight is not even an appropriate activity for the NHS: looking at the way individuals allocate their budget beans we find that as many as three out of ten respondents allocated none of them to the public health option.

Table 5.6 Priorities for NHS spending

	Share (%) of (hypothetical) budget
Increase community nurses to support people with long term health problems in their own homes	38
Reduce hospital waiting times for people who need a hip operation	30
Expand access to counselling and 'talking therapies' for mild/moderate depression	20
Give more help for people who need to lose weight	12

The weighted base is 1113 and the unweighted base is 1096

Ways to improve public health

To investigate further what kinds of public health intervention people consider more or less acceptable, we asked them to say what in their view would be "the best way for the government to help people to lead healthier lifestyles". The options they chose between were:

Leave people to make their own choices without interfering

Provide information (e.g. on healthy diets, how to give up smoking)

Pay people (e.g. to give up smoking or take more exercise)

Use the law (e.g. to ban drinking in public places)

Tax unhealthy things (e.g. alcohol and cigarettes)

The 'softer' approach that almost half say they favour is providing information on healthy diets

In general, as can be seen from Table 5.7, the public is less keen on what might be termed 'hard' interventions – such as using the law (nine per cent) or paying people in return for healthier behaviour (two per cent). The 'softer' approach that almost half say they favour is providing information on healthy diets. Despite the longstanding practice of governments in taxing alcohol and tobacco for avowedly 'health' as well as 'revenue' reasons, we also see that little more than one in five think it offers the best way to promote healthier lifestyles. Just under one in five, meanwhile, take a libertarian view, insisting that people should be left to make their own health choices without government interference.

Table 5.7 Best way for government to help people lead healthier lifestyles

	%
Provide information (e.g. on healthy diets, how to give up smoking)	48
Tax unhealthy things (e.g. alcohol and cigarettes)	22
Leave people to make their own choices without interfering	18
Use the law (e.g. to ban drinking in public places)	9
Pay people (e.g. to give up smoking or take more exercise)	2
Weighted base	*1113*
Unweighted base	*1096*

Conclusions

Undoubtedly the most striking feature of this latest British Social Attitudes survey is the unprecedented drop in public satisfaction with the way the NHS runs compared to the all-time high recorded in 2010 (and following a decade of continuous increase). While satisfaction with many of its component services also fell, these reductions were on a smaller scale than for the NHS overall. This reinforces our hypothesis that the overall decrease in satisfaction reflects an increase in general concern about NHS services and their future augmented by specific worries about the government's controversial organisational reform of the NHS in England.

In line with the sudden drop in satisfaction, there has been a marked increase in the proportion of people saying that the general standard of care in the NHS over the last five years has deteriorated. Moreover, while just over a quarter anticipate that the standard of care in the NHS will get better in the next five years, more than a third think it will get worse.

Given this generally critical picture, it might not seem surprising that more than half the public thinks the NHS needs "a few changes" and another three in ten that it needs "many changes". Few, though, express the stronger view that the system needs to be completely changed. Meanwhile, as we have discussed, the NHS is currently facing major modifications, not least a virtual freeze in real funding growth for health care between 2011/2012 and 2014/2015 in England, and some real reductions for the NHS in Wales and Scotland. This can be considered relatively generous compared with the treatment accorded to other areas of government spending in these austere times, and an indication that government has recognised the public's view (confirmed by this latest survey) that the NHS is a top priority for spending. Nevertheless, a spending standstill amid increasing demands on the service cannot be said to compare favourably with the doubling in real NHS spending that occurred between 2000 and 2010. Hence scope has been created for the kind of public disquiet seen in our survey.

Although health remains the public's top spending priority, 2011 saw a continuation in the decline in the proportion of people according it top priority. An alternative to spending more on the NHS would be to curtail the cost to taxpayers by restricting access to NHS services and moving those who can afford to pay for their health care towards an insurance-based or privately-funded system. However, our findings show that most people (73 per cent) remain opposed to limiting the scope and funding of the NHS in this way, to an extent that is broadly unchanged since the 1980s. Yet we have also seen that mainstream opposition to fundamental changes does not mean that people are convinced that they won't ever happen. On the contrary, a significant minority (44 per cent) do not expect that in 10 years' time the NHS will still be paid for by taxes and free to all – which is almost as many as the 47 per cent who anticipate no change.

Aside from the spending squeeze, one other major change already affecting the NHS is implementation of the government's organisational reforms in England. clinical commissioning groups led by GPs are being created to buy health care services on behalf of their local populations in place of primary care trusts, and thus take control of around 60 per cent of the total NHS budget. Encouragingly for the government, our survey finds that a third of the population think their local GPs are the best people to decide how money is spent on their local NHS, while other options command less support. But this can scarcely be read as a ringing public endorsement of the reforms.

Meanwhile, as the NHS grapples with far-reaching organisational changes and a stringent financial climate, decisions about priorities and how to improve public health assume even greater importance. Local GP commissioners will have to make difficult decisions about how best to allocate a fixed budget between NHS services and patient groups in need of care. Interestingly, the results when we invite the public to tackle this problem (albeit for a much-limited range of services) suggest a marked preference for investing in community health services, exemplified by nursing care at home. In relation to wider government intervention to promote healthier lifestyles we have also seen how people are less keen on 'harder' financial inducements or recourse to the law (for example, to ban drinking in public places) than on 'softer' support, such as advice on healthy diets or how to give up smoking. In addition, little more than one in five of the population view the taxation of 'unhealthy things' (such as alcohol) as the best way to encourage healthy living. As policy makers confront the daunting challenge of extracting greater value from the strictly limited resources now available for the NHS, this is a reminder that the effectiveness and cost-effectiveness of treatments and services cannot be the only consideration. By promoting better public health they might reasonably hope to reduce the need for more expensive medical interventions. But they will also need to acknowledge people's awareness, demonstrated in our survey, of a balance between personal liberty and government action, which it could prove problematic to upset.

We await with interest the satisfaction levels recorded in 2012, which, given our suggested explanations for the precipitous drop in satisfaction in 2011, we might expect to have recovered somewhat as the intense debates surrounding the proposed plans subside. However, while the Health and Social Care Act has now progressed to the statute book, this is just the beginning of changes that will only start to take effect towards the end of 2012. Whether or not public satisfaction levels will return to their high of 70 per cent once the NHS reforms are in place remains to be seen.

Notes

1. The International Social Survey Programme is conducted annually in 48 countries. In Britain it is carried out as part of the British Social Attitudes study, with funding from the Economic and Social Research Council. For more details see the website: www.issp.org/index.php

2. People with experience include those answering "Yes, just me", "Yes, not me, but a close family member or friend", and "Yes, both me and a close family member or friend" to questions about use of inpatients and/or outpatients in the last 12 months

3. The bases for Table 5.4 are as follows:

	Would pay more tax for increased health spending		**Support tax increases to spend more on public services**	
	Weighted base	*Unweighted base*	*Weighted base*	*Unweighted base*
Age				
18–34	*297*	*231*	*948*	*752*
35–54	*335*	*329*	*1171*	*1159*
55–64	*152*	*164*	*496*	*541*
65+	*168*	*212*	*693*	*856*
Political affiliation				
Conservative	*245*	*256*	*881*	*926*
Liberal Democrat	*74*	*78*	*247*	*253*
Labour	*293*	*295*	*1062*	*1039*
Household income (quartiles)				
Lowest quartile	*186*	*229*	*641*	*799*
2nd lowest quartile	*186*	*188*	*571*	*591*
2nd highest quartile	*176*	*170*	*620*	*594*
Highest quartile	*202*	*180*	*657*	*579*
Educational attainment (highest level)				
Degree or equivalent	*313*	*295*	*1005*	*953*
A level	*151*	*137*	*529*	*469*
GCSE or equivalent	*216*	*205*	*787*	*774*
No qualifications	*171*	*197*	*636*	*743*

4. There have been minor variations to this question over the years. From 1983 to 1994 the answer options were "support" and "oppose"; from 1995 to 2010 the answer options were "support a lot", "support a little", "oppose a lot" and "oppose a little", with respondents being prompted to say "a little" or "a lot". In 2011 the same four answer options were retained but presented to respondents on a showcard.

5. Readings are indicated by data marker; the line indicates an overall pattern but where there is no data marker the line cannot be taken as a reading for that year.

References

Appleby, J. (2012a), 'A productivity challenge too far?', *British Medical Journal*, 344: e2416

Appleby, J. (2012b), 'Public satisfaction with the NHS and its services: Headline results from the British Social Attitudes Survey', available at: www.kingsfund.org.uk/current_projects/bsa_survey_results_2011/index.html

Appleby, J., Thompson, J. and Galea, A. (2012), 'How is the NHS performing? May 2012 Quarterly Monitoring Report', available at: www.kingsfund.org.uk/publications/nhs_performance_may.html

Appleby, J. and Alvarez-Rosete, A. (2003), 'Public responses to NHS reform', in Park, A., Curtice, J., Thomson, K., Bromley, C., Phillips, M. and Johnson, M. (eds.), *British Social Attitudes: the 22nd Report – Two terms of New Labour: the public's reaction*, London: Sage

Care Quality Commission (2012a), 'National NHS patient survey programme Survey of adult inpatients 2011: Full national results with 2010 comparisons', available at: www.cqc.org.uk/sites/default/files/media/documents/ip11_national_tables_final.pdf

Care Quality Commission (2012b), 'Outpatient survey 2011', available at: www.cqc.org.uk/outpatientsurvey2011

Clery, E. (2011), 'Taking the pulse: attitudes to the health service', in Park, A., Clery, E., Curtice, J., Phillips, M. and Utting, D. (eds.), *British Social Attitudes: the 28th Report*, London: Sage, available at: www.natcen.ac.uk/BSA28

Curtice, J. and Ormston, R. (2011), 'On the road to divergence? Trends in public opinion in Scotland and England' in Park, A., Clery, E., Curtice, J., Phillips, M. and Utting, D. (eds.), *British Social Attitudes : the 28th Report*, London: Sage, available at: www.natcen.ac.uk/BSA28

Department of Health (2012a), 'The Quarter: Quarter 3, 2011/12: An update from David Flory, Deputy NHS Chief Executive', available at: www.dh.gov.uk/health/files/2012/03/Quarter3_27-March-2011-12.pdf

Department of Health (2012b), *The GP Patient Survey Summary Report July – September 2011*, available at: www.gp-patient.co.uk/results/latest_weighted/summary/

Department of Health (2012c), *NHS staff tracking research – Winter 2011 (Research Wave 6): A research report for Central Office of Information prepared on behalf of the Department of Health*, London: Department of Health

Steele, J. (2009), *NHS Dental Services in England. An independent review led by Professor Jimmy Steele*, London: Department of Health

Timmins, N. (2010), 'NHS reforms run full speed into the unknown', *Financial Times*, 14 December, available at: www.ft.com/cms/s/0/5c23dda2-07b7-11e0-a568-00144feabdc0.html

Acknowledgements

NatCen Social Research would like to thank both The King's Fund and the Economic and Social Research Council (RES-501-25-5002) for funding the questions reported in this chapter. The views expressed here are those of the authors alone.

Appendix

The data for Figures 5.1, 5.2 and 5.3 are shown below.

Table A.1 Satisfaction with the NHS overall, 1983–2011

	83	84	86	87	89	90	91	93	94
	%	%	%	%	%	%	%	%	%
Very/quite satisfied	55	51	40	40	37	37	40	44	44
Neither satisfied nor dissatisfied	20	19	19	20	18	15	19	18	17
Very/quite dissatisfied	26	30	40	40	46	47	41	38	38
Weighted base	*1719*	*1645*	*3066*	*2766*	*2930*	*2698*	*2836*	*2945*	*3469*
Unweighted base	*1719*	*1675*	*3066*	*2847*	*2930*	*2698*	*2918*	*2945*	*3469*

	95	96	97	98	99	00	01	02	03
	%	%	%	%	%	%	%	%	%
Very/quite satisfied	37	36	34	42	46	42	39	40	44
Neither satisfied nor dissatisfied	18	14	15	22	20	19	20	18	18
Very/quite dissatisfied	45	50	50	36	33	39	41	41	37
Weighted base	*3633*	*3620*	*1355*	*3146*	*3143*	*3426*	*1108*	*2285*	*2284*
Unweighted base	*3633*	*3620*	*1355*	*3146*	*3143*	*3426*	*2188*	*2287*	*2293*

	04	05	06	07	08	09	10	11
	%	%	%	%	%	%	%	%
Very/quite satisfied	44	48	49	51	58	64	70	58
Neither satisfied nor dissatisfied	20	20	16	19	16	16	12	18
Very/quite dissatisfied	37	31	34	30	25	19	18	24
Weighted base	*3199*	*3210*	*2151*	*3082*	*3333*	*3421*	*3297*	*1113*
Unweighted base	*3199*	*3193*	*2151*	*3078*	*3358*	*3421*	*3297*	*1096*

Table A.2 First or second priorities for extra government spending, 1983–2011

	83	84	85	86	87	89	90	91	93
	%	%	%	%	%	%	%	%	%
Health	63	76	73	75	78	83	81	74	70
Education	50	49	51	57	55	55	63	62	57
Police and prisons	8	6	5	8	8	7	7	6	11
Housing	20	18	23	21	24	21	20	21	22
Help for industry	29	20	20	16	11	7	6	10	14
Defence	8	6	5	4	4	3	2	4	3
Public transport	3	2	3	2	1	3	6	5	4
Roads	5	4	4	3	3	5	4	5	4
Social security benefits	12	15	12	11	12	14	13	11	13
Overseas aid	1	1	2	1	1	1	1	1	2
(None of these)	1	1	1	1	1	0	0	1	1
Weighted base	*1719*	*1645*	*1769*	*3066*	*2766*	*2930*	*2698*	*2836*	*2945*
Unweighted base	*1761*	*1675*	*1804*	*3100*	*2847*	*3029*	*2797*	*2918*	*2945*

	94	95	96	97	99	00	01	02	03
	%	%	%	%	%	%	%	%	%
Health	72	77	80	78	79	81	83	79	79
Education	60	66	66	70	69	64	67	63	63
Police and prisons	13	10	11	10	8	10	11	14	12
Housing	18	14	12	11	11	11	8	10	10
Help for industry	12	9	9	8	6	5	4	4	4
Defence	4	2	2	3	2	3	3	3	3
Public transport	3	7	6	6	10	10	11	13	13
Roads	4	3	3	3	7	6	5	6	6
Social security benefits	11	11	8	9	7	7	6	5	6
Overseas aid	1	0	1	1	1	1	1	2	1
(None of these)	1	1	0	1	1	1	1	1	1
Weighted base	*1187*	*1199*	*3620*	*1355*	*3143*	*2302*	*3287*	*3435*	*4432*
Unweighted base	*1167*	*1234*	*3620*	*1355*	*3143*	*2292*	*3287*	*3435*	*4432*

	04	05	06	07	08	09	10	11
	%	%	%	%	%	%	%	%
Health	78	75	75	74	72	73	71	68
Education	62	59	61	60	55	59	64	61
Police and prisons	13	14	17	15	19	12	11	15
Housing	12	12	12	15	14	14	13	14
Help for industry	5	5	4	4	5	11	10	12
Defence	5	6	6	7	8	9	8	10
Public transport	11	12	11	11	11	8	7	6
Roads	6	7	5	6	7	6	7	6
Social security benefits	5	5	5	5	5	4	5	4
Overseas aid	2	3	3	2	2	2	2	1
(None of these)	1	1	1	1	1	1	1	1
Weighted base	*3199*	*2167*	*3228*	*3082*	*2184*	*3421*	*3297*	*3311*
Unweighted base	*3199*	*2166*	*3240*	*3094*	*2229*	*3421*	*3297*	*3311*

Table A.3 Support for and opposition to the NHS being made available only to those on lower incomes, 1983–2011

	83	86	89	90	93	94	95	96	98
	%	%	%	%	%	%	%	%	%
Support	29	27	22	22	21	20	23	21	26
Oppose	64	67	74	73	75	78	75	77	72
Weighted base	*1719*	*3066*	*2930*	*2698*	*2945*	*3469*	*3633*	*3620*	*3146*
Unweighted base	*1761*	*3100*	*3029*	*2797*	*2945*	*3469*	*3633*	*3620*	*3146*

	00	01	02	03	04	05	06	10	11
	%	%	%	%	%	%	%	%	%
Support	23	27	24	27	23	24	24	21	26
Oppose	74	71	73	72	76	74	74	77	73
Weighted base	*3426*	*2179*	*2285*	*2284*	*3199*	*3210*	*2151*	*3297*	*1113*
Unweighted base	*3426*	*2188*	*2287*	*2293*	*3199*	*3193*	*2143*	*3297*	*1096*

Multivariate analysis

The multivariate analysis technique used is stepwise logistic regression, about which more details can be found in the Technical details chapter. The dependent variable is satisfaction ("very satisfied" or "satisfied") "with the way in which the National Health Service runs nowadays". A positive coefficient indicates that the group is more likely than the reference group (shown in brackets) to be satisfied, while a negative coefficient indicates that the group is less likely to be satisfied. We controlled for standard demographic factors – sex, age and region – though Table A.4 shows that these were not significant. The independent variables entered into the model were: household income, highest educational qualification, party identification, satisfaction with GPs / Accident and emergency / Dentists / Inpatients / Outpatients, recent contact with Outpatients / Inpatients, views on how NHS performance had changed over the last five years, views on how NHS performance would change over the next five years, and views on whether the NHS would be free to all in 10 years time.

Table A.4 Satisfaction with how the NHS is run nowadays

Category	Coefficient	Standard error	Odds ratio	P value
Baseline odds	-1.718	0.602	0.179	0.004
Sex (Men)				
Women	0.205	0.176	1.228	0.243
Region (North East)				
North West	-0.911	0.504	0.402	0.070
Yorkshire and Humberside	-0.932	0.565	0.394	0.099
East Midlands	-0.111	0.546	0.895	0.839
West Midlands	-0.496	0.534	0.609	0.353
South West	-0.464	0.519	0.629	0.371
Eastern	-0.082	0.694	0.921	0.906
Inner London	-0.054	0.606	0.947	0.928
Outer London	-0.506	0.510	0.603	0.321
South East	-0.537	0.530	0.584	0.311
Wales	-0.334	0.567	0.716	0.556
Scotland	-0.595	0.539	0.552	0.270
Age (18–24)				
25–34	0.106	0.384	1.112	0.783
35–44	0.513	0.384	1.670	0.182
45–54	-0.040	0.384	0.961	0.918
55–64	0.274	0.391	1.316	0.483
65–97	0.012	0.376	1.012	0.974
NHS last 5 years (Worse or no change)				
Better	1.340**	0.200	3.821	0.000
Satisfaction with GPs (Dissatisfied or neither satisfied nor dissatisfied)				
Satisfied	1.214**	0.203	3.366	0.000
Satisfaction with Inpatients (Dissatisfied or neither satisfied nor dissatisfied)				
Satisfied	1.167**	0.181	3.211	0.000
Satisfaction with Outpatients (Dissatisfied or neither satisfied nor dissatisfied)				
Satisfied	1.004**	0.185	2.729	0.000
NHS free to all in next 10 years (Yes)				
No	-0.456*	0.181	0.634	0.012
Don't know	-0.067	0.322	0.935	0.834
Nagelkerke (adjusted) R^2	0.38			

Base: 862

* *= significant at 95% level;* ** *= significant at 99% level*

Work and wellbeing

Hard work? Employment, work-life balance and wellbeing in a changing economy

Job insecurity and poor working conditions can have adverse long-term consequences for employees. In the current recession, we examine the wellbeing of people in work and the balance between their jobs and their non-working lives.

Job quality

Several aspects of job quality have deteriorated since before the recession. People in work are now more likely to be concerned about job security. Many also report receiving pay cuts and that their work has become less interesting.

The proportion of workers saying it is "very true" that their **jobs are secure** has fallen from 32% in 2004 to 23% in 2010.

One in five workers (22%) say they have **taken a pay cut** in the past three years, while one in four (24%) say they have had to do less interesting work over the past three years.

Job satisfaction

Despite this fall in job quality, those in work are glad to have a job. Workers' ratings of satisfaction with work and work-life balance are actually higher on average than before the recession.

On average, workers rate their **satisfaction with their job** as 7.3 out of 10, compared with 6.9 in 2006. This is similar among men (7.2) and women (7.3).

Satisfaction with work-life balance is rated at 6.3 on average. This has also increased slightly from 6.0 in 2006.

Authors

Sally McManus and Jane Perry
Sally McManus is a Research Director at NatCen Social Research. Jane Perry is an independent social researcher

Introduction

While economists and politicians argue over the causes of and potential remedies for the double-dip recession afflicting Britain, its human consequences are most obviously observed in the labour market – through increased unemployment and a heightened sense of insecurity among those who remain in work. Although unemployment rates have fluctuated in Britain during the past four years there are about a million more people out of work than there were before the start of the economic crisis (Office for National Statistics, 2012). We know that people who lose their jobs often experience a decline in their general sense of wellbeing (McManus et al., 2012), and that those who are unemployed or economically inactive tend to experience poorer mental health than people in work (Clark et al., 2011). But having a paid job is by no means a guarantee of wellbeing. It can hold negative as well as positive consequences for the way people feel about themselves (Green, 2012). On the positive side, in addition to income, it may provide opportunities for self-development and social interaction. But it can also be a source of stress. For example, quality of employment is known to impact on people's health, life expectancy and life chances (Coats and Lehki, 2008). Thus, jobs associated with better health and wellbeing are generally those with more variety, autonomy, security and better workplace relationships as well as financial rewards (Bryson et al., 2011). It is possible that these aspects of work might have been influenced by the recession. The balance that people maintain between paid work and their home lives is another aspect of personal wellbeing that might be affected by the economic downturn. On the one hand, it is possible that some individuals who find themselves out of work or working reduced hours will see an improvement in some aspects of their work-life balance; for example, by having more time available for family commitments and leisure activities. Indeed, one recent study found that families eat together more when their level of work becomes less intense (Hall et al., 2011). People who keep their jobs may also find that lower levels of workplace production require them to work less hard. On the other hand, we can anticipate that any increase in job insecurity and reduction in household income will serve to aggravate family tensions and financial strains. And where organisations have cut staffing to achieve efficiency savings, the consequence may well be to increase, not reduce, the demands made of employees who remain.

Quality of employment is known to impact on people's health, life expectancy and life chances

In this chapter we use responses gathered in Britain for the European Social Survey (2004, 2006 and 2010) as well as data from British Social Attitudes (2005, 2009 and 2010) to discover how people's experiences of work have changed and whether they feel that their job quality has improved or declined.[1] In a time of recession, we examine people's working hours, pay and overall sense of security in the workplace. Do more people feel obliged to work harder than they did and has their overall sense of job satisfaction increased or declined? In exploring these issues we pay particular attention to gender differences, and whether certain experiences and views relating to work are more typical of men or women. Has the way in which people think about women's and men's roles in the workplace and at home changed? We also look more generally at people's views concerning work-life balance and how these relate to their satisfaction, happiness and wellbeing.

Employment, economic activity and gender

As a prelude to our exploration of attitudes, we may note that according to the Organisation for Economic Co-operation and Development (OECD) the employment rate among women in the UK and other developed nations remained fairly stable over the past decade until it dropped in almost every OECD country between 2008 and 2009 (Organisation for Economic Co-operation and Development, 2010). In previous recessions, it has been sectors employing more men than women (such as manufacturing and construction) that have been worst affected. However, we know that the current downturn in Britain presents a more complex picture. While employment rates initially fell more rapidly among men than women, men's employment has since showed the stronger signs of recovery (Philpott, 2011). One reason for this appears to be continuing job cuts in the public sector and in part-time jobs, where women predominate.

A longer-term perspective reveals that in previous recessions women were less likely to be economically active and that women's income, on average, made a smaller contribution to overall household finances. The pay gap between men and women in the same household was wider, and there were also fewer lone-parent and other households headed by a female breadwinner (Rake and Rotheroe, 2009). However, Figure 6.1 shows that while there have been signs of recent stabilisation, the level of economic activity among working-age women has progressively increased over the past 40 years, moving ever closer to the declining economic activity levels among working-age men.

Figure 6.1 Proportions of men and women economically active in Britain during recessions, 1971–2008

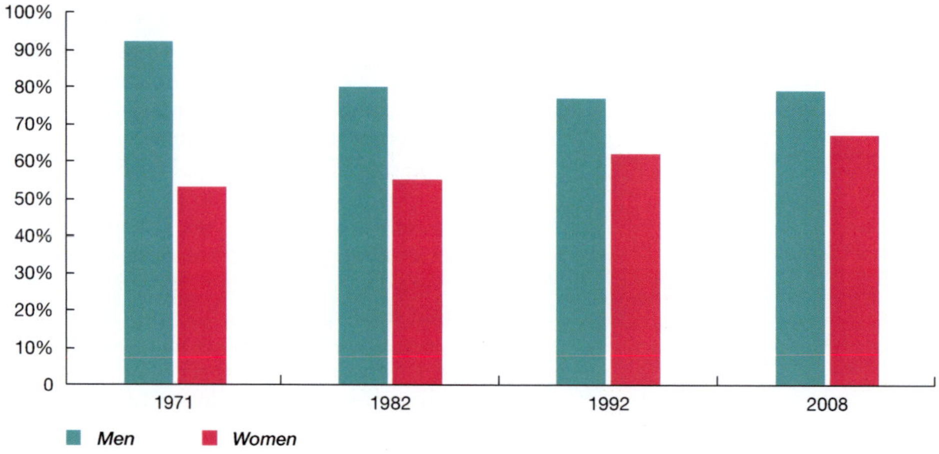

Base: People living in the UK aged 16–64
Source: Labour Force Survey (Spence, 2011)
The data on which Figure 6.1 is based can be found in the appendix to this chapter

Those in education (who tend to be young) and those who are retired (generally past working age) report the greatest levels of happiness

Personal happiness in and out of work

We start our investigation by linking what people say about their personal happiness with whether they are working or not. Using a scale from 0 to 10, the European Social Survey asked people:

> *Taking all things together, how happy would you say you are?*

As we might expect, the results (Table 6.1) show that people's perceptions of their happiness are, indeed, related to the way they spend their time. Those in education (who tend to be young) and those who are retired (generally past working age) report the greatest levels of happiness. This accords with the widely cited 'U-curve' in wellbeing, where levels of happiness and life satisfaction dip during the middle years (Blanchflower and Oswald, 2008). However, we also see that people in paid work (employees and the self-employed) have higher levels of happiness than those who are unemployed or looking after the home or children. The lowest levels of happiness in this comparison are found among people who are permanently sick or disabled. There has been little change in happiness scores in any of these groups since 2004, therefore it seems that the association between economic activity and happiness has not altered during the economic crisis – or, at least, not during its earlier years.

Table 6.1 Self-reported happiness, by main activity, 2010

	Average happiness score	*Weighted base*	*Unweighted base*
Economic activity	**Mean**		
Retired	7.8	*534*	*653*
Education	7.9	*188*	*130*
Paid work	7.5	*1213*	*1148*
Looking after home, children	7.3	*163*	*151*
Unemployed and looking for work	6.6	*124*	*124*
Permanently sick or disabled	6.3	*98*	*118*
All	7.5	*2356*	*2356*

Source: European Social Survey

Views of job security

53%

of employees say that their place of work has experienced "a great deal of financial difficulty" in the past three years

However consistently people rate their personal happiness, we can still expect their opinions about the state of the economy and other employment-related issues to vary over time. For example, when asked how satisfied they are "with the present state of the economy in Britain" on a scale from 0 to 10, people in work give an average score of 3.5; considerably lower than the average of 5.4 recorded among those in work in 2004. The views of men on the economy were more positive than those of women in 2004 (an average of 5.7 compared with 5.0), but the two have since converged (both 3.5 in 2010).

Those in paid work were also asked whether the organisation they work for had experienced changes or difficulties over recent years. Fifty-three per cent of employees say that their place of work has experienced "a great deal of financial difficulty" in the past three years. Reductions in staffing levels are also widely reported, with 39 per cent saying that the number of people employed by the organisation they work for has decreased in the last three years. This compares with 19 per cent who say the workforce in their workplace has expanded. People in work are also more likely to report having experienced a spell of unemployment in the previous five years (49 per cent) than they were in 2004 (42 per cent).

Not surprisingly, given rising experience of recent unemployment and increased awareness among workers of job losses and financial difficulties at work, there is also evidence that people's sense of job insecurity has increased. For example, British Social Attitudes has asked employees since 2005 to say whether they think it would be "difficult or easy" for their employer to replace them if they left. Comparing 2005 with 2010 there has been an increase from 33 per cent to 38 per cent in the proportion who say it would be "easy" or "very easy" to replace them. Women (42 per cent) are more likely to say this than men (34 per cent).

The European Social Survey, meanwhile, invites people who are in work to say whether it is true that their current job is secure. As shown in Table 6.2, only a quarter (23 per cent) say that it is "very true" that their current job is secure, down from a third (32 per cent) in 2004. We can also see that the decline in perceived job security has been almost entirely experienced by women. In 2004, 22 per cent of women thought it "a little true" or "not at all true" that their job was secure, compared with 34 per cent of men. In the latest survey the equivalent figures are 34 per cent for female workers and 33 per cent for male workers.

Table 6.2 Perceived level of job security, by sex, 2004 and 2010

	2004			2010		
	Men	**Women**	**All**	**Men**	**Women**	**All**
"My job is secure"	%	%	%	%	%	%
Very true	25	40	32	23	24	23
Quite true	40	38	39	41	39	40
A little true	22	13	18	19	20	19
Not at all true	12	8	10	14	14	14
Weighted base	*393*	*387*	*780*	*462*	*516*	*978*
Unweighted base	*358*	*386*	*744*	*419*	*512*	*931*

Base: all in paid work
Source: European Social Survey

Income and working hours

1 in 5

have had to take a pay cut in the past three years

Feelings of job insecurity may, of course, relate to people's personal experiences in the workplace, their observations (of colleagues being made redundant, for example), and their concerns about the financial health of their employer. In 2010, the European Social Survey asked workers specifically about changes affecting their own job. This included questions about whether they "had to take a reduction in pay" or "had to work shorter hours" in the past three years. The answers show that just over a fifth (22 per cent) report that they have taken a reduction in pay over the past three years. Men who work full-time (25 per cent) and part-time[2] (34 per cent) are more likely than women (16 per cent full-time,17 per cent part-time) to say this has happened to them (note that the figure for part-time men is based on a sample of fewer than 100). Reports of pay reductions accord with data from the Office for National Statistics showing a continuous fall in average basic earnings in real terms between mid-2008 and the end of 2009. Basic earnings also rose by less than the level of inflation during much of 2010 (Campos et al., 2011).

Reductions in pay will, in some cases, be a direct consequence of reductions in the number of hours worked, so it is also not surprising that 16 per cent of workers say that they have had to reduce their working hours in the past three years. This includes a third of men (32 per cent) and a quarter of women (26 per cent) who are working part-time; but only one in nine men (12 per cent) and women (11 per cent) working full-time.

Respondents were also asked to reflect on the adequacy of their current household income. The answers show that 40 per cent of people in paid employment feel they are "living comfortably" on their income, while another 45 per cent say that they are "coping". One in seven (14 per cent) report that it is "difficult" or "very difficult" to manage on their present income. These figures do not differ significantly from the results obtained in 2004.

We also wanted to find out if recent years had seen fewer or greater demands for night work, weekend working or short-notice overtime. In terms of personal wellbeing, unsocial working hours are known to have an especially negative impact on family relationships (Gallie and Russell, 2009). The European Social Survey asked how often respondents' work involved "working evenings or nights", "having to work overtime at short notice" or "working weekends". By comparing the answers given in 2004 and 2010 we find that, while people report an overall reduction in the working hours for which they are paid, there has been no reduction in the proportion expected to work unsocial hours, at least sometimes (Table 6.3). In fact, for women the proportions reporting that they ever work evenings, nights or weekends have increased, while there has been a modest reduction in the percentage of men who say they work at weekends. Overall, men remain much more likely than women to work unsocial hours.

Table 6.3 Unsocial work hours, by sex, 2004 and 2010

	2004			2010		
	Men	Women	All	Men	Women	All
Working unsocial hours*						
% ever work evenings or nights	67	49	59	71	55	63
% ever work overtime at short notice	67	55	61	71	57	64
% ever work weekends	79	53	67	75	58	67
Weighted base	*393*	*387*	*780*	*462*	*516*	*978*
Unweighted base	*358*	*386*	*744*	*419*	*512*	*931*

Base: all in paid work
Source: European Social Survey

* *Includes respondents who report working unsocial hours "every day", "several times a week", "several times a month", "once a month", or "less than once a month"*

Job quality

Alongside changes to the terms and conditions of their employment, the recession may also have altered people's views about the quality of their jobs. For example, training budgets may have been cut, thereby restricting people's opportunities for continued learning and skill acquisition at work (European Social Survey, 2011). Scope for career progression and pay rises may also have been reduced. There are different theories about what determines job quality. Some researchers have emphasised the negative consequences of stress resulting from an imbalance between the efforts an employee makes and the rewards he or she receives in terms of recognition or payment (Siegrist et al., 2004). Others have focused more on the relationship between the degree of control (or autonomy) that employees feel over their work, the demands being placed on them, and the extent of any social support they receive from the organisation or fellow workers (Karasek et al., 1998). The European Social Survey asks a number of questions related to these issues that have, in turn, been linked to people's overall health and sense of wellbeing (Clark et al., 2011).

Control

In 2004 and 2010, people in work were asked to assess on a scale of 0 to 10 – where 0 is "I have no influence" and 10 is "I have complete influence" – how much they are able to influence how their own daily work is organised. In Britain, the average overall score has barely changed (from 7.1 in 2004 to 7.2 in 2010). However, women's assessment of their level of control has increased, raising their average from 6.9 to 7.2 – the same as men. Here, as in a number of other areas, we see evidence that the employment experiences of men and women have been converging in recent years.

24%

say their work has got less interesting in recent years

Interest and variety

Asked if they have "had to do less interesting work" in the past three years, one in four people with jobs (24 per cent) say they have. In a different, although related, question, workers were asked if there was "a lot of variety" in their work. The replies show a modest decline since 2004 in the proportion agreeing that this is "quite true" or "very true", from 71 per cent to 67 per cent. This reduction is entirely due to a fall in the proportion of male workers who agree that their work provides variety, from 72 per cent to 64 per cent.

Social support

The European Social Survey also asks people in work whether they "can get support and help from co-workers when needed". The results show that there has been little change in employees' perceptions of this since before the recession. Eighty-three per cent say that it is "quite true" or "very true" that they received support from co-workers, compared with 81 per cent in 2004. Men (81 per cent) are now only a little less likely than women (84 per cent) to agree they get help and support – a smaller gap than in 2004 (78 per cent compared with 84 per cent).

Opportunities for advancement

Workers were asked whether "opportunities for advancement are good" at their workplace. Overall the proportion saying this is "quite true" or "very true" has remained stable at 44 per cent since 2004. However, this masks very different trends for men and women. While men have become more likely to feel that their advancement opportunities are good (increasing from 40 per cent in 2004 to 47 per cent in 2010), women have become less likely to feel this way (from 48 per cent to 42 per cent).

Work intensity

Lastly in relation to job quality, we consider the replies from workers to questions concerning work intensity. Respondents were asked how far they agreed with two statements:

> *My job requires that I work very hard*
>
> *I never seem to have enough time to get everything done in my job*

The replies (Table 6.4) reveal a mixed response. Eighty-eight per cent feel that they are required to work very hard, up from 78 per cent in 2004. However, this does not translate into an increase in workers feeling that they are under so much pressure that there is too little time to get everything done. While almost half agree this is the case in 2010, the proportion was the same in 2004, before the recession. Women are more likely than men to say their job requires hard work, and that they don't have enough time to get everything done.

Table 6.4 Perceptions of work intensity, by sex, 2004 and 2010

	2004			2010		
	Men	Women	All	Men	Women	All
% agree job requires that work very hard	76	81	78	85	90	88
% agree never seem to have enough time	47	51	49	45	51	48
Weighted base	*400*	*390*	*789*	*478*	*537*	*1015*
Unweighted base	*364*	*389*	*753*	*435*	*530*	*965*

Base: all in paid work
Source: European Social Survey

When it comes to trends in reported job quality, we have seen that several aspects have deteriorated in recent years, while others have remained stable. None, however, has shown improvement overall. Given our earlier findings on pay and job insecurity, this may reflect a growing perception among workers of an imbalance between workplace efforts and rewards. It is worth noting, however, that some changes in job quality have not affected male and female workers to the same extent. For example, men have become less likely to report variety in their work and more likely to experience social support. Women, meanwhile, report more control in the workplace, but poorer opportunities for advancement. So, what have these changes in job quality and conditions meant for job satisfaction among men and women?

Satisfaction with work and work-life balance

On a scale from 0 to 10, the average job satisfaction rating is 7.3

Previous studies have found a long-term decline in job satisfaction over recent decades, attributed to changes in the characteristics of work (Green and Tsitsianis, 2005). Researchers have also identified competing – though not necessarily contradictory – narratives about what may be happening objectively to the quality of employment. On the one hand, the growth of a 'knowledge economy' where employees are increasingly required to work with their heads rather than their hands has been contributing to an improvement in some measures of job quality. On the other, the globalisation of production and markets has exerted downward pressure on the quality of jobs in developed countries like Britain, leading to inevitable decline (Coats and Lehki, 2008).

As shown in Table 6.5, overall levels of satisfaction with work (scored on a scale of 0 to 10, where 0 is "extremely dissatisfied" and 10 is "extremely satisfied") have been sustained between 2006 and 2010 – and even show a slight increase, from 6.9 to 7.3. In 2006, men were slightly less satisfied with their jobs than women (an average of 6.8 compared with 7.1). Within this figure, the average level of satisfaction with work was similar for both men and women with full-time jobs (6.8), but noticeably higher among women working part-time (7.4). However, we can see that in 2010, the mean scores for men, women, full-time and part-time workers have all converged, (note that the base size for part-time men is less than 100 both in 2006 and in 2010).

It seems that neither the recession, nor the feared impact of globalisation, has yet brought down the overall levels of satisfaction that workers in Britain express about their jobs. In fact, the adverse economic climate may even have bolstered reported satisfaction with current employment among those who have managed to stay in work and appreciate that fact.

Table 6.5 Satisfaction with work and work-life balance among full-time and part-time workers, by sex, 2006 and 2010[3]

	2006			2010		
	Men	**Women**	**All**	**Men**	**Women**	**All**
Satisfied with work	Mean	Mean	Mean	Mean	Mean	Mean
All	6.8	7.1	6.9	7.2	7.3	7.3
Full-time	6.8	6.8	6.8	7.3	7.2	7.3
Part-time	7.0	7.4	7.3	7.1	7.3	7.3
Satisfied with work-life balance	Mean	Mean	Mean	Mean	Mean	Mean
All	5.9	6.1	6.0	6.3	6.4	6.3
Full-time	5.8	5.3	5.6	6.2	5.8	6.0
Part-time	7.3	6.9	7.0	6.9	7.0	6.0

Base: all in paid work
Source: European Social Survey

Turning to people's views about the wider balance between their jobs and the rest of their lives, the survey also asked people to rate on a scale from 0 to 10:

> ***And how satisfied are you with the balance between the time you spend on your paid work and the time you spend on other aspects of your life?***

The bottom three rows of Table 6.5 show us that average overall scores for satisfaction with work-life balance have also increased in recent years (from 6.0 in 2006 to 6.3 in 2010). Satisfaction is highest for women working part-time (7.0), and noticeably lower among women working full-time (5.8). We also see that the increase in overall scores since 2006 is largely attributable to greater satisfaction with work-life balance among women and men in full-time work.

As we might expect, there is a close relationship between job satisfaction and people's satisfaction with their work-life balance. Results from the European Social Survey show this is not only true of Britain. Looking at Figure 6.2 we see that although average levels of satisfaction with work-life balance vary greatly between 20 different European countries, the association with job satisfaction is remarkably consistent.

Figure 6.2 Job satisfaction and satisfaction with work-life balance among people in paid work, by European country

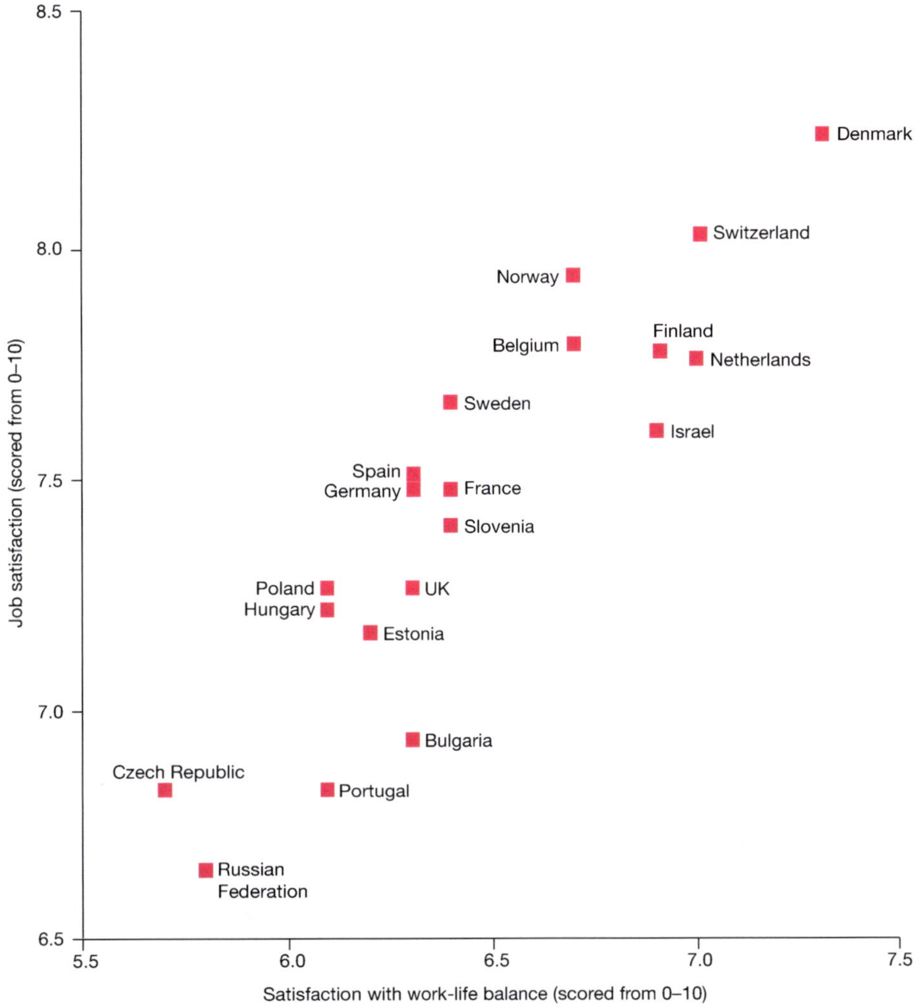

Base: all in paid work
Source: European Social Survey
The data on which Figure 6.2 is based can be found in the appendix to this chapter

Figure 6.2 also strikingly shows that both job satisfaction and satisfaction with work-life balance are lower in Britain than in most other European countries participating in the survey apart from Portugal, Russia and four other former members of the Communist bloc. This is likely to be, in part, the result of the longer (unpaid) working hours culture found in the UK. In 2011, the fourth Work-Life Balance Employee Survey[4] found that just under half (48 per cent) of employees in Britain worked overtime in a typical week, with nearly half (44 per cent) of this overtime being unpaid (Tipping et al., 2012).

Work and home life

Having established that workers in Britain tend to be less content with their work-life balance than workers in neighbouring continental countries such as Belgium, France, Germany and the Netherlands, our next task is to look more closely at what people in Britain say about the relationship between their personal and working lives. On this theme, the European Social Survey asks people in work to say:

how often do you ...

... keep worrying about work problems when you are not working

... feel too tired after work to enjoy things you would like to do at home

89%

say there have been times when they felt too tired after work to enjoy things at home

In 2004 nearly three out of four employed people (73 per cent) said that they had ever worried about work problems when at home,[5] but in the 2010 survey this has risen to 80 per cent. An even higher proportion – 89 per cent – say there have been times when they felt too tired after work to enjoy things at home, although this is close to the proportion in 2004.

By cross-comparing data we can see that a relationship exists between the way people reply to these two questions and their responses to more general questions about their happiness and life satisfaction. Figure 6.3 shows how those who "never" feel too tired after work have an average happiness score of 8.0 out of 10.0, compared with 6.6 among people who "always" feel this way.

Figure 6.3 Average happiness score (0–10), by how often too tired after work

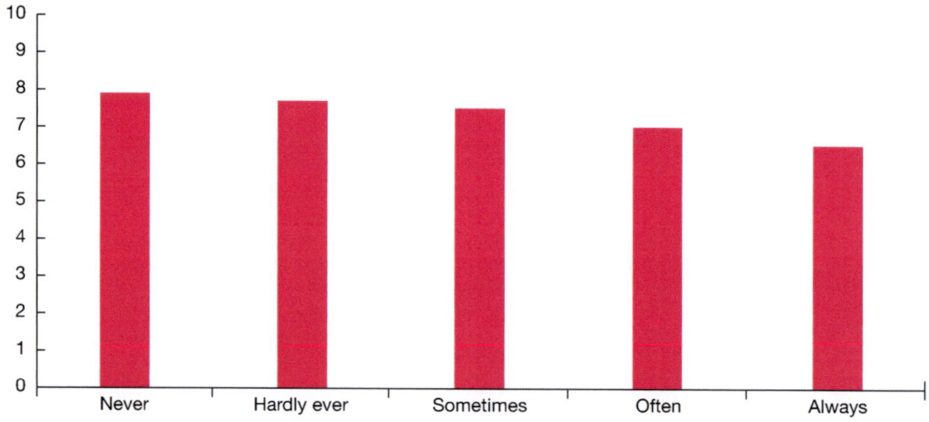

Base: all in paid work
Source: European Social Survey
The data on which Figure 6.3 is based can be found in the appendix to this chapter

However, our analysis finds no association between levels of happiness and whether people work full- or part-time. This matches the findings of another recent study (Pereira and Coelho, 2012), which found that the absolute number of working hours is not the sole determinant of a worker's overall happiness. Rather, happiness seems to be related to the extent to which workers (both full- and part-time) perceive there to be conflicts between work and other aspects of their lives. Such conflicts among respondents are strongly and consistently associated with lower levels of reported happiness.

Gender, work and family

A traditionalist view of men as 'breadwinners' and women as 'homemakers' has declined

European Social Survey data, meanwhile, show us that, alongside changes in labour market participation, a traditionalist view of men as 'breadwinners' and women as 'homemakers' has declined. The survey asks two questions that seek to measure such attitudes. Employed people were asked whether they agree or disagree with the following statements:

When jobs are scarce, men should have more right to a job than women

A woman should be prepared to cut down on her paid work for the sake of her family

Table 6.6 shows that in 2004 only 16 per cent of men in paid work and 14 per cent of women in paid work agreed that men are the primary financial providers by right. In 2010, this view is even less popular: only 10 per cent of working men and nine per cent of working women agree. However, we can also see that a much larger group of workers of both sexes feel that women should be prepared to give family responsibilities greater priority than paid work. The proportion of employed women who agree stands at 40 per cent and has not altered since 2004. Interestingly, it is men – where the level of agreement has declined from 36 per cent to 31 per cent – whose opinions appear to have shifted towards a less traditionalist view of women's roles.

Table 6.6 Gender traditional views among people in paid work, by sex, 2004 and 2010

	2004			2010		
	Men	Women	All	Men	Women	All
% agree a man has more right to work when jobs are scarce	16	14	15	10	9	10
% agree a woman should be prepared to cut down work for the sake of her family	36	40	38	31	40	35
Weighted base	*533*	*442*	*975*	*621*	*613*	*1235*
Unweighted base	*478*	*439*	*917*	*563*	*602*	*1165*

Base: all in paid work
Source: European Social Survey

Clearly a substantial minority of people in work believe that a woman's family responsibilities should come first if there is any conflict with her chosen working hours – this is the view expressed by four out of ten women in work. It is also apparent that the recession and its consequences for household budgets have done nothing to reinforce the traditionalist view of men's and women's work roles, and may even have served to erode it. It should be noted that the survey did not ask respondents whether a man should be prepared to cut down on paid work for the sake of his family. So it is possible that the persistence of this view in relation to women may reflect not the persistence of gender-traditional views about the nurturing role of women, but rather the view that family should take priority over work for everyone.

Conclusions

Demands in the workplace have increased somewhat – workers have become more likely to feel that they have to work "very hard"

In this chapter we have seen that since 2004, many employed people have seen the organisations that they work for encounter financial difficulties and witnessed colleagues being made redundant or failing to have their contracts renewed. Feelings of job insecurity have become more widespread, with women, in particular, feeling more vulnerable than they did before the start of the economic crisis.

Perceptions of job quality have shifted since before the recession among both men and women in work. Demands in the workplace have increased somewhat – workers have become more likely to feel that they have to work "very hard" and more likely to report some types of unsocial working hours. Effort-reward imbalance theory argues that workers can often cope with high demands like this, provided their rewards are commensurate. But we have found that workplace rewards have decreased: people report finding that their work has become less interesting, that it has less variety, and that they have experienced reductions in pay. One thing that has remained stable overall is the level of support provided by colleagues – although it is possible this could reflect a solidarity born of shared insecurity in some of Britain's recession-hit workplaces.

These trends cannot be good news for families. As well as reductions in pay and in average number of paid working hours, and increases in unsocial work hours, between 2004 and 2010 there have also been small but significant increases in people saying that they worry about work-related problems when they are not working. We have observed a drop in the proportion of workers of both sexes who regard men as priority breadwinners, yet found no accompanying drop, at least among women, in the proportion who believe that a woman should be prepared to cut down on paid work for the sake of her family. One interpretation of this is that the dual burden on women – as both economic providers and caregivers – may have intensified.

Self-reported happiness and life satisfaction have remained remarkably stable throughout both good and bad economic times

This presents us with a conundrum. Many of the factors that we know are associated with subjective wellbeing – like job security and managing financially – have deteriorated, yet levels of self-reported life satisfaction and happiness have remained buoyant. Should this surprise us? In Iceland, Gudmundsdottir (2011) uncovered a comparable paradox when she found that the self-reported happiness of people in her country remained pretty much unchanged during its period of extreme economic crisis. American data sources paint a similar picture (for example, Blanchflower and Oswald, 2002). Our findings likewise show that self-reported happiness and life satisfaction have remained remarkably stable throughout both good and bad economic times. Explanations for this phenomenon include a view that individuals have a wellbeing 'set point' that they readily revert to after periods of crisis. However, continuing unemployment is a notable exception to this, being one of the few experiences found to be capable of shifting the 'set point' within an individual for the worse (Lucas et al., 2004). As evidenced by the survey data reported in this chapter, such a 'set point' seems to exist at a societal level as well as at an individual one.

Another lesson we can draw from the findings in this chapter is that the use of satisfaction and subjective wellbeing indicators to evaluate the social impact of a changing economy carries risks. Used in isolation, such measures may be liable to underestimate the real impact of recession on the quality of people's day-to-day lives. The British government's plans to increase the use of subjective wellbeing measures in policy and programme evaluation, as well as for monitoring trends in social progress, have been widely welcomed. But these measures may need to be placed alongside ones that also more directly probe people's specific experiences.

How satisfied people say they are will depend not only on the objective quality of what they are being asked to assess, but also on what their expectations are. In times of economic crisis workers may expect job loss, and so be satisfied with continued employment. In times of economic boom, they may expect promotion and advancement, and be more likely to report dissatisfaction. We should not, therefore, be surprised that reported job satisfaction has increased since before the recession, even though some aspects of job quality have deteriorated. It is important not to assume that high levels of job satisfaction necessarily mean that all is well in the workplace: they might reflect, in part, low expectations.

Notes

1. British Social Attitudes and European Social Survey analysis excludes Northern Ireland, whereas OECD data are based on the whole UK. Various terms are used in this chapter to refer to people in paid work (for example, "workers", "people in paid work", and "employed people"). They all denote everyone who is either an employee or is self-employed, who usually works 10 hours or more a week, and who considers work to be their main activity.

2. Part-time work was defined as working less than 35 hours per week.

3. Bases for Table 6.5 are as follows:

	2004			2010		
	Men	**Women**	**All**	**Men**	**Women**	**All**
All						
Weighted base	*634*	*585*	*1218*	*550*	*585*	*1135*
Unweighted base	*692*	*608*	*1300*	*607*	*594*	*1202*
Full-time						
Weighted base	*564*	*313*	*876*	*465*	*303*	*768*
Unweighted base	*620*	*320*	*940*	*503*	*304*	*807*
Part-time						
Weighted base	*62*	*265*	*327*	*70*	*273*	*343*
Unweighted base	*63*	*282*	*345*	*86*	*280*	*366*

4. The fourth Work-Life Balance Employee Survey was conducted by NatCen Social Research for the Department for Business, Innovation and Skills.

5. This includes people who say they "always", "often", "sometimes" or "hardly ever" do this, but excludes those who say they "never" do.

References

Blanchflower, D.G. and Oswald, A.J. (1999), 'Well-Being, Insecurity and the Decline of American Job Satisfaction', presented at Cornell University conference May 1999, available at: www.dartmouth.edu/~blnchflr/papers/JobSat.pdf

Blanchflower, D.G. and Oswald, A.J. (2002), 'Well-being over time in Britain and the USA', *Journal of Public Economics*, **88**: 1359–1386

Blanchflower, D.G. and Oswald, A. J., (2008), 'Is Wellbeing U-Shaped over the Life Cycle?', *Social Science & Medicine*, **66(8)**: 1733-1749

Bryson, A., Green, F., Bridges, S. and Craig, R. (2011), 'Wellbeing, health and work', in Craig, R. and Mindell J. (eds.), *Health Survey for England – 2010: Respiratory Health*, Leeds: NHS Information Centre

Campos, C., Dent, A., Fry, R. and Reid, A. (2011), *Impact of the Recession*, London: Office for National Statistics

Clark, C., Pike, C., McManus, S., Harris, J., Bebbington, P., Brugha, T., Jenkins, R., Meltzer, H., Weich, S. and Stansfeld, S. (2011), 'The contribution of work and non-work stressors to common mental disorders in the 2007 Adult Psychiatric Morbidity Survey', *Psychological Medicine*, **42(4)**: 829–42

Coats, D. and Lehki, R. (2008), *'Good Work': Job Quality in a Changing Economy*, London: The Work Foundation

European Social Survey (2011), *Round 5 Module on Work, Family and Wellbeing – Final Question Design Template*, London: Centre for Comparative Social Surveys, City University London

Gallie, D. and Russell, H. (2009), 'Work-Life Conflict and Working Conditions in Western Europe', *Social Indicators Research*, **93(3)**: 445–467

Green, F. (2012), 'Work, Job Attributes and Subjective Wellbeing: Evidence from the Health Survey for England 2010', Presentation to NatCen/NIESR Workshop, *Linking Paid Work, Health and Wellbeing*

Green, F. and Tsitsianis, N. (2005), 'An Investigation of National Trends in Job Satisfaction in Britain and Germany', *British Journal of Industrial Relations*, **43(3)**: 401-429

Gudmundsottir, D.G. (2011), 'The impact of economic crisis on happiness', *Social Indicators Research*, available at: www.springerlink.com/content/x20g311m55404r66/

Hall, J., d'Ardenne, J., Barnes, M., Roberts, C. and McManus, S. (2011), *Food choices and behaviour: trends and the impact of life events*, London: NatCen Social Research

Karasek, R., Brisson, C., Kawakami, N., Houtman, I., Bongers, P. and Amick, B. (1998), 'The Job Content Questionnaire (JCQ): An instrument for internationally comparative assessments of psychosocial job characteristics', *Journal of Occupational Health Psychology*, **3(4)**: 322–355

Lucas, R.E., Clark, A.E., Georgellis, Y., and Diener, E. (2004), 'Unemployment alters the set point for life satisfaction', *Psychological Sciences* **15(1)**: 8–13

McManus, S., Mowlam, A., Wollny, I., Dorsett, R., Stansfeld, S., Clark C., Morrell, G., Rahmen, N. and Meltzer, H. (forthcoming, 2012), *Mental health in context: the national study of work-search and wellbeing*, London: Department for Work and Pensions

Office for National Statistics (2012), *Labour Market Statistic: March 2012*, Office for National Statistics, available at: www.ons.gov.uk/ons/dcp171778_257901.pdf

Organisation for Economic Co-operation and Development (2010), *Database on Labour Force Statistics*, Paris, France: OECD Publishing

Pereira, M.C. and Coelho, F. (2012), 'Work Hours and Well Being: An Investigation of Moderator Effects', *Social Indicators Research*, available at: www.springerlink.com/content/c24188u16r511l4q

Philpott, J. (2011), 'How men and women have fared in the post-recession UK jobs market', London: Chartered Institute of Personnel and Development

Rake, K. and Rotheroe, A. (2009), *Are women bearing the burden of the recession?* London: Fawcett Society

Siegrist, J., Starke, D., Chandola, T., Godin, I., Marmot, M., Niedhammer, I. and Peter, R. (2004), 'The measurement of effort-reward imbalance at work: European comparisons', *Social Sciences and Medicine*, **58(8)**:1483–1499

Spence, A. (2011), *Social Trends 41: Labour Market*, London: Office for National Statistics

Tipping, S., Chanfreau, J., Perry, J. and Tait, C. (2012), *The Fourth Work-Life Balance Employee Survey*, London: Department for Business, Innovation and Skills

Acknowledgements

The European Social Survey is funded jointly by the European Commission, the European Science Foundation and academic funding bodies in participating countries. NatCen Social Research is also grateful to the Department for Business, Innovation and Skills for their financial support which enabled us to ask the British Social Attitudes questions reported in the chapter. The views expressed are those of the authors alone.

Appendix

The data on which Figure 6.1 is based are shown below.

Table A.1 Proportion of men and women economically active during recessions, 1971–2008

	1971	1982	1992	2008
	%	%	%	%
Men	92	80	77	79
Women	53	55	62	67

Base: People living in the UK aged 16-64
Source: Labour Force Survey (Spence, 2011)

The data on which Figure 6.2 is based are shown below.

Table A.2 Job satisfaction and satisfaction with work-life balance among people in paid work, by European country

	Job satisfaction	Satisfaction with work-life balance	*Weighted base*	*Unweighted base*
Country	**Mean**	**Mean**		
Russian Federation	6.7	5.8	*1363*	*1325*
Czech Republic	6.8	5.7	*1181*	*1257*
Portugal	6.8	6.1	*826*	*798*
Bulgaria	6.9	6.3	*904*	*969*
Estonia	7.2	6.2	*854*	*854*
Hungary	7.2	6.1	*745*	*740*
Poland	7.3	6.1	*837*	*548*
UK	7.3	6.3	*1172*	*1241*
Slovenia	7.4	6.4	*616*	*531*
France	7.5	6.4	*626*	*626*
Germany	7.5	6.3	*1502*	*1510*
Spain	7.5	6.3	*899*	*903*
Israel	7.6	6.9	*989*	*992*
Sweden	7.7	6.4	*797*	*797*
Netherlands	7.7	7.0	*954*	*921*
Finland	7.8	6.9	*884*	*884*
Belgium	7.8	6.7	*830*	*830*
Norway	7.9	6.7	*886*	*916*
Switzerland	8.0	7.0	*853*	*853*
Denmark	8.2	7.3	*823*	*823*

Base: All in paid work
Source: European Social Survey

The data on which Figure 6.3 is based are shown below.

Table A.3 Average happiness score, by how often too tired after work

	How often too tired after work to enjoy things at home				
	Never	Hardly ever	Some-times	Often	Always
Mean happiness score	8.0	7.8	7.6	7.1	6.6
Weighted base	*237*	*351*	*872*	*550*	*136*
Unweighted base	*216*	*336*	*836*	*515*	*128*

Base: All in paid work
Source: European Social Survey

Scottish independence

The state of the Union: public opinion and the Scottish question

The Scottish National Party's (SNP) success in the 2011 Scottish Parliament elections has renewed and invigorated the long-running debate on Scotland's constitutional status. In the near future, it seems certain that people in Scotland will be asked to decide whether they wish to become independent and leave the UK. But does the SNP's electoral success reflect a desire for independence among people in Scotland? And is there any sign of weakening support in England for Scotland's current position within the Union?

Scottish support for independence

Only a minority of people in Scotland currently support independence, while there is no evidence of a long-term increase in support for Scotland leaving the UK. People's willingness to back the idea depends more on whether they think it would make Scotland's economy stronger than on whether they have a strong Scottish identity.

Around a third of people in Scotland favour independence, and there is no consistent evidence of an increase in support over time. At 32% **support for independence** is up 9 points on 2010, when it was at a record low of 23%, but is still lower than in 2005, when it stood at 35%.

Only just over half (53%) of those who say they are "Scottish, not British" support independence, compared with over three-quarters of those who say that Scotland's economy would be a lot stronger if the country left the UK. But at present only 34% in Scotland think the economy would be stronger.

The English perspective

There is evidence of increasing unhappiness in England about the 'anomalies' thrown up by the current asymmetric devolution settlement, and of greater willingness to question its continuation.

Although less than half (44%) of people in England think that Scotland gets more than its **fair share of public spending**, that is double the proportion who were of that view little more than a decade ago.

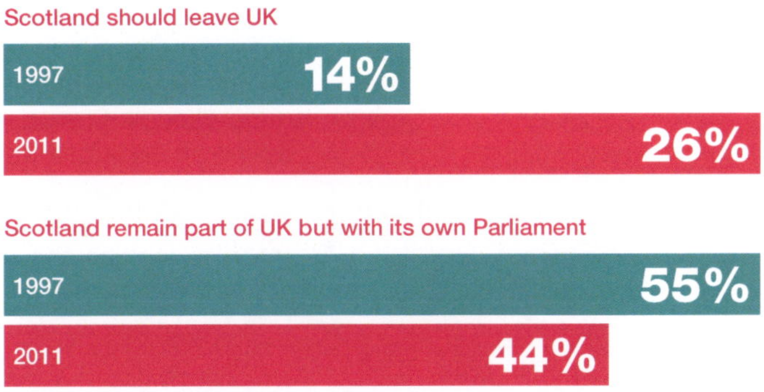

26% of people in England now believe **Scotland should leave the UK** compared with 14% in 1997. Conversely, support for Scotland remaining part of the UK but with its own Parliament has declined from 55% in 1997 to 44% in 2011.

Authors

John Curtice and Rachel Ormston
John Curtice is Professor of Politics at the University of Strathclyde and Research Consultant at NatCen Social Research. Rachel Ormston is a Senior Research Director at ScotCen Social Research

Commentators and politicians have advocated 'devolution plus' or 'devolution max'

Introduction

The success of the Scottish National Party (SNP) in securing an overall majority in the 2011 Scottish Parliament election has had profound implications for the long-running debate about Scotland's constitutional status. The SNP's election manifesto included a commitment to hold a referendum on whether Scotland should become a separate country, independent from the rest of the UK.[1] Although there remain question marks over whether the Scottish Parliament has the legal authority to hold a ballot, the SNP's opponents have accepted that their electoral success has given the nationalists the moral right to do so. Meanwhile, the UK government has signalled a willingness to give the Edinburgh institution explicit authority to hold a vote (Scotland Office, 2012). Given these developments, it now looks inevitable that in the next couple of years, people in Scotland will be asked to decide whether they wish to dissolve the 300-year Union between their country and the rest of the UK.

However, current debates about Scotland's constitutional future are not focused solely on the merits or otherwise of independence. The SNP's victory in 2011 has also sparked renewed discussion about whether Scotland should have increased rights and responsibilities within the United Kingdom. This debate does not appear to have been quelled by the passage through the UK Parliament of the Scotland Act 2012. Prompted in part by the SNP's earlier success in forming a minority government in 2007, that Act grants the Scottish Parliament increased powers, including taxation powers. But even before the Scotland Act received Royal Assent, the debate about Scotland's powers within the Union already appeared to have moved on. Commentators and politicians have variously advocated 'devolution plus' (under which the Scottish Parliament would be responsible for raising more or less all of its own revenues (Thomson et al., 2011)) or 'devolution max' (under which most welfare benefits would also be devolved (Scottish Government, 2009)) as better reflecting the aspirations of Scotland for further self-government within the UK. Interestingly, discussion of these possibilities has in part been promoted by the SNP themselves, who have repeatedly shown a willingness to consider including some such option on the referendum ballot as an alternative to full independence. In contrast, the UK government, together with the Labour opposition, have opposed the inclusion of a 'second question' on the referendum ballot paper, although they have indicated they are open to considering options for further devolution should Scotland opt to remain within the Union (Cameron, 2012; Lamont, 2012).

While the future of the Union is currently being questioned most openly north of the border, ultimately the future stability of the UK depends on public opinion in England too. The current devolution settlement is already highly asymmetric. Many of Scotland's domestic affairs – health, education and public transport, for example – are determined by Scotland's devolved institutions, on which England is unrepresented. Yet public policy for England itself continues to be decided by UK-wide institutions in which Scotland does have a say. It has long been argued that this situation would eventually lead to an 'English backlash' – that people in England would be increasingly unhappy about the apparently advantaged position that Scotland enjoys within the Union. The risk of such a backlash might well be thought to be heightened if the rights of the Scottish Parliament were further extended. Meanwhile, maintaining Scotland's membership of the UK would certainly be made more difficult if people in England decided they would prefer the two countries to go their own separate ways.

This chapter addresses these three issues. First, we examine the level and character of support north of the border for Scottish independence. In particular, we assess how far the demand for independence appears to reflect a desire to express a distinctive sense of Scottish national identity, and how far it appears to be contingent on expectations of what independence might bring, including not least its material consequences. Second, we consider whether there is support north of the border for some form of 'devolution plus' or 'devolution max', that would extend Scotland's say over its own domestic affairs while retaining its membership of the UK. Finally we consider whether there is any evidence of increasing unhappiness south of the border with the current asymmetric devolution settlement – an unhappiness that might perhaps lead people to regard Scottish independence as preferable to a Union that leaves England at a disadvantage.

The first two questions are addressed using data from the Scottish Social Attitudes survey. This survey is conducted in much the same way as British Social Attitudes but interviews sufficient people living in Scotland to provide robust estimates of public opinion there. The third question is answered using British Social Attitudes data but looking only at the views of those living in England.

Does Scotland want independence?

Since its inception in 1999, Scottish Social Attitudes has asked respondents the same question each year about how they would prefer Scotland to be governed. This question was first asked in two other surveys carried out by NatCen Social Research: one fielded immediately after the 1997 UK general election, and one conducted following the 1997 referendum on Scottish devolution. This means Scottish Social Attitudes is a unique source of evidence on trends in support for independence since the advent of devolution. The survey invites respondents to say which of five options is closest to their view about how Scotland should be governed:

> *Scotland should become independent, separate from the UK and the European Union*
>
> *Scotland should become independent, separate from the UK but part of the European Union*
>
> *Scotland should remain part of the UK, with its own elected parliament which has **some** taxation powers*
>
> *Scotland should remain part of the UK, with its own elected parliament which has **no** taxation powers*
>
> *Scotland should remain part of the UK **without** an elected parliament*

The first two responses refer to independence, either within or outside the European Union. The next two refer to devolution – Scotland having its own devolved parliament – either with or without taxation powers. The last option describes the status quo prior to devolution, that is, Scotland being part of the UK without its own parliament. In Figure 7.1 we have combined the responses to each of the first two pairs of options, so that we can see clearly the level of overall support each year for independence (middle line), devolution (top) and not having any Scottish Parliament at all (bottom line).

There has been remarkably little change since 1997 in the level of support for independence

There has in fact been remarkably little change since 1997 in the level of support for independence. In most years it has been somewhere between one quarter and one third. It reached a peak of 37 per cent in the immediate wake of the 1997 referendum on devolution and another of 35 per cent in 2005. But more recently support has, if anything, been on the low side, falling as low as 23 per cent in 2010.

Far from stimulating support for independence, the experience of having the SNP in power after 2007 seemed, if anything, to have depressed it (Ormston and Curtice, 2010; Curtice and Ormston, 2011). That drop appears to have been reversed in the immediate wake of the SNP's second and more spectacular electoral success in 2011. However, at 32 per cent the level of support for independence now is still in the range within which it has oscillated during the last dozen or so years, and still trails that for devolution (58 per cent) by some considerable margin. It is also clear that far fewer people currently support independence than were willing to vote SNP in the 2011 Scottish Parliament elections; indeed only 51 per cent of those who said they voted SNP in 2011 also favoured independence.

Figure 7.1 Attitudes in Scotland to how Scotland should be governed, 1997–2011

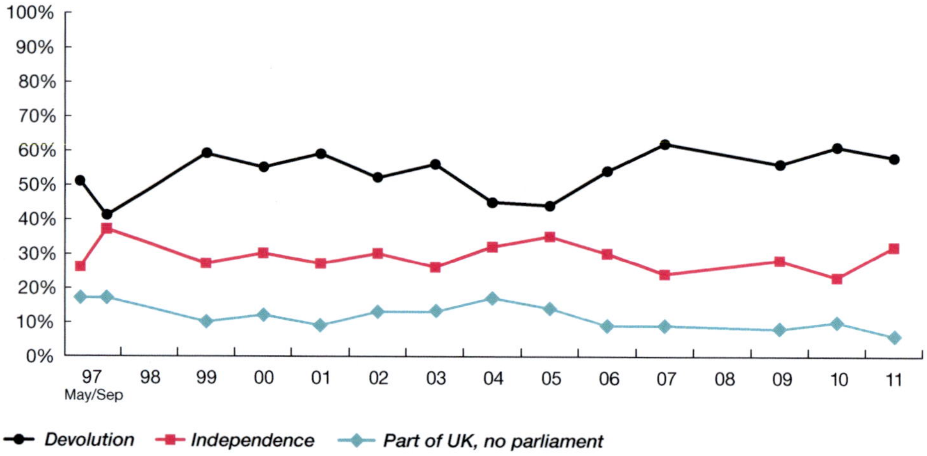

The data on which Figure 7.1 is based can be found in the appendix to this chapter
Sources: 1997 May: Scottish Election Study; 1997 Sept: Scottish Referendum Study; 1999–2011: Scottish Social Attitudes survey
In 1997 two readings were taken, one before the general election and one after

What leads people to support independence or not?

So support for independence remains a minority position, despite the SNP's electoral success. But what leads people to support independence or not? One possibility is that attitudes reflect people's sense of national identity. Perhaps people who feel Scottish rather than British are inclined to feel that Scotland should enjoy the full status of an independent state, just like any other nation (Gellner, 1983). However, previous research into levels of support for 'secessionist' movements around the world suggests that support also depends on perceptions of economic wealth and access to natural resources (Hechter, 2000; Sorens, 2005; Sambanis, 2006). Research on the basis of public support for Quebec sovereignty, for example, finds that while it is rooted in part in questions of identity and language, those who take a favourable view of the economic consequences of leaving Canada are also more likely to back the idea (Blais and Nadeau, 1992; Howe, 1998; Nadeau et al., 1999). Meanwhile in Scotland, the perceived material consequences of constitutional change have been cited as key influences on whether people voted 'Yes' in the 1997 referendum on devolution (Surridge et al., 1998; Surridge and McCrone, 1999; though see also Curtice, 1999). So we clearly need to examine how far support for independence is linked to perceptions of its consequences, and particularly its material consequences, as well as how far it appears to reflect a distinctive Scottish sense of national identity.

Table 7.1 shows what impact people in Scotland currently think independence would have, not only on various aspects of the country's material wellbeing but also on its sense of pride and its voice in the world (the full question text can be found in the appendix to this chapter). In each case, much the same question was also asked about devolution shortly after the 1997 referendum, in which a majority voted in favour of creating a Scottish Parliament. This means we can compare current levels of optimism about independence with the hopes and expectations people had for devolution when it had just been given the green light.

Table 7.1 Expectations in Scotland of devolution in 1997 and of independence in 2011[2]

		Devolution, 1997			Independence, 2011		
		Better/ stronger	No difference	Worse/ weaker	Better/ stronger	No difference	Worse/ weaker
Pride in country	%	77	20	1	67	27	2
Voice in the world*	%	60	22	11	51	27	19
Standard of health service	%	65	28	6	37	35	19
Standard of living	%	n/a	n/a	n/a	34	34	23
Economy	%	64	24	12	34	26	29
Taxes**	%	3	20	76	10	29	53

n/a = not asked

In 1997 the question referred to "voice in Europe"

***Those who thought taxes would be "higher" are classified as saying things would be 'worse', while those who thought they would be "lower" are classified as saying things would be 'better'*

Sources: 1997: Scottish Referendum Study; 2011: Scottish Social Attitudes

With the exception of taxation, more people think things would be better under independence than would be worse

For the most part the balance of expectations appears to be relatively favourable towards independence. With the exception of taxation, where there is a widespread feeling that taxes would be higher, more people think that things would be better under independence than think they would be worse. However, the excess of optimists over pessimists is much greater in respect of the less immediately material consequences than it is when it comes to the material (and especially the economic) ones. For example, while 67 per cent feel that people in Scotland would have more pride in their country as a result of independence, just 34 per cent feel the standard of living would improve, while 23 per cent think it will get worse. Moreover, people are much less optimistic about the prospect of independence now than they were about devolution in 1997. Again, this is especially so with respect to the anticipated material consequences. While then, 64 per cent thought Scotland's economy would be stronger as a result of devolution, now just 34 per cent feel it would be stronger if Scotland became independent. While independence is far from being widely regarded as a wholly disastrous prospect, it would appear that most people in Scotland have yet to be persuaded that it would bring significant material benefits.

Moreover, despite the generally favourable balance of opinion on some of the anticipated consequences of independence, the prospect of independence is widely regarded with a degree of unease. This emerges most clearly in responses to the following question:

> ***If Scotland were to become independent, would you feel confident about Scotland's future, worried, or neither confident nor worried?***

No less than 46 per cent say that they would be worried (either "very" or "quite"). Just 31 per cent indicate that they would feel confident (again either "very" or "quite"), while a further 22 per cent state that they would be neither confident nor worried. It would seem that above and beyond its anticipated specific consequences, independence is regarded as something of a risk by a substantial section of the population.

But how far are any of these expectations linked with people's attitudes towards independence? Are people only likely to support the idea if they think it would benefit Scotland's economy or standard of living? And do any of these expectations make much difference once we take into account people's sense of national identity? These questions are best answered by using multivariate analysis (described in more detail in the Technical details chapter). This enables us to assess and summarise the strength of the relationships between a variety of expectations about independence and national identity on the one hand, and levels of support for independence on the other. We can also check whether there are any demographic differences in attitudes, above and beyond any differences relating to national identity or expectations.

The results of our analyses are summarised in Table 7.2. First though, we should note that how confident or worried people feel about independence is strongly associated with support for the idea. No less than 85 per cent of those who feel very confident about independence support the idea, while only six per cent of those who are very worried about the prospect wish to leave the UK. As a result our measure of confidence dominates the results if it is included in any model of support for independence. This means that any such model might be regarded as simply re-describing rather than explaining support for independence. We therefore model support for independence (as measured by our long-standing question reported in Figure 7.1) and confidence separately, in the knowledge that having confidence in independence appears to play an important role in fostering support for the idea.[3]

Table 7.2 Summary of attitudes, expectations and characteristics associated with support for and confidence in independence, in Scotland

More likely to support independence if	More likely to feel confident about independence if
– Think Scotland's **economy** would be better under independence – Have a strong Scottish rather than British **national identity** – Think people in Scotland would have more **pride in their country** under independence – Think Scotland would have a stronger **voice in the world** under independence – **Age** is less than 65	– Think Scotland's **economy** would be better under independence – Think people in Scotland would have more **pride in their country** under independence – Think Scotland would have a stronger **voice in the world** under independence – Think **taxes** would be lower under independence – Think the **standard of living** would be higher under independence – A **man** – **Age** is 18–34 or 45–64

This table summarises the results of regression analyses that are reported in full in Tables A.2 and A.3. In the case of the 'Independence' model, variables are listed in the order in which they were entered into the model. In the case of the 'Confidence' model variables are listed in the order of the strength of their relationship in the final model[4]

Source: Scottish Social Attitudes

So far as support for independence is concerned, expectations about the impact of independence both on the economy and on national identity appear in our multivariate model. However, economic expectations are more closely related to support than is national identity, a finding illustrated by Table 7.3. There is a 43 percentage point difference in the level of support for independence between those who say they feel Scottish not British and those who say they are British not Scottish. But there is no less than a 74 point difference in support for independence between those who feel Scotland's economy would be a lot stronger and those who think it would be a lot weaker if the country were to leave the Union. By this measure, at least, material expectations appear to be the more important of the two considerations in voters' minds.

Table 7.3 Support in Scotland for independence by national identity and economic expectations[5]

National identity	% support independence	Economic expectations	% support independence
Scottish, not British	53	Lot stronger	78
More Scottish than British	32	Little stronger	46
Equally Scottish and British	12	No difference	32
More British than Scottish	11	Little weaker	10
British, not Scottish	10	Lot weaker	4

Source: Scottish Social Attitudes

Economic expectations prove to be unambiguously the most important correlate

Economic expectations are not, however, the only expectations about independence associated with support for the idea. So too are beliefs about some less immediately material considerations – in particular, views about whether independence would mean people in Scotland had more pride in their country, and whether it would bring Scotland a stronger voice in the world. The former in particular might be regarded as a more 'affective' or 'emotional' consideration, in much the same way as national identity. Meanwhile, younger people are somewhat keener on independence than their older counterparts, irrespective of their expectations about the consequences or their national identity. Overall, as Table 7.4 shows, 42 per cent of 18–24 year olds support independence, compared with 24 per cent of those aged 65 and older.

Nevertheless, the critical importance of economic expectations in shaping attitudes towards independence is further underlined by our model of whether people feel confident or worried about independence. In this case economic expectations prove to be unambiguously the most important correlate, while expectations of what would happen to taxes and living standards under independence matter too. At the same time, perceptions that independence would enhance national pride and strengthen Scotland's voice in the world are once again significant. National identity, however, is not. It would seem that while some people support independence simply because they feel Scottish, such feelings do not necessarily translate into a sense of confidence in the prospect.

Meanwhile, we should also note that just as younger people are more likely to support independence, they are also more likely to feel confident about it (see Table 7.4). In addition, we find that men are more likely to feel confident about independence than women, irrespective of their expectations of what consequences it would bring. This latter difference may well help explain why, as Table 7.4 demonstrates, men appear more willing than women to support independence, a pattern that has been identified by many previous surveys (McCrone and Paterson, 2002), though it is one that disappears once we take into account where people stand on the variables that appear in our model of support for independence.

Table 7.4 Support for and confidence in independence by sex and age, in Scotland

	% support independence	% feel confident about independence	*Weighted base*	*Unweighted base*
Sex				
Men	36	37	*573*	*528*
Women	29	25	*625*	*669*
Age group				
18–24	42	33	*143*	*81*
25–34	36	37	*189*	*143*
35–44	31	38	*207*	*212*
45–54	35	27	*220*	*227*
55–64	31	26	*186*	*193*
65 plus	24	26	*245*	*337*

Source: Scottish Social Attitudes

So far our findings have shown that independence remains the preference of a minority in Scotland, albeit a considerable one. This is despite the fact that around three-fifths (62 per cent) of people in Scotland say that they are "Scottish, not British" or "More Scottish than British". For many people then, feeling a strong sense of Scottish national identity is not sufficient reason for backing independence. Even among those who deny they are British at all, only just over half (53 per cent) back leaving the UK. To be willing to support independence, most people also need to be convinced it would bring some benefit, including above all some economic advantage; otherwise they are inclined to feel worried about the prospect. And at present, although only a minority reckon an independent Scotland would be economically weaker than it is now, optimism about the material consequences of independence is far from being widespread either. It seems unlikely that a majority of people in Scotland will decide to vote in favour of independence unless they can be persuaded that leaving the UK would be an economically advantageous course of action.

More devolution for Scotland *within* the UK?

While support for leaving the Union may only be a minority position at present, and as we saw earlier (Figure 7.1) a majority (58 per cent) favour some form of devolved government, this does not necessarily mean the Scottish public are happy with the current devolution settlement. After all, Scottish Social Attitudes has persistently found that far fewer people (in 2011, 38 per cent) feel that the Scottish Government has most influence over the way that Scotland is run than feel it should have most influence (in 2011, 78 per cent) (Ormston and Reid, 2012).[6] This contrast would certainly suggest that a move towards more powerful devolved institutions would be in step with the broad thrust of public opinion.

Views in Scotland on who "ought to make most of the important decisions for Scotland" in various policy areas provide more precise evidence for that assertion. As Table 7.5 shows, in 2010 two-thirds of Scottish Social Attitudes respondents said that the Scottish Parliament ought to have that role so far as the health service is concerned, while almost as many said the same about schools. These of course are both areas where primary responsibility already lies with the Scottish Parliament. However, as many said the same of welfare benefits, and nearly three in five said so for taxes, both of which are still largely the preserve of Westminster. The one policy area where a majority of people in Scotland feel that decisions should be made by the UK government is defence and foreign affairs, where only around three in ten reckon the Scottish Parliament should make the decisions.

Table 7.5 Views in Scotland about who should make important decisions for Scotland, 2010

		Scottish Parliament	UK government at Westminster	Local councils in Scotland	European Union
Who ought to make important decisions about ...					
... health service	%	66	26	5	*
... schools	%	62	14	23	*
... welfare benefits	%	62	25	9	1
... level of taxes	%	57	37	3	*
... defence and foreign affairs	%	31	63	1	3

In each case the weighted and unweighted base is 1495
Source: Scottish Social Attitudes

Responsibility for defence and foreign affairs is, of course, arguably the essence of being an independent state. This last finding is thus in line with our earlier evidence on the level of support for independence, at around three in ten. But otherwise, it would seem that the instinctive reaction of the majority of people in Scotland is that decisions about the country's domestic affairs, including the financially crucial areas of taxation and welfare benefits, should be made in Edinburgh. It is often argued that these two areas – and especially welfare benefits – should remain primarily a UK-wide responsibility because the resources for insuring individuals and communities against the risks (such as unemployment) to which they are subject are best pooled across the country as a whole. At the same time, opponents of devolving benefits argue that a common welfare system is crucial to ensuring that all UK citizens enjoy exactly the same social rights (see, for example, Commission on Scottish Devolution, 2009). However, it seems that these arguments cut little ice with the Scottish public.

68%

in Scotland say the Scottish Parliament should decide the basic rate of income tax

A critical reader of these findings might wonder whether references in our questions to "taxation" and "welfare benefits" are rather abstract. Perhaps some survey respondents do not fully appreciate the implications of the proposition that decisions about these areas should primarily be made by the Scottish Parliament rather than the UK government. Maybe if we referred explicitly to specific, high profile taxes and benefits, the pattern of response might look different. These considerations prompted us to ask on our 2011 survey who should make most of the important decisions for Scotland about "the basic rate of income tax" and "the old age pension paid out by government".[7] However, in practice the answers proved to be little different from those shown in Table 7.5. Sixty-eight per cent say the Scottish Parliament should make decisions about the basic rate of income tax, while 65 per cent say the same of the old age pension. Just 29 and 33 per cent respectively nominate the UK government.[8] So it appears that – whatever way the question is asked – there is majority support in Scotland for devolving responsibility for the bulk of the country's domestic affairs, including the key areas of taxes and benefits, to the devolved institutions.

However, this does not mean that some form of 'devolution max' is necessarily the option for Scotland's future that is most preferred by a majority living north of the border. This becomes apparent in the pattern of responses to a question on Scotland's constitutional future that has been asked on Scottish Social Attitudes in the last two years. Unlike the question summarised in Table 7.1, this more recent question includes an option intended to refer to 'devolution max'. The question reads as follows:

> *Which of the statements on this card comes closest to your view about who should make government decisions for Scotland?*
>
> *The **Scottish Parliament** should make all the decisions for Scotland*
>
> *The **UK government** should make decisions about defence and foreign affairs; the **Scottish Parliament** should decide everything else*
>
> *The **UK government** should make decisions about taxes, benefits and defence and foreign affairs; the **Scottish Parliament** should decide the rest*
>
> *The **UK government** should make all decisions for Scotland*

The first statement is intended to imply independence (without referring explicitly to that word). The second is intended to describe 'devolution max', while the third and fourth statements refer to the status quo and no devolution at all respectively.

Table 7.6 Constitutional preferences in Scotland with 'devolution max' option, 2010 and 2011

	2010	2011
Preferred distribution of decision-making authority	%	%
Scottish Parliament make all decisions (independence)	28	43
UK government decide defence/foreign affairs; Scottish Parliament the rest (devolution max)	32	29
UK government decide taxes, benefits & defence/foreign affairs; Scottish Parliament the rest (status quo)	27	21
UK government make all decisions (no devolution)	10	5
Weighted base	*1495*	*1197*
Unweighted base	*1495*	*1197*

Source: Scottish Social Attitudes

As Table 7.6 shows, in fact the principle of 'home rule' or 'devolution max' appears to be the first preference of only around three in ten people in Scotland and is apparently only a little more popular than the status quo. Meanwhile, in our most recent survey at least, it appears to be less popular than independence which, when described as it is here, attracts rather more support than it did at the question reported in Figure 7.1 (albeit still only from a minority).[9] Evidently there is something of a puzzle to be unravelled here.

The solution is, in fact, relatively simple. Most people who believe that Scotland should be independent also believe taxation and welfare benefits should be decided by the Scottish Parliament.[10] But so too do over half of those who oppose independence.[11] Thus the responses reported in Table 7.5 give the impression that 'devolution max' has majority support not because it is necessarily the single most popular option, but rather because it is the one option around which both 'nationalists' and many 'unionists' can seemingly potentially coalesce. It is perhaps not so surprising after all that the SNP have been willing to keep open the possibility that a 'second question' on more devolution might appear on the ballot paper, while both the UK government and some Labour politicians have indicated a willingness to contemplate further devolution too.

What about England?

We have seen that some form of 'devolution max' may be the constitutional option that best meets the aspirations of the majority in Scotland. Yet whatever Scotland's preferences may be, any move to introduce further devolution in Scotland also needs to be acceptable to the public in England – otherwise it may put the stability of the Union at risk. But the more that is devolved to Scotland, the greater the apparent risk that the anomalies created by asymmetric devolution will come to be unacceptable to the public south of the border. Such a risk might be considered even more serious if there are already signs of an 'English backlash' taking place in response to the existing devolution settlement. And there are indeed some signs of such a development (for a more extended discussion see Ormston, 2012).

4 in 10

in England think Scotland gets more than its fair share of public spending

This is perhaps most evident in respect of views about the current financial arrangements, under which funding of the devolved institutions is primarily via a block grant from Westminster. These arrangements, which in fact pre-date the Scottish Parliament, result in public spending per head in Scotland being some 20 per cent or so higher than in England (HM Treasury, 2011). In popular debate, this has sometimes been presented as an arrangement that enables Scots to enjoy free university tuition, free personal care for older people, and free prescriptions, all at England's expense at a time when England itself is unable to afford such policies (see, for example, Heathcoat Amory, 2007; Heffer, 2007). Table 7.7 shows the pattern of responses in England over the last 10 years or so on the question of whether Scotland gets more or less than its fair share of public spending.
Until 2007, a little over two in ten in England were of the view that Scotland secured more (either "much" or "a little") than its fair share. But in 2007 that proportion increased to around three in ten, and since 2008 it has consistently been about four in ten. Although there is no evidence of a further increase since 2008, it is nonetheless the case that nowadays more people in England think that Scotland gets more than its fair share of public spending than believe it does not.

On the other hand, in spite of this increase, the perception that Scotland receives an unfair share of public spending remains a minority one. One reason for this is that, when asked this question, around one in four people in England say they do not know. This suggests that Scotland's share of public spending is not a particularly salient issue for many people in England. It is also arguable that the more responsibility the Scottish Parliament is given for raising its own tax revenues, the less it will be possible to present any higher level of public spending in Scotland as the result of an unfair subsidy provided by English taxpayers. So, in this instance at least, more devolution for Scotland could be regarded as increasing the fairness of constitutional arrangements for both Scotland and England.

Table 7.7 Attitudes in England towards Scotland's share of public spending 2000–2011

	00	01	02	03	07	08	09	10	11
Compared with other parts of the UK, Scotland's share of government spending is …	%	%	%	%	%	%	%	%	%
… much more than its fair share	8	9	9	9	16	21	18	21	22
… a little more than its fair share	13	15	15	13	16	20	22	17	22
… pretty much its fair share	42	44	44	45	38	33	30	29	30
… a little less than its fair share	10	8	8	8	6	3	4	3	3
… much less than its fair share	1	1	1	1	1	*	*	1	*
Don't know	25	23	22	25	22	23	25	28	23
Weighted base	*1956*	*2786*	*2931*	*1929*	*870*	*1001*	*992*	*928*	*974*
Unweighted base	*1928*	*2761*	*2897*	*1917*	*859*	*982*	*980*	*913*	*967*

Base: British Social Attitudes respondents living in England

65%

in England in 2010 agreed Scottish MPs should no longer be allowed to vote on laws that only affect England

However, the same could certainly not be said of the so-called 'West Lothian' question – the name coined for the argument that it is unfair that Scottish MPs can continue to vote in the House of Commons on English laws when, since devolution, MPs representing England cannot vote on similar laws for Scotland (Conservative Democracy Task Force, 2008). In this case, the more power and responsibility that is devolved to the Scottish Parliament, the more such an imbalance may appear to be an unfair anomaly. In any event, as can be seen from Table 7.8, the current position on this issue is widely regarded with disapproval in England. Around three-fifths in 2010 agreed that Scottish MPs should no longer be allowed to vote on laws that only affect England. Moreover, there are signs that feelings about this issue have become somewhat more intense – the proportion who "agree strongly" that the situation is unfair has gradually increased from 18 per cent in 2000 to 31 per cent in 2010 (our most recent reading). Given this, it is perhaps not surprising that in January 2012 the UK government created a commission chaired by a former House of Commons clerk, Sir William McKay, to see whether the procedures of the House of Commons could be amended to address concern on this issue – although it is widely regarded as difficult to solve, both technically and politically (Hazell, 2006).[12]

Table 7.8 Attitudes in England towards the West Lothian question, 2000–2010

	2000	2001	2003	2007	2010
Now that Scotland has its own parliament, Scottish MPs should no longer be allowed to vote in the UK House of Commons on laws that only affect England	%	%	%	%	%
Strongly agree	18	19	22	25	31
Agree	45	38	38	36	35
Neither agree nor disagree	19	18	18	17	17
Disagree	8	12	10	9	6
Strongly disagree	1	2	1	1	1
Weighted base	*1721*	*2387*	*1548*	*752*	*794*
Unweighted base	*1695*	*2341*	*1530*	*739*	*773*

Base: British Social Attitudes respondents living in England

Do people in England think that England too should enjoy some measure of devolution?

Do these signs that people in England are growing rather more concerned about the apparent unfairness of the current devolution settlement mean that they are also coming to the conclusion that England too should enjoy some measure of devolution? Whether, though, such a development would make it easier or more difficult for the Union to be maintained is the subject of continued debate (Hazell, 2006). We asked respondents for their views as follows:

> *With all the changes going on in the way the different parts of Great Britain are run, which of the following do you think would be best for England ...*
>
> *... for England to be governed as it is now, with laws made by the UK parliament,*
>
> *for each region of England to have its own assembly that runs services like health,*
>
> *or, for England as a whole to have its own new parliament with law-making powers?*[13]

As Figure 7.2 shows, in practice there is little sign that England has come to embrace devolution for itself. A little over half (56 per cent) believe England's laws should continue to be made by the UK Parliament, in line with most of our readings since the advent of devolution in 1999. Support for the creation of an English Parliament similar to that which now exists in Scotland (the third option in our question) stands at just one in four (25 per cent), though it garners rather more support nowadays than it did between 1999 and 2007. Even less popular, favoured by one in eight (12 per cent), is a more limited form of devolution to each of the regions of England; the popularity of this idea has clearly waned since the defeat in a referendum in November 2004 of proposals to create an elected regional assembly in the north-east of England (Sandford, 2009).[14] There seems to be little immediate prospect of building a majority consensus for a system of devolution for England that would in any way match the apparent desire for self-government north of the border.

Figure 7.2 Attitudes in England to how England should be governed, 1999–2011

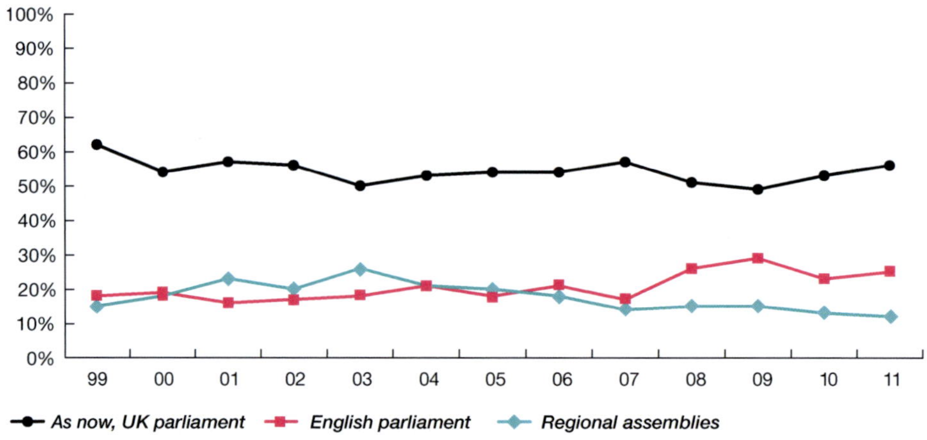

The data on which Figure 7.2 is based can be found in the appendix to this chapter
Base: British Social Attitudes respondents living in England

26%

in England support the idea that Scotland should leave the UK

However, the most important question about public opinion in England, at least as far as the future stability of the Union is concerned, is whether people are sufficiently dissatisfied with the apparent privileges enjoyed by Scotland that they are beginning to think it might be better if Scotland were to become independent after all. In Table 7.9, we show how people in England have responded when asked the question about how Scotland should be governed that has been asked regularly on Scottish Social Attitudes (reported in Figure 7.1). This shows there is some evidence of increased support in England for the idea that Scotland should leave the UK. Between 1999 and 2007 the proportion who supported that proposition was around one fifth, but in 2011 increased to about one quarter (26 per cent).[15] So while the idea that the Union should be broken up remains even more clearly a minority view in England than it is in Scotland, it seems that support in England for the continuation of the UK is potentially vulnerable to erosion.

Table 7.9 Attitudes in England to how Scotland should be governed, 1997–2011

	97+	99	00	01	02	03	07	11
How Scotland should be governed	%	%	%	%	%	%	%	%
Independent, separate from UK and EU, or separate from UK but part of EU	14	21	19	19	19	17	19	26
Part of UK, with own parliament either with or without some taxation powers	55	57	52	59	51	59	47	44
Part of UK, without an elected parliament	23	14	17	11	15	13	18	19
Don't know	8	8	11	10	14	11	15	11
Weighted base	*2492*	*905*	*1956*	*2786*	*1948*	*1929*	*870*	*974*
Unweighted base	*3150*	*902*	*1928*	*2761*	*1924*	*1917*	*859*	*967*

+*Source: British Election Study*

Base: British Social Attitudes respondents living in England

Conclusions

There is no doubt the Union between Scotland and the rest of the UK is closer to being dissolved than at any time in its 300-year history. Its future looks set to rest in the hands of the Scottish public, who will make their opinion known via a referendum within the next couple of years. However, at present it appears that leaving the UK remains a minority preference, not least because people in Scotland are doubtful that it would bring them much material benefit.

But the demand for outright independence is not the only challenge facing the Union. A majority of people in Scotland may currently be disinclined to vote to leave the UK, but many who support the Union nonetheless want Scotland to be responsible for most of its domestic affairs, including taxation and welfare benefits. As a result, it appears a scheme of devolution that goes considerably further than the current settlement, even as amended by the 2012 Scotland Act, may be able to generate a widespread consensus. Any such scheme would constitute a much looser Union than has hitherto been in place.

Yet a potential question mark remains over how England would react to such a development. England continues to show little sign of wanting devolution for itself. But there is evidence of growing discontent with the asymmetries of the current devolution settlement, a discontent that may now be beginning to be accompanied by some erosion of previous support for the Union. Some of England's discontent, such as that over finance, might in fact be addressed via more devolution for Scotland. But other areas of concern, such as the West Lothian question, would be likely to become more pressing. Ensuring that both Scotland and England continue to remain happy with the Union could well require an ability and willingness to find some constitutionally imaginative solutions.

Notes

1. Such a commitment had also been included in the SNP's 2007 election manifesto. However, as a minority government between 2007 and 2011, the SNP lacked the votes in the Scottish Parliament needed to pass legislation authorising a ballot.

2. In the case of the first two items the unweighted and weighted sample size in 1997 is 676. In the case of the remaining items the unweighted size is 657 and the weighted 659. The unweighted sample size for all items in 2011 is 1156 and the weighted 1167.

3. Support for independence has been modelled using binary logistic regression in which the dependent variable is support for independence (either inside or outside the European Union) versus any other response. Confidence in independence has been modelled using ordinal logistic regression in which the dependent variable is a five-point scale ranging from "very confident" to "very worried".

4. In contrast to binary logistic regression, the ordinal logistic procedure in SPSS does not provide a stepwise facility. This means we do not know the order in which the variables would be entered using such an approach. However, an alternative analysis of the data on confidence in independence using stepwise binary logistic regression revealed that the order in which the variables were entered using that approach was much the same as the order of the Wald scores reported by the ordinal regression.

5. Bases for Table 7.3 are as follows:

National identity	*Weighted base*	*Unweighted base*	**Economic expectations**	*Weighted base*	*Unweighted base*
Scottish, not British	*351*	*346*	Lot stronger	*114*	*110*
More Scottish than British	*391*	*381*	Little stronger	*286*	*286*
Equally Scottish and British	*270*	*278*	No difference	*307*	*296*
More British than Scottish	*56*	*62*	Little weaker	*198*	*204*
British, not Scottish	*56*	*68*	Lot weaker	*147*	*149*

6. The full question wording was as follows:

   Which of the following do you think has most influence over the way Scotland is run?

   And which do you think ought to have most influence over the way Scotland is run?

   [the Scottish Government, the UK government at Westminster, local councils in Scotland, the European Union]

7. Note that, unlike the questions reported in Table 7.5, these questions did not offer the answer options "local councils in Scotland" or "European Union". As so few respondents chose these options when they were offered, their exclusion will have made little or no material difference to the pattern of response.

8. We should note though that the balance in favour of decisions being made in Edinburgh rather than London is in both cases somewhat less than for the already devolved area of university tuition fees, where no less than 86 per cent think decisions should be taken by the Scottish Parliament and only 10 per cent say responsibility should lie with Westminster.

9. Note that in contrast to the question reported at Figure 7.1, independence is not referred to here as involving 'separation' from the rest of the UK. In general, survey questions that include 'separation' in their description of independence have tended to elicit lower levels of support than those that do not.

10. In the case of welfare benefits, the relevant figure in 2010 was 82 per cent while in the case of taxes it was 83 per cent.

11. The relevant 2010 figures are 61 per cent for welfare benefits and 54 per cent for taxes.

12. Debarring Scottish MPs from voting on English laws would not necessarily prove unpopular with the general public north of the border either. When the question presented in Table 7.8 was last asked by Scottish Social Attitudes, in 2009, 47 per cent agreed that Scottish MPs should not vote on English laws, while only 22 per cent disagreed.

13. In 2004–2006 the second option read "that makes decisions about the region's economy, planning and housing". The 2003 survey carried both versions of this option and demonstrated that the difference of wording did not make a material difference to the pattern of response. In Figure 7.2 the figures shown for 2003 are those for the two versions combined.

14. It has also been suggested that the creation of directly elected mayors in the major cities of England might provide a focus for greater devolution in a manner that, along with the creation of the Greater London Assembly, it has already done. However, as the Constitutional reform chapter shows, public opinion towards directly elected mayors is somewhat equivocal and, in practice, when 10 of England's largest provincial cities were asked in May 2012 to vote in a referendum on whether they should have such a mayor, only one voted in favour.

15. This increase would appear to be attributable to the increased concern about Scotland's share of public spending, albeit not wholly so. Those who think that Scotland secures more than its fair share are markedly more likely to support Scottish independence (33 per cent) than are those who do not think it secures more than its fair share (19 per cent). The increase in support for Scottish independence between 2007 and 2011 among those who say that Scotland secures more than its fair share is, at five points, a little less than the seven point increase in the population as a whole. At the same time, the equivalent figure among those who feel Scotland does not secure more than its fair share is, at two points, well below the general increase of seven. Some of that overall increase of seven points must therefore have arisen because of the rise between 2007 and 2011 in the proportion who think that Scotland secures more than its fair share.

References

Blais, A. and Nadeau, R. (1992), 'To Be or Not To Be Sovereigntist: Quebeckers' Perennial Dilemma', *Canadian Public Policy*, **28**: 89–103

Cameron, D. (2012), PM Scotland Speech 16 February 2012, available at: www.number10.gov.uk/news/transcript-pm-scotland-speech/

Commission on Scottish Devolution (2009), *Serving Scotland Better: Scotland and the United Kingdom in the 21st Century*, Edinburgh: Commission on Scottish Devolution

Conservative Democracy Task Force (2008), *Answering the Question: Devolution, the West Lothian Question and the Future of the Union*, London: Conservative Party

Curtice, J. (1999), 'Is Scotland a Nation and Wales Not?', in Taylor, B. and Thomson, K. (eds.), *Scotland and Wales: Nations Again?,* Cardiff: University of Wales Press

Curtice, J. and Ormston, R. (2011), 'So who is winning the debate? Constitutional preferences in Scotland after four years of nationalist government', *Scottish Affairs*, **74** : 24–44

Gellner, E. (1983), *Nations and Nationalism*, Ithaca, NY: Cornell University Press

Hazell, R. (ed.) (2006), *The English Question*, Manchester: Manchester University Press

Heathcoat Amory, E. (2007), 'The new apartheid', *Daily Mail*, 16 June

Hechter, M. (2000), *Containing Nationalism*, Oxford: Oxford University Press

Heffer, S. (2007), 'The Union of England and Scotland is over', *The Daily Telegraph*, 14 November

HM Treasury (2011), *Public Expenditure Statistical Analyses 2011*, Cm 8104, London: The Stationery Office

Howe, P. (1998), 'Rationality and Sovereign Support in Quebec', *Canadian Journal of Political Science*, **31**: 31–59

Lamont, J. (2012), Speech to Scottish Labour Party Conference 2012, available at: www.labourhame.com/archives/3024

McCrone, D. and Paterson, L. (2002), 'The Conundrum of Scottish Independence', *Scottish Affairs*, **40**: 54–75

Nadeau, R., Martin, P. and Blais, A. (1999), 'Attitude towards Risk-Taking and Individual Choice in the Quebec Referendum on Sovereignty', *British Journal of Political Science*, **29**: 523–39

Ormston, R. (2012), *The English Question: How is England responding to devolution?* London: NatCen Social Research, available at: www.natcen.ac.uk/media/816007/the-english-question-final.pdf

Ormston, R. and Curtice, J. (2010), 'Resentment or Contentment? Attitudes towards the Union 10 years on', in *British Social Attitudes: the 27th Report – Exploring Labour's legacy*, London: Sage

Ormston, R. and Reid, S. (2012), *Scottish Social Attitudes Survey 2011 Core Module: Attitudes to Government, The Economy and Public Services in Scotland*, Edinburgh: Scottish Government, available at: www.scotland.gov.uk/Publications/2012/06/3902

Sambanis, N. (2006), 'Globalization, Secession and Autonomy: A review of the literature and some conjectures', in Cameron, D., Ranis, G. and Zinn, A. (eds.), *Globalization and Self-Determination: Is the nation state under siege?*, London: Routledge

Sandford, M. (2009), *The Northern Veto*, Manchester: Manchester University Press

Scotland Office (2012), *Scotland's Constitutional Future*, Cm 8203, London: The Stationery Office

Scottish Government (2009), *Your Scotland, Your Voice: A National Conversation*, Edinburgh: Scottish Government

Sorens, J. (2005), 'The Cross-Sectional Determinants of Secessionism in Advanced Democracies', *Comparative Political Studies*, **38**: 304–26

Surridge, P., Paterson, L., Brown, A. and McCrone, D. (1998), 'The Scottish Electorate and the Scottish Parliament', *Scottish Affairs*, Special Issue on Constitutional Change: 38–60

Surridge, P. and McCrone, D. (1999), 'The 1997 Scottish Referendum Vote', in Taylor, B. and Thomson, K. (eds.), *Scotland and Wales: Nations Again?*, Cardiff: University of Wales Press

Thomson, B., Blackett, G., Aitken, J., Mawdsley, G. and Payne, A. (2011), *Devolution Plus*, Edinburgh: Reform Scotland. Available at: www.reformscotland.com/index.php/publications/details/1148

Acknowledgements

NatCen Social Research is grateful to the Nuffield Foundation for the financial support that enabled us to ask the 2010 and 2011 Scottish Social Attitudes questions reported in this chapter. The views expressed are those of the authors alone.

Appendix

The data for Figure 7.1 are shown below:

Table A.1 Attitudes in Scotland to how Scotland should be governed, 1997–2011

	May 97	Sep 97	99	00	01	02	03	04	05	06	07	09	10	11
	%	%	%	%	%	%	%	%	%	%	%	%	%	%
Independent, separate from UK and EU, or separate from UK but part of EU	26	37	27	30	27	30	26	32	35	30	24	28	23	32
Part of UK, with own parliament either with or without some taxation powers	51	41	59	55	59	52	56	45	44	54	62	56	61	58
Part of UK, without an elected parliament	17	17	10	12	9	13	13	17	14	9	9	8	10	6
Don't know	5	4	5	3	4	6	6	5	8	7	5	7	5	5
Weighted base	*882*	*676*	*1482*	*1663*	*1605*	*1665*	*1508*	*1637*	*1549*	*1594*	*1508*	*1482*	*1495*	*1197*
Unweighted base	*882*	*676*	*1482*	*1663*	*1605*	*1665*	*1508*	*1637*	*1549*	*1594*	*1508*	*1482*	*1495*	*1197*

Sources: 1997 May: Scottish Election Study; 1997 Sept: Scottish Referendum Study; 1999–2011: Scottish Social Attitudes survey

The full question text for the 2011 questions reported in Table 7.1 is given below. In each case there were five answer options: in addition to the middle option of "no difference", respondents could choose "a lot" or "a little" to indicate the strength of their positive or negative view. In the table these two sets of responses have been combined.

Thinking now about what might happen if Scotland were to become an independent country, separate from the rest of the United Kingdom but part of the European Union.

Do you think that, as a result of independence, taxes in Scotland would become higher, lower or would it make no difference?

As a result of independence would Scotland's economy become better, worse, or would it make no difference?

As a result of independence would the standard of the health service in Scotland become better, worse, or would it make no difference?

As a result of independence would people in Scotland have more pride in their country, less pride or would it make no difference?

As a result of independence would the standard of living in Scotland be higher, lower, or would it make no difference?

As a result of independence would Scotland have a stronger voice in the world, a weaker voice, or would it make no difference?

Tables A.2 and A.3 report full details of the multivariate modelling, the results of which are summarised in Table 7.2.

This model is based on a stepwise regression with insignificant variables not entered. Dependent variable is support independence versus not doing so based on responses to the question detailed at Table A.1. Independent variables are shown in the order of entry into the model. All such variables apart from age are entered as interval level variables. In the case of the 'impact on independence' variables the higher the score, the more positive the evaluation. In the case of national identity, the higher the score the more Scottish and less British someone feels. In the case of age, the coefficients are simple contrast coefficients with the reference category shown in brackets.

Table A.2 Binary logistic regression of support in Scotland for independence

	Coefficient	Standard error	p value
Impact of independence on economy	0.52	0.10	0.000
National identity: Scottish rather than British identity	0.58	0.09	0.000
Impact of independence on pride	0.52	0.11	0.000
Impact of independence on voice in the world	0.37	0.09	0.000
Age (65 plus)			
18–24	0.84	0.29	0.003
25–34	0.55	0.26	0.038
35–44	0.26	0.26	0.323
45–54	0.56	0.25	0.000
55–64	0.63	0.27	0.025
Constant	3.64		
Nagelkerke (adjusted) R^2	0.39		

Unweighted base: 1096

Source: Scottish Social Attitudes 2011

This model is based on an ordinal regression of a five-point scale ranging from 'very confident' to 'very worried'. The higher the score on the dependent variable, the more confident and less worried someone was about independence. Independent variables are listed in rank order of their Wald scores, with variables that proved to be insignificant at the 5% level removed. In the case of the 'impact on independence' evaluations, all of which are entered as interval level variables, the higher the score the more positive the evaluation; in the case of impact on taxes, a high score represents a belief that taxes would be lower. In the case of age and sex coefficients are simple contrast coefficients with the reference category shown in brackets.

Table A.3 Ordinal logistic regression of confidence in independence

	Coefficient	Standard error	p value
Impact of independence on economy	0.80	0.08	0.000
Impact of independence on pride	0.47	0.08	0.000
Impact of independence on voice in the world	0.39	0.07	0.000
Impact of independence on taxes	0.40	0.07	0.000
Impact of independence on standard of living	0.28	0.08	0.001
Sex (Women)			
Men	0.47	0.11	0.000
Age (65 plus)			
18–24	1.01	0.11	0.000
25–34	0.43	0.19	0.023
35–44	0.32	0.18	0.078
45–54	0.16	0.18	0.370
55–64	0.01	0.19	0.950
Thresholds (Very confident)			
Very worried	-6.67		
Quite worried	-3.93		
Neither confident nor worried	-2.34		
Quite confident	-0.23		
Nagelkerke (adjusted) R^2	0.54		

Weighted base: 1161

Source: Scottish Social Attitudes 2011

The data for Figure 7.2 are shown below:

Table A.4 Attitudes in England to how England should be governed, 1999–2011

	99	00	01	02	03*	04	05	06	07	08	09	10	11
How England should be governed	%	%	%	%	%	%	%	%	%	%	%	%	%
As it is now, with laws made by the UK Parliament	62	54	57	56	50	53	54	54	57	51	49	53	56
Each region of England to have own assembly that runs services like health	15	18	23	20	26	21	20	18	14	15	15	13	12
England to have its own new parliament with law-making powers	18	19	16	17	18	21	18	21	17	26	29	23	25
Weighted bases	*2722*	*1956*	*2786*	*2931*	*3742*	*2721*	*1815*	*936*	*870*	*1001*	*992*	*928*	*974*
Unweighted bases	*2718*	*1928*	*2761*	*2897*	*3709*	*2684*	*1794*	*928*	*859*	*982*	*980*	*913*	*967*

Base: British Social Attitudes respondents living in England

In 2004–2006 the second option read "that makes decisions about the region's economy, planning and housing". The 2003 survey carried both versions of this option and demonstrated that the difference of wording did not make a material difference to the pattern of response. The figures shown for 2003 are those for the two versions combined

Armed Forces
The UK's Armed Forces: public support for the troops but not their missions?

Since the deployment of UK Armed Forces personnel to Afghanistan and Iraq, relations between the military, the government and the public have been placed under scrutiny. Politicians and Armed Forces leaders have expressed concern that public disapproval of these missions might have damaged civil-military relations. But are fears that the public may be losing its respect for the military justified?

Opinions of the Armed Forces

Most people in Britain, especially older people, have a high opinion of the Armed Forces.

Eight out of ten say they have a **high or very high opinion** of the Armed Forces.

Nine out of ten people aged over 65, compared with seven out of ten aged 18–34 have a high opinion.

Support for missions

There is considerable public opposition to the UK's military interventions in Afghanistan and Iraq, with the 2003 Iraq War being more unpopular than the continuing mission in Afghanistan. Yet more than nine in ten support the personnel who have recently served in the two conflicts.

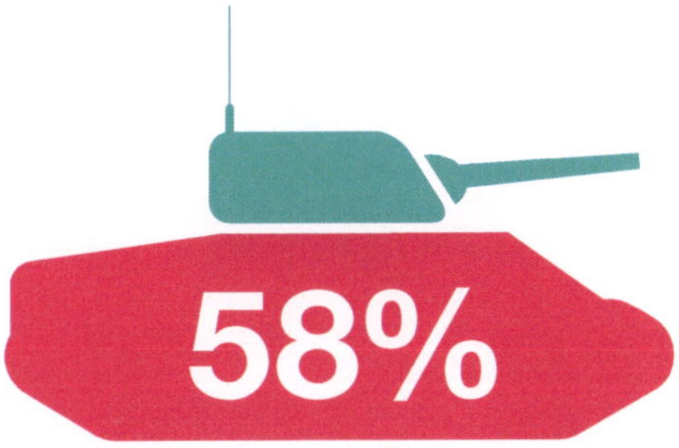

Almost six out of ten agree that the UK was **wrong to go to war in Iraq** while almost half (48%) say it was **wrong for the UK to send its Armed Forces to Afghanistan.**

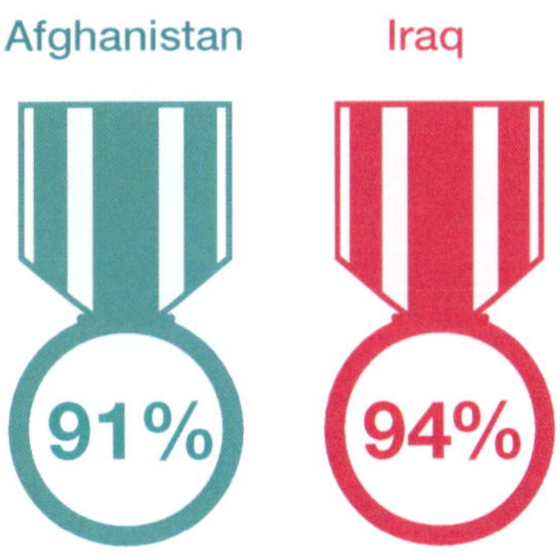

Nine out of ten people declare their **support for Armed Service personnel who have recently served in Iraq and Afghanistan** regardless of their opinions about the actual military deployment.

Authors

Rachael Gribble, Simon Wessely, Susan Klein, David A. Alexander, Christopher Dandeker & Nicola T. Fear
Rachael Gribble is Research Assistant, King's Centre for Military Health Research (KCMHR) at King's College London. Simon Wessely is Professor of Psychological Medicine, Head of the Department of Psychological Medicine, and Director, KCMHR. Susan Klein is Professor of Trauma Research and Director, Aberdeen Centre for Trauma Research, Institute for Health & Welfare Research, Robert Gordon University. David A. Alexander is Emeritus Professor of Mental Health, Former Director, Aberdeen Centre for Trauma Research, Institute for Health & Welfare Research, Robert Gordon University. Christopher Dandeker is Professor of Military Sociology, Department of War Studies, and Co-Director, KCMHR. Nicola T. Fear is a Reader in Military Epidemiology, and Co-Director, KCMHR

Introduction

Since the UK Armed Forces were deployed to Iraq (from 2003 until the end of combat operations in 2009) and Afghanistan (since 2001, but especially since the deployment in Helmand province in 2006), relationships between the military, the British government and the public have come under scrutiny. Fierce political and public debate has reflected expressions of widespread public dissent regarding the justifications for military operations, as well as doubts raised about the quality and quantity of equipment being provided for deployed personnel. Afghanistan and Iraq have become the most controversial conflicts since the Vietnam War, both in the UK (which was not militarily engaged in Vietnam) and globally. In 2001, around 20,000 people protested publicly against the UK's contribution towards the initial air strikes of the Afghanistan conflict[1] and, on a global day of demonstrations against the Iraq War in February 2003, more than 750,000 people marched in protest through London alone.[2] One consequence of this debate has been the concern expressed by some politicians and military leaders that a loss of mutual understanding between civil society and the military could not only lead to a decline in support for the missions conducted by the Armed Forces, but to a reduction in both public respect for the Armed Forces themselves and recruitment figures. This, in turn, could damage the morale and operational effectiveness of deployed troops, while creating pressure on the government to reduce its expenditure on defence. Another feared potential consequence of public indifference or hostility towards the military is that service personnel might face an inhospitable environment for their reintegration into civilian society following discharge. In the United States, research has suggested that personnel returning from Vietnam faced stigmatisation as a direct consequence of the overwhelming negative opinion of the public towards that war (Borus, 1973; Boman, 1982; Yager et al., 1984).

In Britain, one prominent way in which the current government has acknowledged these concerns and the importance of the relationships among government, society and the Armed Forces has been through legislation. Five-yearly Armed Forces Acts are the constitutional tool through which Parliament renews the basis on which the military are recruited and maintained as disciplined services. But the 2011 Armed Forces Act also gives legal force, for the first time, to the so-called Military Covenant whose core principles insist that members of the Armed Forces community should not suffer disadvantage as a result of their service and may receive special treatment where appropriate. The new law requires the Defence Secretary to make an annual report to Parliament on the state of the Covenant and the condition of civil-military relationships in the UK. According to the Prime Minister, David Cameron:

> **...the principles of the Covenant are now part of the law of our land and the value we place on our Armed Forces is clear for all to see.**[3]

Even so, while a considerable fund of knowledge exists concerning public attitudes towards the military in the United States and in some continental European countries, there is relatively little empirical evidence available about British people's perceptions of their Armed Forces. Given the capacity for public opinion to influence when and where the Armed Forces can operate in pursuit of government policy (Foyle, 2004), and affect political decisions about defence budgets, this is a notable gap that this chapter will fill.[4] Based largely on questions included for the first time in the latest British Social Attitudes survey, it explores people's views of the UK Armed Forces in general and of the military operations in Iraq and Afghanistan in particular.

We begin by examining overall perceptions of the Armed Forces; what is people's general opinion of them, how respected are they, and has this changed at all in recent years? More specifically, are there differences between the views of particular demographic groups? Previous research has found that men are more positive towards military conflicts and military spending than women (Eichenberg, 2003; Rohall et al., 2006; Caforio, 2007; Schoen, 2007; Burris, 2008; Clements, 2011) and that younger age groups are generally less supportive than older people (Gonzalez, 1996; Vennesson, 2003; Leal, 2005; Burris, 2008). They also suggest that people with higher education qualifications and those who place themselves on the left of the political spectrum tend to be more critical (Gonzalez, 1996; Holsti, 2004). But does opinion in contemporary Britain conform to the same patterns? Might we, for example, expect supporters of the Liberal Democrats and nationalist parties that were opposed to British involvement in Iraq to take a less sympathetic view of the Armed Forces generally than those of Labour, whose government sanctioned it? Or might the deployment of the Armed Forces on a 'mission impossible' lead to an increase in sympathy?

We next consider how far the public agrees (in principle) with the UK's military deployments in Iraq and Afghanistan, and whether their general opinion of the Armed Forces is coloured by their view of these two controversial missions. Although other surveys have found majority opposition to the military operations in both Iraq and Afghanistan (Clements, 2011), there has been little previous evidence about whether this affects public support for Armed Forces personnel returning from these operations. Finally, we also use British Social Attitudes data, dating back to 1983, to look at the priority people attach to spending on defence and whether this has altered in response to military operations over time. Our guiding aim, throughout the chapter, is to cast light on how far the concerns of political and military leaders about a disconnection between civil society and the Armed Forces are justified.

Public opinion of the UK Armed Forces

To gauge people's overall view we asked them:

> *What is your general opinion of the UK Armed Forces?*

More than eight out of ten people say they hold a "high" or "very high" opinion of the Armed Forces

We also invited them to say whether, on the whole, they respected the Armed Forces as a profession based on what they knew or had heard about them. As seen in Table 8.1 the response to both questions was very positive indeed. More than eight out of ten people say they hold a "high" or "very high" opinion of the Armed Forces. By contrast, only three per cent express negative opinions ("low" or "very low"), while another 13 per cent describe their opinion as "neither high nor low". It is, similarly, evident that most people (75 per cent) have "a great deal of respect" for the Armed Forces, with another 20 per cent stating they have "some respect". Just two per cent say they have "not a lot" of respect.

The responses reveal only small gender differences – and not in any consistent direction. Men are a little more likely to express a "very high" opinion of the Armed Forces, while women are slightly more likely to say they have "a great deal" of respect for them. However, attitudes do vary somewhat between age groups. Although seven out of ten people aged 18–34 (73 per cent) say they have a "high" or "very high" opinion of the Armed Forces, this is considerably lower than the nine out of ten respondents aged 65 and over taking the same view (92 per cent). Indeed, the percentage among the oldest age group that report a "very high" opinion (50 per cent) is almost double that reported in the youngest age group (30 per cent). The public's good opinion of the military is seen to increase steadily with age, while there is a decline in the very small proportions expressing a low opinion (from five per cent to just one per cent). Similarly, the proportion saying their opinion is "neither high nor low" drops from 21 per cent to six per cent. However, this may represent a cohort effect (with today's younger generations being generally less supportive of the Armed Forces than their predecessors) rather than indicating that views about the Armed Forces grow more positive over time.

The age gradient for replies to our question about respect is less marked. Seven out of ten respondents aged 18–34 say they respect the Armed Forces, compared with almost eight out of ten in the two oldest age groups. The proportion saying they don't have a lot of respect falls from just four per cent of the youngest respondents to only one per cent among those aged 35 and over.

Table 8.1 Public opinion of the UK Armed Forces, by age

	Age				
	18–34	35–54	55–64	65+	All
Opinion of the UK Armed Forces	%	%	%	%	%
Very high	30	43	49	50	42
High	43	41	40	42	41
Neither high nor low	21	13	9	6	13
Low	4	1	1	1	2
Very low	1	1	1	-	1
No opinion	1	1	1	*	1
Weighted base	*948*	*1171*	*496*	*693*	*3311*
Unweighted base	*752*	*1159*	*541*	*856*	*3311*
Degree of respect for the UK Armed Forces	%	%	%	%	%
A great deal	71	75	79	78	75
Some	21	21	18	17	20
Not a lot	4	2	1	1	2
No respect at all	*	1	*	*	*
Weighted base	*799*	*1015*	*445*	*580*	*2841*
Unweighted base	*640*	*1006*	*488*	*710*	*2845*

Examining people's views by educational qualification (Table 8.2), we also find strong support for the Armed Forces across all groups. Almost eight out of ten graduates (79 per cent) declare a "high" or "very high" opinion, moving closer to nine out of ten (87 per cent) among those without qualifications. Our second question about respect for the Armed Forces produces a wider difference of view between the six out of ten graduates (62 per cent) who answer "a great deal" and the eight out of ten with lower (78 per cent) or no qualifications (81 per cent) who say the same. However, only four per cent of graduates state they have "not a lot" or "no respect at all", falling to two per cent or less among those with lower qualifications. Most people holding higher qualifications are far from dismissive of the military but their responses do indicate a more mixed evaluation of the Armed Forces than other educational groups.

Table 8.2 Public opinion of the UK Armed Forces, by level of education

	Level of education				
	Degree or equivalent	A level	GCSE or equivalent	No qualifications	All
Opinion of the UK Armed Forces	%	%	%	%	%
Very high	33	41	42	35	41
High	46	43	41	9	13
Neither high nor low	18	13	15	2	2
Low	2	1	1	1	1
Very low	1	1	*	1	1
No opinion	1	*	1	*	1
Weighted base	*656*	*860*	*787*	*800*	*3311*
Unweighted base	*610*	*798*	*774*	*928*	*3311*
Degree of respect for the UK Armed Forces	%	%	%	%	%
A great deal	62	78	78	81	75
Some	32	18	18	13	20
Not a lot	4	1	2	1	2
No respect at all	1	1	-	*	*
Weighted base	*591*	*759*	*685*	*649*	*2841*
Unweighted base	*552*	*714*	*678*	*752*	*2845*

When it comes to political sympathies, Table 8.3 shows that a higher proportion of those who identify with the Conservatives (five out of ten) express a very high opinion of the Armed Forces than of those (around four out of ten) who support Labour, the Liberal Democrats, or smaller parties. But the differences are not as great as some might expect. When people claiming a "high" or "very high" opinion are combined, we see than nine out of ten Conservative and Liberal Democrat supporters take a positive view, as do eight out of ten who identify with Labour or other parties. Conversely, there are larger proportions of supporters of Labour and minority parties than Conservatives and Liberal Democrats who say their opinion of the Armed Forces is "neither high nor low". Meanwhile, eight out of ten Conservative supporters say they have "a great deal" of respect for the Armed Forces, compared with seven out of ten supporters of all other parties, including the Liberal Democrats. Liberal Democrat sympathisers are also a little more likely than others to adopt a restrained view, saying they have "some" respect.

Table 8.3 Public opinion of the UK Armed Forces, by party identification

	Party identification				
	Conservative	Labour	Liberal Democrat	Other parties	All
Opinion of the UK Armed Forces	%	%	%	%	%
Very high	49	41	38	39	42
High	42	39	52	41	41
Neither high nor low	8	15	8	18	13
Weighted bases	*881*	*1062*	*247*	*215*	*3309*
Unweighted bases	*926*	*1039*	*253*	*215*	*3309*
Degree of respect for the UK Armed Forces	%	%	%	%	%
A great deal	82	73	70	71	75
Some	16	20	29	24	20
Not a lot	1	3	1	3	2
Weighted base	*783*	*893*	*224*	*201*	*2839*
Unweighted base	*822*	*881*	*227*	*202*	*2843*

Percentages may not add to 100% due to omission of options with low response rates

'Other party' supporters are those who identify with the Scottish National Party, Plaid Cymru, UKIP, Scottish Socialist Party, Respect, Green Party or the British National Party

Although as many as one in three say they have limited or no respect for lawyers, only one in fifty say the same about the Armed Forces and doctors, and less than one in ten about the police

Having established that most people – irrespective of age, educational qualifications or political affiliation – hold the military in high regard, it is interesting to see how this compares with their attitudes towards other professions. Do other groups inspire a comparable or even higher expression of goodwill? When inviting respondents to gauge their respect for the Armed Forces, we also asked them about three other prominent types of profession: doctors, police and lawyers. In Table 8.4 we see that the Armed Forces elicit the most enthusiastic response, although the level for doctors is similar if the totals for "a great deal" and "some" respect are combined. Moreover, although as many as one in three say they have limited or no respect for lawyers, only one in fifty say the same about the Armed Forces and doctors, and less than one in ten about the police. It seems, therefore, that the Armed Forces are popular with the public in relative as well as absolute terms.

Table 8.4 Respect for the Armed Forces and other professions

	Armed Forces	Doctors	Police	Lawyers
Degree of respect	%	%	%	%
A great deal	75	63	48	12
Some	20	33	41	50
Not a lot	2	2	7	25
None at all	*	*	2	7
Weighted base	*2841*	*2841*	*2841*	*2841*
Unweighted base	*2845*	*2845*	*2845*	*2845*

Public opinion over time

Another contextual question that arises from our findings about the popularity of the Armed Forces is whether the public's goodwill has remained constant or altered over time. Given the extent of controversy over the deployment in Iraq, we might wonder whether attitudes towards the military have improved at all since UK Armed Forces personnel were withdrawn in 2009. As the British Social Attitudes survey has not previously asked the public for their general opinion of the Armed Forces, we asked respondents to say if they thought their view had changed over the last few years. Their answers show that while a majority of people, almost eight in ten, report that their attitude has stayed the same, a significant minority (18 per cent) say their opinion has improved (Table 8.5). By contrast, only five per cent say they have formed a lower opinion of the military in recent years. Older people and those without qualifications are the least likely to report that their attitude has changed. Among political sympathisers, Conservative supporters are somewhat less likely to say their view has changed, while those who incline towards the Liberal Democrats are a little more likely than others to report that their opinion has become more positive (Table 8.5).

Table 8.5 Recent changes in opinion about the UK Armed Forces, by party identification

	Party identification				
	Conservative	Labour	Liberal Democrat	Other parties	All
Change in opinion	%	%	%	%	%
No change	80	74	72	78	77
Higher opinion	17	20	23	16	18
Lower opinion	3	5	5	5	5
Weighted base	*881*	*1062*	*247*	*215*	*3309*
Unweighted base	*926*	*1039*	*253*	*215*	*3309*

Another possible way of examining changes in people's perceptions is to compare responses to our new question about respect for the military with replies to a question in earlier surveys about pride in the Armed Forces. Respondents in 1995 and 2003 were invited to say how proud they felt of Britain in different ways, including the military. Clearly pride and respect are not identical concepts and the questions were asked in different contexts. Comparisons must, therefore, be treated with caution. It is, nevertheless, interesting that the questions about pride in the Armed Forces were asked at the time of multilateral peace-keeping operations in Bosnia (1995) and in Iraq and Afghanistan (2003), while replies to our question about respect were gathered after the British military mission in Iraq had ended but the Afghanistan campaign continued. We can cautiously estimate how public opinion responds to the active engagement of the UK Armed Forces in military conflicts.

In both 1995 and 2003, around half of all respondents said they were "very proud" of the Armed Forces, with only a slight upward increase between the two years. In the latest survey, three out of four people said they had "a great deal of respect". While we cannot accurately estimate public esteem for the military prior to 2012 from these data, it is likely that goodwill towards the UK Armed Forces previously stood at a lower level than it does now and that there has been a strengthening of public support for the military throughout the duration of the Iraq and Afghanistan missions.

Thus far we have seen that public opinion is generally very supportive towards the Armed Forces. We have also found evidence from two different sources that people's respect for the military is likely to have increased in recent years. However, we have also discovered interesting nuances in the way that people in different demographic groups react to different questions concerning their views. In particular, the discernible differences between younger and older people in their general opinion of the military are less marked when it comes to the concept of respect. One possible explanation is that responses to the latter question may be more indicative of attitudes towards the men and women who serve in the Armed Forces, while the former tells us more about people's opinions of the military as an institution. This leads usefully towards our next group of questions concerning British military intervention in Iraq and Afghanistan. Here it will be important to find out whether similar or even greater distinctions exist between the public's view of the Armed Forces and the controversial combat missions in which they have been deployed.

Support for the missions in Iraq and Afghanistan

To gauge people's views on the two military missions, half our sample was asked about Iraq and the other half about Afghanistan. This was done to avoid the possibility that people might feel prompted by their opinion about one military conflict into expressing an identical view about the other. People were asked if they agreed or disagreed that:

The UK was wrong to send its Armed Forces to Afghanistan

or that:

The UK was wrong to go to war with Iraq in 2003

58%

object to the Iraq War – while the proportion who say it was wrong to send UK Forces to Afghanistan is just below half

Table 8.6 shows substantial public opposition to both of the military deployments. However, those who object to the Iraq War (agree with the statement) are in the majority – almost six out of ten – while the proportion who say it was wrong to send UK Forces to Afghanistan is just below half. The percentages of men and women who say that British military intervention was wrong are similar, although women are slightly more likely to object (agree) than men. However, men are more likely to indicate support (disagree with the statement) for UK military involvement. We also see among both groups that people are more likely to express a neutral attitude about the Afghanistan campaign than about Iraq, suggesting greater uncertainty or confusion about the UK's role in this conflict.

Table 8.6 View of the Iraq/Afghanistan missions, by sex

	Sex		
	Male	**Female**	**All**
UK wrong to go to war with Iraq	%	%	%
Agree	56	60	58
Neither agree nor disagree	15	18	16
Disagree	28	19	24
Weighted base	*827*	*827*	*1654*
Unweighted base	*739*	*934*	*1673*
UK wrong to send its Armed Forces to Afghanistan	%	%	%
Agree	46	50	48
Neither agree nor disagree	18	21	20
Disagree	34	25	29
Weighted base	*785*	*872*	*1657*
Unweighted base	*711*	*927*	*1638*

When investigating general attitudes to the Armed Forces we found that older people were more positive in their views than younger people. We might, therefore, expect younger age groups to be more opposed to the two military deployments. However, previous research points in the other direction, suggesting that it is older people who tend to be more opposed to armed conflict (Gonzalez, 1996; van der Meulen and de Konink, 2001; Scotto et al., 2011), possibly reflecting the influence on succeeding generations of significant world events – such as the Vietnam War or the terrorist attacks of 9/11 in 2001– rather than being a simple consequence of advancing age (Holsti, 2004; Schoen, 2007). In our own survey, it is certainly clear that opposition to the UK's military operations in Iraq and Afghanistan increases with age (Table 8.7). Disapproval of the Iraq War rises steadily from 47 per cent among 18–34 year olds to 66 per cent among the over-65s and, in the case of Afghanistan, increases from 42 per cent among the youngest age group to 60 per cent among the oldest. However, the highest levels of positive support for British military involvement can be found in the middle age range of 35–54 year olds, particularly for Afghanistan, where 34 per cent support the mission. Neutral attitudes towards the two military operations are noticeably highest among younger age groups.

Table 8.7 View of the Iraq/Afghanistan missions, by age group

	Age				
	18–34	35–54	55–64	65+	All
UK wrong to go to war with Iraq	%	%	%	%	%
Agree	47	57	64	66	58
Neither agree nor disagree	24	16	11	12	16
Disagree	25	26	24	19	24
Weighted base	*446*	*586*	*256*	*366*	*1654*
Unweighted base	*353*	*585*	*280*	*454*	*1673*
UK wrong to send its Armed Forces to Afghanistan	%	%	%	%	%
Agree	42	44	55	60	48
Neither agree nor disagree	25	20	16	15	20
Disagree	30	34	28	21	29
Weighted base	*502*	*585*	*240*	*327*	*1657*
Unweighted base	*399*	*574*	*261*	*402*	*1638*

People without qualifications are one of the groups most strongly opposed to both the continuing military mission in Afghanistan, and to UK involvement in the Iraq War

Historical analyses of the relationship between people's levels of education and their opinions concerning military interventions has indicated that this is not a straightforward relationship (Gartner et al., 1997; Gelpi et al., 2009). Data from the United States suggest that people with higher levels of education are more likely to disapprove of the mission in Iraq but support Afghanistan (Burris, 2008). This is replicated in the UK, with graduates more supportive of the mission in Afghanistan, while only those whose highest qualification is at GSCE level are more supportive of the mission in Iraq (Clements, 2011). This apparent discrepancy is thought to be related to a greater understanding of the missions' particular objectives and individual merits, arrived at through an increased interest in current events and politics, among those with a university-level education (Holsti, 2004; Sirin, 2011).

Somewhat contrary to these points, the results of our survey show that people without qualifications are one of the groups most strongly opposed to both the continuing military mission in Afghanistan, and to UK involvement in the Iraq War (Table 8.8). In both cases, six out of ten people without qualifications say that UK involvement was wrong. A slightly higher proportion of graduates (64 per cent) take a similar view of Iraq, but only four out of ten express opposition in relation to Afghanistan (42 per cent). Moreover, while the (minority) levels of support for British involvement in Iraq are much the same regardless of educational qualifications, the proportions supporting the Afghanistan mission range from a fifth of people without qualifications to more than a third of graduates.

Table 8.8 View of the Iraq/Afghanistan missions, by level of education

	Level of education				
	Degree or equivalent	A level	GCSE or equivalent	No qualifications	All
UK wrong to go to war with Iraq	%	%	%	%	%
Agree	64	53	56	60	58
Neither agree nor disagree	11	23	17	13	16
Disagree	25	23	25	23	24
Weighted base	*330*	*436*	*404*	*387*	*1654*
Unweighted base	*301*	*405*	*408*	*465*	*1673*
UK wrong to send its Armed Forces to Afghanistan	%	%	%	%	%
Agree	42	43	47	60	48
Neither agree nor disagree	21	24	21	16	20
Disagree	36	32	30	20	29
Weighted base	*326*	*425*	*384*	*413*	*1657*
Unweighted base	*309*	*393*	*366*	*463*	*1638*

Existing research has also found that people's views of armed intervention are linked to political partisanship (Burris, 2008) and that this operates primarily through people holding core values that favour or criticise the use of military action (Holsti, 2004). But what differences of opinion should we expect between supporters of the various parties in Britain, given that the involvement in the Iraq invasion was initiated by a Labour government with Conservative support – and that the Conservatives' current coalition partners, the Liberal Democrats, like the Scottish and Welsh nationalist parties, were opposed to the war? Might views also differ about Afghanistan, given that the Conservatives, in opposition, were especially critical about the helicopters and other equipment being provided for the Armed Forces?

Agreement that the Iraq War was wrong extends across the political spectrum

Perhaps surprisingly, we find that agreement that the Iraq War was wrong extends across the political spectrum (Table 8.9), with the majority of people opposed to the mission despite their political affiliation. Around six out of ten people who identify with each of the three main parties at Westminster say Britain was wrong to go to war, rising to seven out of ten supporters of the nationalists and other smaller parties. However, levels of endorsement for the campaign are higher among those who lean towards Labour or the Conservatives (one in four) than Liberal Democrat supporters (one in five) and those of other parties (one in seven). While providing some evidence of a link between party political affiliations and support for military intervention, these findings also suggest that other factors are responsible for the antipathy towards British involvement in Iraq, which are shared by supporters of different parties. These may include continuing doubts about the legality of the invasion and its strategic value, as well as the consequent loss of military and civilian lives.

Opposition to the continuing Afghanistan campaign is also spread fairly evenly among supporters of the three main parties, but at a lower level. Around half of Labour supporters and a slightly smaller proportion of Conservative and Liberal supporters (45 per cent) agree that the UK was wrong to send its forces there. People who identify with minority parties are more likely to disagree with British involvement (55 per cent), including supporters of nationalist parties such as Plaid Cymru, which consistently opposed the deployment. Active support for military involvement is also lower among the supporters of other parties than those who identify with the Conservatives, Labour and, in this particular instance, the Liberal Democrats.

Table 8.9 View of the Iraq/Afghanistan missions, by party identification

	Party identification				
	Conservative	Labour	Liberal Democrat	Other parties	All
UK wrong to go to war with Iraq	%	%	%	%	%
Agree	59	57	61	70	58
Neither agree nor disagree	16	15	18	15	16
Disagree	25	26	18	15	24
Weighted base	*479*	*512*	*121*	*110*	*1652*
Unweighted base	*502*	*507*	*123*	*114*	*1671*
UK wrong to send its Armed Forces to Afghanistan	%	%	%	%	%
Agree	45	49	45	55	48
Neither agree nor disagree	20	17	19	17	20
Disagree	33	31	35	27	29
Weighted base	*402*	*550*	*126*	*105*	*1657*
Unweighted base	*424*	*532*	*130*	*101*	*1638*

While it is evident from these findings that more people disapprove than approve of UK involvement in both military missions, public support for the Afghanistan campaign is greater than for operations in Iraq. This may suggest the public considers the core mission in Afghanistan – a declared act of self-defence to root out the planners of the 9/11 terrorist attacks – to have greater legitimacy. United Nations authorisation of the International Security Assistance Force in Afghanistan, and the mission's broader focus on state building and improving living standards for the local population, may also have improved its palatability for the public. Conversely, confusion around the legality of the Iraq War and the justifications proposed for the invasion – not least the notorious claims concerning 'weapons of mass destruction' – may account for the higher level of public disapproval.

Support for returning service personnel

Since we earlier found that the public generally holds the Armed Forces in high regard, we are left with the interesting question of how far people's support for the military has been influenced – for better or worse – by their opinions about the missions in Iraq and Afghanistan. As previously noted, public opposition in the United States to the war in Vietnam contributed to the poor treatment of returning veterans. To assess whether anything comparable might be happening to UK military personnel, we first of all compare responses to the questions about opinions of and respect for the Armed Forces, discussed earlier, with those measuring opposition to and support for the missions in Iraq and Afghanistan. These comparisons are presented in Table 8.10 below. Although the numbers of respondents who report a low opinion or lack of respect for the Armed Forces are often too small to enable us to draw firm conclusions, there is some evidence that those expressing the most positive views of the Armed Forces are less likely to oppose the two missions. Less than six in ten of those who report having "a great deal of respect" for the Armed Forces agree the UK was wrong to go to war with Iraq in 2003; this proportion rises to almost seven in ten of those who express just "some respect" for the Armed Forces. On the other hand, less than five out of ten people with a "very high" opinion of the Armed Forces agree that the UK was wrong to send its Armed Forces to Afghanistan – a proportion which rises to almost six in ten of those who express a "low" opinion or an opinion which is "neither high nor low". Clearly, those who hold less positive views of the Armed Forces are more likely to oppose its recent missions, although care must be taken in interpreting the small number of respondents in some categories. Nonetheless, around half of the public report the highest levels of support and respect for the Armed Forces despite opposing the mission they were asked about. Therefore, opposition to the missions the Armed Forces have recently been involved in does not appear to produce an automatic decline in an individual's opinion of, or respect for, this institution or its personnel.

Table 8.10 View of the Iraq/Afghanistan missions, by opinion of the Armed Forces

	General opinion			Respect			
	Very high opinion	High opinion	Neither high nor low/low/ very low opinion	A great deal of respect	Some respect	Not a lot/no respect	All
UK wrong to go to war with Iraq	%	%	%	%	%	%	%
Agree	55	59	61	56	67	71	58
Neither agree nor disagree	15	18	17	16	14	7	16
Disagree	28	21	18	26	18	20	24
Weighted base	*723*	*690*	*222*	*1077*	*287*	*32*	*1654*
Unweighted base	*758*	*691*	*203*	*1113*	*273*	*26*	*1673*
UK wrong to send its Armed Forces to Afghanistan	%	%	%	%	%	%	%
Agree	48	45	58	47	50	71	48
Neither agree nor disagree	16	23	22	19	23	14	20
Disagree	35	29	18	32	25	15	29
Weighted base	*656*	*676*	*291*	*1056*	*279*	*36*	*1657*
Unweighted base	*681*	*661*	*268*	*1060*	*267*	*32*	*1638*

To explore the issue of support for returning personnel directly with the public, we invited the half of our sample who were asked for their views about the Iraq War (see earlier) to agree or disagree with the statement:

> *Regardless of what I think about the mission to Iraq, I support members of the UK Armed Forces who have recently served there*

The public is overwhelmingly supportive of the men and women who have served in Iraq and Afghanistan, irrespective of opinions about whether UK military personnel should have been deployed there

The same proposition was put to the other half of the sample in relation to Afghanistan.

As can be seen in Table 8.11 the public proves to be overwhelmingly supportive of the men and women who have served with the Armed Forces in Iraq and Afghanistan, irrespective of individual opinions about whether UK military personnel should have been deployed there in the first place. More than nine out of ten people say they support members of the Armed Forces regardless of what they think about those missions, while less than five per cent disagree (one per cent for Iraq, three per cent for Afghanistan). There are few differences between age groups, although younger people are a little less firm in their positive view and slightly more likely to express no opinion either way.

Table 8.11 Support for recently serving personnel, by age

	Age				
Military mission	**18–34**	**35–54**	**55–64**	**65+**	**All**
Iraq	%	%	%	%	%
Agree	88	96	95	95	94
Neither agree nor disagree	8	3	4	4	5
Disagree	2	*	-	*	1
Weighted base	*446*	*586*	*256*	*366*	*1654*
Unweighted base	*353*	*585*	*280*	*454*	*1673*
Afghanistan	%	%	%	%	%
Agree	87	90	96	95	91
Neither agree nor disagree	8	6	2	3	5
Disagree	3	3	2	2	3
Weighted base	*502*	*585*	*240*	*327*	*1657*
Unweighted base	*399*	*574*	*261*	*402*	*1638*

Further analysis shows the views given by women and men to be almost identical, and that there are only small differences according to educational attainment. While graduates express a slightly lower level of agreement with the statement than non-graduates, the proportions are still 91 per cent positive in relation to service personnel returning from Iraq and 89 per cent in relation to Afghanistan veterans. There are, similarly, only minor differences between the views expressed by people according to political affiliation, although those identifying with the Conservative Party are the most emphatic in their endorsement of service men and women who have recently served in Iraq (97 per cent) or Afghanistan (96 per cent).

Earlier we noted the possibility that the public takes somewhat different views of the Armed Forces as an institution and the men and women who serve with them. Even clearer from the findings reported above is the distinction people make between the UK military missions in Iraq and Afghanistan (more likely to be negative than positive) and their support for personnel who have served there (overwhelmingly positive). From these data, it would appear that concerns about the consequences of two unpopular deployments on public support for individual service personnel are unfounded. The coalition government might also conclude from these findings that its decision to reinforce the Armed Forces Covenant through legislation matches the broad thrust of public opinion.

Public support for defence spending

Finally, we look at changes in public attitudes to defence spending over time to see if they may have been influenced by high-profile military missions, and especially the deployments of UK Armed Forces to Iraq and Afghanistan given the debates around adequate resourcing for personnel. Since 1983, British Social Attitudes has collected data on people's priorities for government spending by asking them to select the public service that would be their highest priority for extra spending. The choices offered are between education, defence, health, housing, public transport, roads, police and prisons, social security benefits, help for industry and overseas aid. A full set of first and second priorities for extra spending are presented in the chapter on Health. Figure 8.1 shows the trend for the proportion of the public selecting defence as their first priority.

Figure 8.1 Prioritisation of extra government spending on defence, 1983–2011

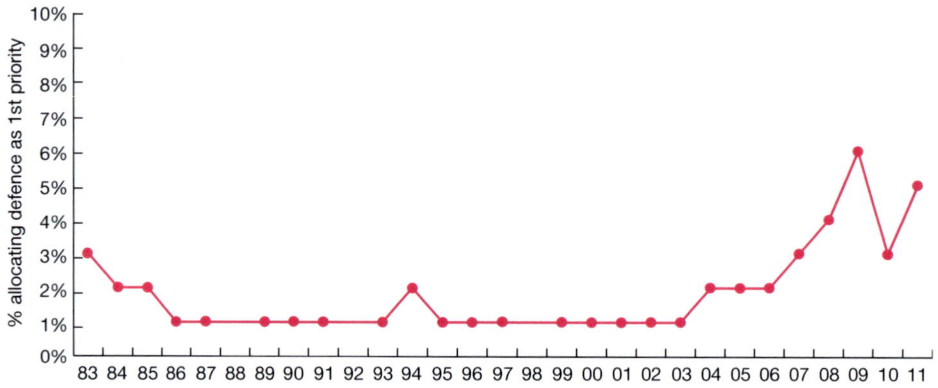

The data on which Figure 8.1 is based can be found in the appendix to this chapter

Only a small minority have ever said that defence is their top priority for additional government spending

We see that only a small minority have ever said that defence is their top priority for additional government spending. But while the first British Social Attitudes survey, conducted a year after the Falklands War, shows three per cent choosing defence, the proportion falls to just one per cent three years later and hovers around that level until 2003. It then increases to six per cent in 2009, before falling again. In the latest survey, five per cent regard defence as their top priority for extra spending.

It therefore seems there was no great public clamour for more money to be spent on defence near the start of either the Afghanistan or the Iraq deployments. Nor does it seem likely that the increase in support for defence spending that occurred between 2003 and 2009 is a response to the increasing number of deaths that have occurred among UK service personnel as this has continued to increase while the priority awarded to extra defence spending has decreased. It is more probable that the modest spike we see in support for increased defence spending is a response to the public debate that peaked in 2009 around claims that the UK Armed Forces were experiencing shortages of vital equipment – an interpretation supported by other recent studies (McCartney, 2010; Edmunds, 2012; Forster, 2012).

More generally, we may conclude that while the majority of the British public hold the Armed Forces in high esteem, only a small number regard defence as a top priority for additional public spending. It may be that the public supports the Armed Forces but is unwilling to provide additional spending at the expense of other government sectors if current spend levels are widely considered to be sufficient and resourcing problems seen to be due to poor financial organisation and planning. Other sectors, especially health and education, which regularly emerge as the top two priorities, are generally considered more pressing concerns and possibly more deserving of extra funding.

Conclusions

High public esteem for the Armed Forces is, as we have seen, in considerable contrast to the opposition that many people express towards the 2003–2009 deployment of troops in Iraq and, to a lesser degree, the continuing mission in Afghanistan. Given the extent of people's objections to these military campaigns, a striking feature of our survey findings is the public's overwhelming support for the Armed Service personnel who have served in Iraq and Afghanistan. This subtlety in public thinking and opinion about the Armed Forces and their deployment in specific military operations has not been sufficiently acknowledged previously. People clearly find little difficulty in separating the politics of military deployments from attitudes towards the service men and women who take part in them. It remains to be seen what effect the final withdrawal of military personnel from active operations in Afghanistan, due in 2014, will have on public opinion. Yet it seems highly probable from our survey findings that Armed Service personnel will be warmly welcomed home by most of the public, no matter what people think of the mission they have been asked to fulfil.

Notes

1. See news.bbc.co.uk/1/hi/uk/1596810.stm
2. A police estimate of numbers. Protest organisers suggested a figure nearer two million. See news.bbc.co.uk/1/hi/2765041.stm
3. 'Armed Forces Covenant recognised in law for first time', Ministry of Defence, Defence News, 3rd November, 2011, available at www.mod.uk/DefenceInternet/DefenceNews/DefencePolicyAndBusiness/ArmedForcesCovenantRecognisedInLawForFirstTime.htm
4. A report by the former Liberal Democrat leader and career soldier Lord Ashcroft (2012) recently cast some light on public attitudes towards the Armed Forces, but owing to its sampling strategy the findings were not necessarily representative of the UK population as a whole.

References

Boman, B. (1982), 'The Vietnam Veteran Ten Years On', *Australian and New Zealand Journal of Psychiatry*, **16(3)**: 107–127

Borus, J. (1973), 'Reentry I. Adjustment Issues Facing the Vietnam Returnee', *Archives of General Psychiatry*, **28(4)**: 501–506

Burris, V. (2008), 'From Vietnam to Iraq: Continuity and Change in Between-Group Differences in Support for Military Action', *Social Problems*, **55(4)**: 443–479

Caforio, G. (2007), 'Media and Public Opinion', in Caforio, G. (ed.), *Cultural Differences between the Military and Parent Society in Democratic Countries (Contributions to Conflict Management, Peace Economics and Development, Volume 4)*, Bingley: Emerald Group Publishing

Clements, B. (2011), 'Examining Public Attitudes towards Recent Foreign Policy Issues: Britain's Involvement in the Iraq and Afghanistan Conflicts', *Politics*, **31(2)**: 63–71

Edmunds, T. (2012), 'British civil-military relations and the problem of risk', *International Affairs*, **88(2)**: 265–282

Eichenberg, R. (2003), 'Gender Differences in Public Attitudes toward the Use of Force by the United States,1990-2003', *International Security*, **28(1)**: 110–141

Forster, A. (2012), 'The Military Covenant and British Civil-Military Relations: Letting the Genie out of the Bottle', *Armed Forces & Society*, **38(2)**: 273–290

Foyle, D. (2004), 'Leading the Public To War? The Influence of American Public Opinion on the Bush Administration's Decision to go to War in Iraq', *International Journal of Public Opinion Research,* **16(3)**: 269–294

Gartner, S., Segura, G.M. and Wilkening, M. (1997), 'All Politics Are Local: Local Losses and Individual Attitudes toward the Vietnam War', *The Journal of Conflict Resolution*, **41(5)**: 669–694

Gelpi, C., Feaver, P.D. and Reifler, J. (2009), 'Theories of American Attitudes to Warfare', in Gelpi, C., Feaver, P.D. and Reifler, J. (eds.), *Paying the Human Costs of War: American Public Opinion and Casualties in Military Conflicts*, Princeton, New Jersey: Princeton University Press

Gonzalez, A. (1996), 'Spanish attitudes towards Multinational Defense', in Manigart, P. (ed.), *Future Roles, Missions and Structures of Armed Forces in the New World Order: The Public View*, Commack, New York: Nova Science Publishers

Holsti, O. (2004), 'Sources of Foreign Policy Attitudes' in Holsti, O. (ed.), *Public Opinion and American Foreign Policy*, Ann Arbor, Michigan: University of Michigan Press

Leal, D. (2005), 'American Public Opinion toward the Military: Differences by Race, Gender, and Class?', *Armed Forces & Society*, **32(1)**: 123–138

McCartney, H. (2010), 'The military covenant and the civil-military contract in Britain', *International Affairs*, **86(2)**: 411–428

Rohall, D., Ender, M.G. and Matthews, M.D. (2006), 'The Effects of Military Affiliation, Gender, and Political Ideology on Attitudes toward the Wars in Afghanistan and Iraq', *Armed Forces & Society*, **33(1)**: 59–77

Schoen, H. (2007), 'Personality Traits and Foreign Policy Attitudes in German Public Opinion', *Journal of Conflict Resolution*, **51(3)**: 408–430

Scotto, T., Reifler, J., Clarke, H.D., Diaz Lopez, J.A., Saunders, D., Stewart, M. and Whiteley, P. (2011), 'Attitudes towards British Involvement in Afghanistan – Institute for Democracy & Conflict Resolution Briefing Paper 03/11', available at: www.idcr.org.uk/wp-content/uploads/2010/09/03_11.pdf

Sirin, C. (2011), 'Public Support for Military Interventions across Levels of Political Information and Stages of Intervention: The Case of the Iraq War', *Armed Forces & Society*, **38(2)**: 252–272

van der Meulen, J. and de Konink, M. (2001), 'Risky missions: Dutch public opinion on peace-keeping in the Balkans', in Everts, P. and Isernia, P. (eds.), *Public opinion and the international use of force*, London: Routledge

Vennesson, P. (2003), 'Civil-military relations in France: is there a gap?', *Journal of Strategic Studies*, **26(2)**: 29–42

Yager, T., Laufer, R. and Gallops, M. (1984), 'Some problems associated with war experience in men of the Vietnam generation', *Archives of General Psychiatry*, **41(4)**: 327–33

Acknowledgements

NatCen Social Research is grateful to the Economic and Social Research Council (RES-062-23-2878) for their financial support which enabled us to ask the questions reported in this chapter. The views expressed are those of the authors alone.

Appendix

Table A.1 Prioritisation of government spending on defence, 1983–2011

	1983	1984	1985	1986	1987	1989	1990	1991	1993	1994	1995	1996	1997
Defence top spending priority (%)	3	2	2	1	1	1	1	1	1	2	1	1	1
Weighted base	*1719*	*1645*	*1769*	*3066*	*2766*	*2930*	*2698*	*2836*	*2945*	*1187*	*1199*	*3620*	*1355*
Unweighted base	*1761*	*1675*	*1804*	*3100*	*2847*	*3029*	*2797*	*2918*	*2945*	*1167*	*1234*	*3620*	*1355*

	1999	2000	2001	2002	2003	2004	2005	2006	2007	2008	2009	2010	2011
Defence top spending priority (%)	1	1	1	1	1	2	2	2	3	4	6	3	5
Weighted base	*3143*	*2302*	*3287*	*3435*	*4432*	*3199*	*2167*	*3228*	*3082*	*2184*	*3421*	*3297*	*3311*
Unweighted base	*3143*	*2292*	*3287*	*3435*	*4432*	*3199*	*2166*	*3240*	*3094*	*2229*	*3421*	*3297*	*3311*

Technical details

In 2011, the sample for the British Social Attitudes survey was split into three equally-sized portions. Each portion was asked a different version of the questionnaire (versions A, B and C). Depending on the number of versions in which it was included, each 'module' of questions was thus asked either of the full sample (3,311 respondents) or of a random third or two-thirds of the sample. The structure of the questionnaire can be found at www.natcen.ac.uk/bsa.

Sample design

The British Social Attitudes survey is designed to yield a representative sample of adults aged 18 or over. Since 1993, the sampling frame for the survey has been the Postcode Address File (PAF), a list of addresses (or postal delivery points) compiled by the Post Office.[1]

For practical reasons, the sample is confined to those living in private households. People living in institutions (though not in private households at such institutions) are excluded, as are households whose addresses were not on the PAF.

The sampling method involved a multi-stage design, with three separate stages of selection.

Selection of sectors

At the first stage, postcode sectors were selected systematically from a list of all postal sectors in Great Britain. Before selection, any sectors with fewer than 500 addresses were identified and grouped together with an adjacent sector; in Scotland all sectors north of the Caledonian Canal were excluded (because of the prohibitive costs of interviewing there). Sectors were then stratified on the basis of:

- 37 sub-regions;
- population density, with variable banding used in order to create three equal-sized strata per sub-region; and
- ranking by percentage of homes that were owner occupied.

This resulted in the selection of 226 postcode sectors, with probability proportional to the number of addresses in each sector.

Selection of addresses

Thirty addresses were selected in each of the 226 sectors or groups of sectors. The issued sample was therefore 226 x 30 = 6,780 addresses, selected by starting from a random point on the list of addresses for each sector, and choosing each address at a fixed interval. The fixed interval was calculated for each sector in order to generate the correct number of addresses.

The Multiple-Occupancy Indicator (MOI) available through PAF was used when selecting addresses in Scotland. The MOI shows the number of accommodation spaces sharing one address. Thus, if the MOI indicated more than one accommodation space at a given address, the chances of the given address being selected from the list of addresses would increase so that it matched the total number of accommodation spaces. The MOI is largely irrelevant in England and Wales, as separate dwelling units (DUs) generally appear as separate entries on PAF. In Scotland, tenements with many flats tend to appear as one entry on PAF. However, even in Scotland, the vast majority (98.9 per cent) of MOIs had a value of one. The remainder were incorporated into the weighting procedures (described below).

Selection of individuals

Interviewers called at each address selected from PAF and listed all those eligible for inclusion in the British Social Attitudes sample – that is, all persons currently aged 18 or over and resident at the selected address. The interviewer then selected one respondent using a computer-generated random selection procedure. Where there were two or more DUs at the selected address, interviewers first had to select one DU using the same random procedure. They then followed the same procedure to select a person for interview within the selected DU.

Weighting

The weights for the British Social Attitudes survey correct for the unequal selection of addresses, DUs and individuals, and for biases caused by differential non-response. The different stages of the weighting scheme are outlined in detail below.

Selection weights

Selection weights are required because not all the units covered in the survey had the same probability of selection. The weighting reflects the relative selection probabilities of the individual at the three main stages of selection: address, DU and individual. First, because addresses in Scotland were selected using the MOI, weights were needed to compensate for the greater probability of an address with an MOI of more than one being selected, compared with an address with an MOI of one. (This stage was omitted for the English and Welsh data). Secondly, data were weighted to compensate for the fact that a DU at an address that contained a large number of DUs was less likely to be selected for inclusion in the survey than a DU at an address that contained fewer DUs. (We used this procedure because in most cases where the MOI is greater than one, the two stages will cancel each other out, resulting in more efficient weights). Thirdly, data were weighted to compensate for the lower selection probabilities of adults living in large households, compared with those in small households.

At each stage the selection weights were trimmed to avoid a small number of very high or very low weights in the sample; such weights would inflate standard errors, reducing the precision of the survey estimates and causing the weighted sample to be less efficient. Less than one per cent of the selection weights were trimmed at each stage.

Non-response model

It is known that certain subgroups in the population are more likely to respond to surveys than others. These groups can end up over represented in the sample, which can bias the survey estimates. Where information is available about non-responding households, the response behaviour of the sample members can be modelled and the results used to generate a non-response weight. This non-response weight is intended to reduce bias in the sample resulting from differential response to the survey.

The data was modelled using logistic regression, with the dependent variable indicating whether or not the selected individual responded to the survey. Ineligible households2 were not included in the non-response modelling. A number of area-level and interviewer observation variables were used to model response. Not all the variables examined were retained for the final model: variables not strongly related to a household's propensity to respond were dropped from the analysis.

The variables found to be related to response were: Government Office Region (GOR), percentage of owner-occupied households in the area, dwelling type, relative condition of the address, and whether there were entry barriers to the selected address. The model shows that response increases if there are no barriers to entry (for instance, if there are no locked gates around the address and no entry phone) and if the general condition of the address is the same or better than other addresses in the area. Response is also higher for addresses in the North, but lower for those in a terraced house or flat or maisonette. The full model is given in Table A.1.

Table A.1 The final non-response model

Variable	B	S.E.	Wald	df	Sig.	Odds
Region			48.54	10	0.00	
North East	0.40	0.13	10.44	1	0.00	1.50
North West	0.35	0.09	14.20	1	0.00	1.42
Yorks. and Humber	-0.03	0.10	0.08	1	0.78	0.97
East Midlands	0.28	0.11	6.86	1	0.01	1.32
West Midlands	0.16	0.10	2.81	1	0.09	1.18
East of England	0.25	0.10	6.81	1	0.01	1.29
London	-0.01	0.09	0.03	1	0.87	0.99
South East	0.08	0.09	0.78	1	0.38	1.08
South West	-0.05	0.10	0.30	1	0.58	0.95
Wales	0.14	0.11	1.42	1	0.23	1.15
Scotland	(baseline)					
Barriers to address						
No barriers	0.31	0.09	11.10	1	0.00	1.36
One or more	(baseline)					
Relative condition of the address			32.79	2	0.00	
Better	0.60	0.12	25.72	1	0.00	1.83
About the same	0.16	0.09	3.25	1	0.07	1.18
Worse	(baseline)					
Owner occupied	0.00	0.00	5.77	1	0.02	1.00
Dwelling type			20.91	5	0.00	
Semi-detached house	-0.11	0.06	3.67	1	0.06	0.90
Terraced house	-0.26	0.06	18.25	1	0.00	0.77
Flat – purpose built	-0.18	0.09	3.58	1	0.06	0.84
Flat – conversion	-0.22	0.14	2.26	1	0.13	0.81
Other	0.17	0.22	0.59	1	0.44	1.18
Detached house	(baseline)					
Constant	-0.31	0.18	3.09	1	0.08	0.73

The response is 1 = individual responding to the survey, 0 = non-response
Only variables that are significant at the 0.05 level are included in the model
The model R^2 is 0.02 (Cox and Snell)
B** is the estimate coefficient with the standard error **S.E

*The **Wald**-test measures the impact of the categorical variable on the model with the appropriate number of degrees of freedom (**df**). If the test is significant (**sig.** < 0.05), then the categorical variable is considered to be 'significantly associated' with the response variable and therefore included in the model*

The non-response weight was calculated as the inverse of the predicted response probabilities saved from the logistic regression model. The non-response weight was then combined with the selection weights to create the final non-response weight. The top one per cent of the weight were trimmed before the weight was scaled to the achieved sample size (resulting in the weight being standardised around an average of one).

Calibration weighting

The final stage of weighting was to adjust the final non-response weight so that the weighted sample matched the population in terms of age, sex and region.

Table A.2 Weighted and unweighted sample distribution, by Region, age and sex

	Population	Unweighted respondents	Respondents weighted by selection weight only	Respondents weighted by un-calibrated non-response weight	Respondents weighted by final weight
Region	%	%	%	%	%
North East	4.4	5.0	4.7	4.2	4.4
North West	11.4	12.5	12.7	11.6	11.4
Yorks. and Humber	8.8	7.9	7.7	8.2	8.8
East Midlands	7.4	8.2	8.3	7.6	7.4
West Midlands	8.9	9.7	9.8	9.5	8.9
East of England	9.6	10.7	10.7	10.1	9.6
London	12.8	10.4	10.8	12.3	12.8
South East	14.0	13.7	14.0	14.2	14.0
South West	8.8	8.4	8.2	8.6	8.8
Wales	5.0	5.4	5.2	5.1	5.0
Scotland	8.8	8.2	8.0	8.7	8.8
Age & sex	%	%	%	%	%
M 18–24	6.2	2.7	3.9	3.9	6.2
M 25–34	8.4	6.8	7.3	7.7	8.4
M 35–44	8.9	7.7	7.7	7.9	8.9
M 45–54	8.6	7.7	8.2	8.1	8.6
M 55–59	3.6	3.4	3.4	3.4	3.6
M 60–64	3.8	4.5	4.6	4.5	3.8
M 65+	9.3	11.1	10.3	10.1	9.3
F 18–24	5.9	4.1	5.2	5.3	5.9
F 25–34	8.1	9.2	9.0	9.5	8.1
F 35–44	9.1	10.4	10.0	10.0	9.1
F 45–54	8.8	9.2	10.3	10.2	8.8
F 55–59	3.7	3.7	3.8	3.7	3.7
F 60–64	3.9	4.7	4.4	4.3	3.9
F 65+	11.8	14.9	11.8	11.6	11.8
Base	*47,754,569*	*3311*	*3311*	*3311*	*3311*

Only adults aged 18 or over are eligible to take part in the survey, therefore the data have been weighted to the British population aged 18+ based on the 2010 mid-year population estimates from the Office for National Statistics/General Register Office for Scotland.

The survey data were weighted to the marginal age/sex and GOR distributions using raking-ratio (or rim) weighting. As a result, the weighted data should exactly match the population across these three dimensions. This is shown in Table A.2.

The calibration weight is the final non-response weight to be used in the analysis of the 2011 survey; this weight has been scaled to the responding sample size. The range of the weights is given in Table A.3.

Table A.3 Range of weights

	N	Minimum	Mean	Maximum
DU and person selection weight	3311	0.55	1.00	2.21
Un-calibrated non-response weight	3311	0.43	1.00	2.50
Final calibrated non-response weight	3311	0.36	1.00	4.32

Effective sample size

The effect of the sample design on the precision of survey estimates is indicated by the effective sample size (neff). The effective sample size measures the size of an (unweighted) simple random sample that would achieve the same precision (standard error) as the design being implemented. If the effective sample size is close to the actual sample size, then we have an efficient design with a good level of precision. The lower the effective sample size is, the lower the level of precision. The efficiency of a sample is given by the ratio of the effective sample size to the actual sample size. Samples that select one person per household tend to have lower efficiency than samples that select all household members. The final calibrated non-response weights have an effective sample size (neff) of 2,677 and efficiency of 81 per cent.

All the percentages presented in this report are based on weighted data.

Questionnaire versions

Each address in each sector (sampling point) was allocated to one of the portions of the sample: A, B or C. As mentioned earlier, a different version of the questionnaire was used with each of the three sample portions. If one serial number was version A, the next was version B and the third version C. Thus, each interviewer was allocated ten cases from each of versions A, B and C. There were 2,260 issued addresses for each version.

Fieldwork

Interviewing was mainly carried out between June and September 2011, with a small number of interviews taking place in October and November.

Fieldwork was conducted by interviewers drawn from NatCen Social Research's regular panel and conducted using face-to-face computer-assisted interviewing.[3] Interviewers attended a one-day briefing conference to familiarise them with the selection procedures and questionnaires, with the exception of very experienced interviewers who completed a self-briefing containing updates to the questionnaire and procedures.

The mean interview length was 67 minutes for version A of the questionnaire, 72 minutes for version B and 70 minutes for version C.4 Interviewers achieved an overall response rate of between 53.8 and 54.3 per cent. Details are shown in Table A.4.

Table A.4 Response rate[1] on British Social Attitudes, 2011

	Number	Lower limit of response (%)	Upper limit of response (%)
Addresses issued	6780		
Out of scope	673		
Upper limit of eligible cases	6107	100.0	
Uncertain eligibility	51	0.8	
Lower limit of eligible cases	6056		100.0
Interview achieved	3311	54.2	54.7
With self-completion	2845	46.6	47.0
Interview not achieved	2745	44.9	45.3
Refused[2]	2032	33.3	33.6
Non-contacted[3]	322	5.3	5.3
Other non-response	391	6.4	6.5

1 Response is calculated as a range from a lower limit where all unknown eligibility cases (for example, address inaccessible, or unknown whether address is residential) are assumed to be eligible and therefore included in the unproductive outcomes, to an upper limit where all these cases are assumed to be ineligible and therefore excluded from the response calculation

2 'Refused' comprises refusals before selection of an individual at the address, refusals to the office, refusal by the selected person, 'proxy' refusals (on behalf of the selected respondent) and broken appointments after which the selected person could not be recontacted

3 'Non-contacted' comprises households where no one was contacted and those where the selected person could not be contacted

As in earlier rounds of the series, the respondent was asked to fill in a self-completion questionnaire which, whenever possible, was collected by the interviewer. Otherwise, the respondent was asked to post it to NatCen Social Research. If necessary, up to three postal reminders were sent to obtain the self-completion supplement.

A total of 466 respondents (14 per cent of those interviewed) did not return their self-completion questionnaire. Version A of the self-completion questionnaire was returned by 85 per cent of respondents to the face-to-face interview, version B of the questionnaire was returned by 86 per cent and version C by 87 per cent. As in previous rounds, we judged that it was not necessary to apply additional weights to correct for non-response to the self-completion questionnaire.

Advance letter

Interviewers were supplied with letters describing the purpose of the survey and the coverage of the questionnaire, which they posted to sampled addresses before making any calls.[5]

Analysis variables

A number of standard analyses have been used in the tables that appear in this report. The analysis groups requiring further definition are set out below. For further details see Stafford and Thomson (2006). Where there are references to specific question numbers, the full question text, including frequencies, can be found at www.natcen.ac.uk/bsa

Region

The dataset is classified by the 12 Government Office Regions.

Standard Occupational Classification

Respondents are classified according to their own occupation, not that of the 'head of household'. Each respondent was asked about their current or last job, so that all respondents except those who had never worked were coded. Additionally, all job details were collected for all spouses and partners in work.

With the 2011 survey, we began coding occupation to the new Standard Occupational Classification 2010 (SOC 2010) instead of the Standard Occupational Classification 2000 (SOC 2000). The main socio-economic grouping based on SOC 2010 is the National Statistics Socio-Economic Classification (NS-SEC). However, to maintain time-series, some analysis has continued to use the older schemes based on SOC 90 – Registrar General's Social Class and Socio-Economic Group - though these are now derived from SOC 2000 (which is derived from SOC 2010).

National Statistics Socio-Economic Classification (NS-SEC)

The combination of SOC 2010 and employment status for current or last job generates the following NS-SEC analytic classes:

- Employers in large organisations, higher managerial and professional
- Lower professional and managerial; higher technical and supervisory
- Intermediate occupations
- Small employers and own account workers
- Lower supervisory and technical occupations
- Semi-routine occupations
- Routine occupations

The remaining respondents are grouped as "never had a job" or "not classifiable". For some analyses, it may be more appropriate to classify respondents according to their current socio-economic status, which takes into account only their present economic position. In this case, in addition to the seven classes listed above, the remaining respondents not currently in paid work fall into one of the following categories: "not classifiable", "retired", "looking after the home", "unemployed" or "others not in paid occupations".

Registrar General's Social Class

As with NS-SEC, each respondent's social class is based on his or her current or last occupation. The combination of SOC 90 with employment status for current or last job generates the following six social classes:

I	Professional etc. occupations	'Non-manual'
II	Managerial and technical occupations	
III (Non-manual)	Skilled occupations	
III (Manual)	Skilled occupations	'Manual'
IV	Partly skilled occupations	
V	Unskilled occupations	

They are usually collapsed into four groups: I & II, III Non-manual, III Manual, and IV & V.

Socio-Economic Group

As with NS-SEC, each respondent's Socio-Economic Group (SEG) is based on his or her current or last occupation. SEG aims to bring together people with jobs of similar social and economic status, and is derived from a combination of employment status and occupation. The full SEG classification identifies 18 categories, but these are usually condensed into six groups:

- Professionals, employers and managers
- Intermediate non-manual workers
- Junior non-manual workers
- Skilled manual workers
- Semi-skilled manual workers
- Unskilled manual workers

As with NS-SEC, the remaining respondents are grouped as "never had a job" or "not classifiable".

Industry

All respondents whose occupation could be coded were allocated a Standard Industrial Classification 2007 (SIC 07). Two-digit class codes are used. As with social class, SIC may be generated on the basis of the respondent's current occupation only, or on his or her most recently classifiable occupation.

Party identification

Respondents can be classified as identifying with a particular political party on one of three counts: if they consider themselves supporters of that party, closer to it than to others, or more likely to support it in the event of a general election. The three groups are generally described respectively as partisans, sympathisers and residual identifiers. In combination, the three groups are referred to as 'identifiers'. Responses are derived from the following questions:

Generally speaking, do you think of yourself as a supporter of any one political party? [Yes/No]

[If "No"/"Don't know"]
Do you think of yourself as a little closer to one political party than to the others? [Yes/No]

[If "Yes" at either question or "No"/"Don't know" at 2nd question]
Which one?/If there were a general election tomorrow, which political party do you think you would be most likely to support?

[Conservative; Labour; Liberal Democrat; Scottish National Party; Plaid Cymru; Green Party; UK Independence Party (UKIP)/Veritas; British National Party (BNP)/National Front; RESPECT/Scottish Socialist Party (SSP)/Socialist Party; Other party; Other answer; None; Refused to say]

Income

Two variables classify the respondent's earnings [REarn] and household income [HHInc] (see www.natcen.ac.uk/bsa). The bandings used are designed to be representative of those that exist in Britain and are taken from the Family Resources Survey (see http://research.dwp.gov.uk/asd/frs/). Four derived variables give income deciles/quartiles: [RearnD], [REarnQ], [HHIncD] and [HHIncQ]. Deciles and quartiles are calculated based on individual earnings and household incomes in Britain as a whole.

Attitude scales

Since 1986, the British Social Attitudes surveys have included two attitude scales which aim to measure where respondents stand on certain underlying value dimensions – left–right and libertarian–authoritarian.6 Since 1987 (except in 1990), a similar scale on 'welfarism' has also been included. Some of the items in the welfarism scale were changed in 2000–2001. The current version of the scale is shown below.

A useful way of summarising the information from a number of questions of this sort is to construct an additive index (Spector, 1992; DeVellis, 2003). This approach rests on the assumption that there is an underlying – 'latent' –attitudinal dimension which characterises the answers to all the questions within each scale. If so, scores on the index are likely to be a more reliable indication of the underlying attitude than the answers to any one question.

Each of these scales consists of a number of statements to which the respondent is invited to "agree strongly", "agree", "neither agree nor disagree", "disagree" or "disagree strongly".

The items are:

Left–right scale

Government should redistribute income from the better off to those who are less well off. [Redistrb]

Big business benefits owners at the expense of workers. [BigBusnN]

Ordinary working people do not get their fair share of the nation's wealth. [Wealth][7]

There is one law for the rich and one for the poor. [RichLaw]

Management will always try to get the better of employees if it gets the chance. [Indust4]

Libertarian–authoritarian scale

Young people today don't have enough respect for traditional British values. [TradVals]

People who break the law should be given stiffer sentences. [StifSent]

For some crimes, the death penalty is the most appropriate sentence. [DeathApp]

Schools should teach children to obey authority. [Obey]

The law should always be obeyed, even if a particular law is wrong. [WrongLaw]

Censorship of films and magazines is necessary to uphold moral standards. [Censor]

Welfarism scale

The welfare state encourages people to stop helping each other. [WelfHelp]

The government should spend more money on welfare benefits for the poor, even if it leads to higher taxes. [MoreWelf]

Around here, most unemployed people could find a job if they really wanted one. [UnempJob]

Many people who get social security don't really deserve any help. [SocHelp]

Most people on the dole are fiddling in one way or another. [DoleFidl]

If welfare benefits weren't so generous, people would learn to stand on their own two feet. [WelfFeet]

Cutting welfare benefits would damage too many people's lives. [DamLives]

The creation of the welfare state is one of Britain's proudest achievements. [ProudWlf]

The indices for the three scales are formed by scoring the leftmost, most libertarian or most pro-welfare position, as 1 and the rightmost, most authoritarian or most anti-welfarist position, as 5. The "neither agree nor disagree" option is scored as 3. The scores to all the questions in each scale are added and then divided by the number of items in the scale, giving indices ranging from 1 (leftmost, most libertarian, most pro-welfare) to 5 (rightmost, most authoritarian, most anti-welfare). The scores on the three indices have been placed on the dataset.[8]

The scales have been tested for reliability (as measured by Cronbach's alpha). The Cronbach's alpha (unstandardised items) for the scales in 2011 are 0.81 for the left–right scale, 0.73 for the welfarism scale and 0.80 for the libertarian–authoritarian scale. This level of reliability can be considered "good" for the left–right and libertarian–authoritarian scales and "respectable" for the welfarism scale (DeVellis, 2003: 95–96).

Other analysis variables

These are taken directly from the questionnaire and to that extent are self-explanatory (see www.natcen.ac.uk/bsa). The principal ones are:

- Sex (Q. 48)
- Age (Q. 45)
- Household income (Q. 1141)
- Economic position (Q. 703)
- Religion (Q. 909)
- Highest educational qualification obtained (Q. 1033)
- Marital status (Qs. 143–149)
- Benefits received (Qs. 1096–1114)

Sampling errors

No sample precisely reflects the characteristics of the population it represents, because of both sampling and non-sampling errors. If a sample were designed as a random sample (if every adult had an equal and independent chance of inclusion in the sample), then we could calculate the sampling error of any percentage, p, using the formula:

$$\text{s.e. (p)} = \sqrt{\frac{p(100 - p)}{n}}$$

where n is the number of respondents on which the percentage is based. Once the sampling error had been calculated, it would be a straightforward exercise to calculate a confidence interval for the true population percentage. For example, a 95 per cent confidence interval would be given by the formula:

$$p \pm 1.96 \times \text{s.e. (p)}$$

Clearly, for a simple random sample (srs), the sampling error depends only on the values of p and n. However, simple random sampling is almost never used in practice, because of its inefficiency in terms of time and cost.

As noted above, the British Social Attitudes sample, like that drawn for most large-scale surveys, was clustered according to a stratified multi-stage design into 226 postcode sectors (or combinations of sectors). With a complex design like this, the sampling error of a percentage giving a particular response is not simply a function of the number of respondents in the sample and the size of the percentage; it also depends on how that percentage response is spread within and between sample points.

The complex design may be assessed relative to simple random sampling by calculating a range of design factors (DEFTs) associated with it, where:

$$\text{DEFT} = \sqrt{\frac{\text{Variance of estimator with complex design, sample size n}}{\text{Variance of estimator with srs design, sample size n}}}$$

and represents the multiplying factor to be applied to the simple random sampling error to produce its complex equivalent. A design factor of one means that the complex sample has achieved the same precision as a simple random sample of the same size. A design factor greater than one means the complex sample is less precise than its simple random sample equivalent. If the DEFT for a particular characteristic is known, a 95 per cent confidence interval for a percentage may be calculated using the formula:

p ± 1.96 x complex sampling error (p)

$$= p \pm 1.96 \times \text{DEFT} \times \sqrt{\frac{p(100 - p)}{n}}$$

Table A.5 gives examples of the confidence intervals and DEFTs calculated for a range of different questions. Most background questions were asked of the whole sample, whereas many attitudinal questions were asked only of a third or two-thirds of the sample; some were asked on the interview questionnaire and some on the self-completion supplement.

Table A.5 Complex standard errors and confidence intervals of selected variables

Classification variables	% (p)	Complex standard error of p	95% confi-dence interval	DEFT	*Base*
Q. 249 Party identification (full sample)					
Conservative	26.6	1.1	24.4–28.9	1.465	*3311*
Labour	32.1	1.1	29.8–34.4	1.411	*3311*
Liberal Democrat	7.5	0.6	6.4–8.7	1.261	*3311*
Q. 923 Housing tenure (full sample)					
Owns	65.1	1.3	62.4–67.7	1.615	*3311*
Rents from local authority	11.5	0.9	9.9–13.3	1.550	*3311*
Rents privately/HA	21.7	1.1	19.7–23.9	1.494	*3311*
Q. 934 Religion (full sample)					
No religion	45.7	1.2	43.4–48.1	1.374	*3311*
Church of England	21.1	0.9	19.3–23.0	1.305	*3311*
Roman Catholic	8.7	0.6	7.6–9.8	1.142	*3311*
Q. 993 Age of completing continuous full-time education (full sample)					
16 or under	50.0	1.3	47.4–52.5	1.484	*3311*
17 or 18	18.7	0.7	17.3–20.2	1.069	*3311*
19 or over	26.2	1.1	24.0–28.5	1.474	*3311*
Q. 237 Home internet access (full sample)					
Yes	82.2	0.8	80.5–83.7	1.190	*3311*
No	17.8	0.8	16.3–19.4	1.196	*3311*
Q. 924 Urban or rural residence (full sample)					
A big city	12.2	1.4	9.7–15.3	2.491	*3311*
The suburbs or outskirts of a big city	24.1	1.8	20.7–27.9	2.449	*3311*
A small city/town	42.2	2.3	37.7–46.8	2.687	*3311*
Country village	18.3	1.6	15.4–21.7	2.354	*3311*
Farm/home in the country	2.4	0.5	1.7–3.6	1.800	*3311*

Table A.5 Complex standard errors and confidence intervals of selected variables (continued)

Attitudinal variables (face-to-face interview)	% (p)	Complex standard error of p	95% confidence interval	DEFT	*Base*
Q. 270 Benefits for the unemployed are ... (full sample)					
... too low	18.6	0.8	17.1–20.2	1.178	*3311*
... too high	62.2	1.1	60.1–64.4	1.289	*3311*
Q. 391 How serious a problem is traffic congestion in towns, cities (full sample)					
A very serious problem	11.2	0.6	10.0–12.6	1.180	*3311*
A serious problem	29.5	0.9	27.8–31.2	1.107	*3311*
Not a very serious problem	39.8	0.9	38.0–41.7	1.110	*3311*
Not a problem at all	19.3	0.9	17.6–21.1	1.306	*3311*
Q. 277 Who should mainly be responsible for ensuring that people have enough to live on if they become unemployed (full sample)					
Mainly the government	59.3	1.2	57.0–61.6	1.367	*3311*
Mainly a person's employer	4.6	0.4	3.9–5.5	1.098	*3311*
Mainly a person themselves and their family	33.4	1.1	31.3–35.5	1.297	*3311*
Q. 568 Being respected by wider society more likely to be found in ex-Service personnel or general population (half sample)					
Ex-Service personnel more likely	51.8	1.4	48.9–54.6	1.170	*1646*
Civilians more likely	6.6	0.7	5.4–8.1	1.115	*1646*
Ex-Service personnel and civilians equally likely	38.3	1.4	35.5–41.1	1.170	*1646*
Attitudinal variables (self-completion)					
A48a Government should redistribute income from the better off to those who are less well off (full sample)					
B25a Agree strongly	8.0	0.6	6.9–9.2	1.127	*2845*
C24a Agree	29.3	1.0	27.3–31.3	1.189	*2845*
Neither agree nor disagree	27.5	0.9	25.8–29.3	1.067	*2845*
Disagree	27.5	1.0	25.6–29.4	1.155	*2845*
Disagree strongly	6.1	0.6	5.1–7.3	1.241	*2845*
B16 C15 Which of these statements comes closest to your view about general elections? (2/3 sample)					
It's not really worth voting	16.3	1.0	14.4–18.5	1.209	*1909*
People should vote only if they care who wins	20.7	1.1	18.8–22.8	1.137	*1909*
It's everyone's duty to vote	62.0	1.4	59.1–64.8	1.292	*1909*
Q. 365 Whether support or oppose National Health Service should be available only to those with lower incomes (1/3 sample)					
Support this idea a lot	6.4	0.9	4.8–8.4	1.216	*1096*
Support this idea a little	19.9	1.2	17.5–22.4	1.032	*1096*
Oppose this idea a little	20.0	1.4	17.4–22.9	1.151	*1096*
Oppose this idea a lot	52.7	1.7	49.4–56.0	1.102	*1096*
A38a People should be able to travel by plane as much as they like (1/3 sample)					
Agree	61.5	1.8	57.9–64.9	1.113	*936*
Neither agree nor disagree	22.0	1.5	19.2–25.2	1.113	*936*
Disagree	10.5	1.0	8.7–12.7	0.996	*936*

The table shows that most of the questions asked of all sample members have a confidence interval of around plus or minus two to three per cent of the survey percentage. This means that we can be 95 per cent certain that the true population percentage is within two to three per cent (in either direction) of the percentage we report.

Variables with much larger variation are, as might be expected, those closely related to the geographic location of the respondent (for example, whether they live in a big city, a small town or a village). Here, the variation may be as large as six or seven per cent either way around the percentage found on the survey. Consequently, the design effects calculated for these variables in a clustered sample will be greater than the design effects calculated for variables less strongly associated with area. Also, sampling errors for percentages based only on respondents to just one of the versions of the questionnaire, or on subgroups within the sample, are larger than they would have been had the questions been asked of everyone.

Analysis techniques

Regression

Regression analysis aims to summarise the relationship between a 'dependent' variable and one or more 'independent' variables. It shows how well we can estimate a respondent's score on the dependent variable from knowledge of their scores on the independent variables. It is often undertaken to support a claim that the phenomena measured by the independent variables cause the phenomenon measured by the dependent variable. However, the causal ordering, if any, between the variables cannot be verified or falsified by the technique. Causality can only be inferred through special experimental designs or through assumptions made by the analyst.

All regression analysis assumes that the relationship between the dependent and each of the independent variables takes a particular form. In linear regression, it is assumed that the relationship can be adequately summarised by a straight line. This means that a one percentage point increase in the value of an independent variable is assumed to have the same impact on the value of the dependent variable on average, irrespective of the previous values of those variables.

Strictly speaking the technique assumes that both the dependent and the independent variables are measured on an interval-level scale, although it may sometimes still be applied even where this is not the case. For example, one can use an ordinal variable (e.g. a Likert scale) as a dependent variable if one is willing to assume that there is an underlying interval-level scale and the difference between the observed ordinal scale and the underlying interval scale is due to random measurement error. Often the answers to a number of Likert-type questions are averaged to give a dependent variable that is more like a continuous variable. Categorical or nominal data can be used as independent variables by converting them into dummy or binary variables; these are variables where the only valid scores are 0 and 1, with 1 signifying membership of a particular category and 0 otherwise.

The assumptions of linear regression cause particular difficulties where the dependent variable is binary. The assumption that the relationship between the dependent and the independent variables is a straight line means that it can produce estimated values for the dependent variable of less than 0 or greater than 1. In this case it may be more appropriate to assume that the relationship between the dependent and the independent variables takes the form of an S-curve, where the impact on the dependent variable of a one-point increase in an independent variable becomes progressively less the closer the value of the dependent variable approaches 0 or 1. Logistic regression is an alternative form of regression which fits such an S-curve rather than a straight line. The technique can also be adapted to analyse multinomial non-interval-level dependent variables, that is, variables which classify respondents into more than two categories.

The two statistical scores most commonly reported from the results of regression analyses are:

A measure of variance explained: This summarises how well all the independent variables combined can account for the variation in respondents' scores in the dependent variable. The higher the measure, the more accurately we are able in general to estimate the correct value of each respondent's score on the dependent variable from knowledge of their scores on the independent variables.

A parameter estimate: This shows how much the dependent variable will change on average, given a one-unit change in the independent variable (while holding all other independent variables in the model constant). The parameter estimate has a positive sign if an increase in the value of the independent variable results in an increase in the value of the dependent variable. It has a negative sign if an increase in the value of the independent variable results in a decrease in the value of the dependent variable. If the parameter estimates are standardised, it is possible to compare the relative impact of different independent variables; those variables with the largest standardised estimates can be said to have the biggest impact on the value of the dependent variable.

Regression also tests for the statistical significance of parameter estimates. A parameter estimate is said to be significant at the five per cent level if the range of the values encompassed by its 95 per cent confidence interval (see also section on sampling errors) are either all positive or all negative. This means that there is less than a five per cent chance that the association we have found between the dependent variable and the independent variable is simply the result of sampling error and does not reflect a relationship that actually exists in the general population.

Factor analysis

Factor analysis is a statistical technique which aims to identify whether there are one or more apparent sources of commonality to the answers given by respondents to a set of questions. It ascertains the smallest number of factors (or dimensions) which can most economically summarise all of the variation found in the set of questions being analysed. Factors are established where respondents who gave a particular answer to one question in the set tended to give the same answer as each other to one or more of the other questions in the set. The technique is most useful when a relatively small number of factors are able to account for a relatively large proportion of the variance in all of the questions in the set.

The technique produces a factor loading for each question (or variable) on each factor. Where questions have a high loading on the same factor, then it will be the case that respondents who gave a particular answer to one of these questions tended to give a similar answer to each other at the other questions. The technique is most commonly used in attitudinal research to try to identify the underlying ideological dimensions which apparently structure attitudes towards the subject in question.

International Social Survey Programme

The International Social Survey Programme (ISSP) is run by a group of research organisations in different countries, each of which undertakes to field annually an agreed module of questions on a chosen topic area. Since 1985, an International Social Survey Programme module has been included in one of the British Social Attitudes self-completion questionnaires. Each module is chosen for repetition at intervals to allow comparisons both between countries (membership is currently standing at 48) and over time. In 2011, the chosen subject was Health and Health Care, and the module was carried on the A version of the self-completion questionnaire (Qs. 1a–29).[9]

Notes

1. Until 1991 all British Social Attitudes samples were drawn from the Electoral Register (ER). However, following concern that this sampling frame might be deficient in its coverage of certain population subgroups, a 'splicing' experiment was conducted in 1991. We are grateful to the Market Research Development Fund for contributing towards the costs of this experiment. Its purpose was to investigate whether a switch to PAF would disrupt the time-series – for instance, by lowering response rates or affecting the distribution of responses to particular questions. In the event, it was concluded that the change from ER to PAF was unlikely to affect time trends in any noticeable ways, and that no adjustment factors were necessary. Since significant differences in efficiency exist between PAF and ER, and because we considered it untenable to continue to use a frame that is known to be biased, we decided to adopt PAF as the sampling frame for future British Social Attitudes surveys. For details of the PAF/ER 'splicing' experiment, see Lynn and Taylor (1995).

2. This includes households not containing any adults aged 18 or over, vacant dwelling units, derelict dwelling units, non-resident addresses and other deadwood.

3. In 1993 it was decided to mount a split-sample experiment designed to test the applicability of Computer-Assisted Personal Interviewing (CAPI) to the British Social Attitudes survey series. CAPI has been used increasingly over the past decade as an alternative to traditional interviewing techniques. As the name implies, CAPI involves the use of a laptop computer during the interview, with the interviewer entering responses directly into the computer. One of the advantages of CAPI is that it significantly reduces both the amount of time spent on data processing and the number of coding and editing errors. There was, however, concern that a different interviewing technique might alter the distribution of responses and so affect the year-on-year consistency of British Social Attitudes data.

   Following the experiment, it was decided to change over to CAPI completely in 1994 (the self-completion questionnaire still being administered in the conventional way). The results of the experiment are discussed in The 11th Report (Lynn and Purdon, 1994).

4. Interview times recorded as less than 20 minutes were excluded, as these timings were likely to be errors.

5. An experiment was conducted on the 1991 British Social Attitudes survey (Jowell et al., 1992) which showed that sending advance letters to sampled addresses before fieldwork begins has very little impact on response rates. However, interviewers do find that an advance letter helps them to introduce the survey on the doorstep, and a majority of respondents have said that they preferred some advance notice. For these reasons, advance letters have been used on the British Social Attitudes surveys since 1991.

6. Because of methodological experiments on scale development, the exact items detailed in this section have not been asked on all versions of the questionnaire each year.

7. In 1994 only, this item was replaced by: Ordinary people get their fair share of the nation's wealth. [Wealth1]

8. In constructing the scale, a decision had to be taken on how to treat missing values ("Don't know" and "Not answered"). Respondents who had more than two missing values on the left-right scale and more than three missing values on the libertarian–authoritarian and welfarism scales were excluded from that scale. For respondents with fewer missing values, "Don't know" was recoded to the midpoint of the scale and "Not answered" was recoded to the scale mean for that respondent on their valid items.

9. See www.natcen.ac.uk/bsa.

References

DeVellis, R.F. (2003), *Scale Development: Theory and Applications*, 2nd edition, Applied Social Research Methods Series, 26, Thousand Oaks, Calif.: Sage

Jowell, R., Brook, L., Prior, G. and Taylor, B. (1992), *British Social Attitudes: the 9th Report*, Aldershot: Dartmouth

Lynn, P. and Purdon, S. (1994), '*Time-series and lap-tops: the change to computer- assisted interviewing*', in Jowell, R., Curtice, J., Brook, L. and Ahrendt, D. (eds.), British Social Attitudes: the 11th Report, Aldershot: Dartmouth

Lynn, P. and Taylor, B. (1995), '*On the bias and variance of samples of individuals: a comparison of the Electoral Registers and Postcode Address File as sampling frames*', The Statistician, **44**: 173–194

Spector, P.E. (1992), *Summated Rating Scale Construction: An Introduction, Quantitative Applications in the Social Sciences*, 82, Newbury Park, Calif.: Sage

Stafford, R. and Thomson, K. (2006), *British Social Attitudes and Young People's Social Attitudes surveys* 2003: Technical Report, London: NatCen Social Research